Get the eBooks FREE!

(PDF, ePub, Kindle, and liveBook all included)

We believe that once you buy a book from us, you should be able to read it in any format we have available. To get electronic versions of this book at no additional cost to you, purchase and then register this book at the Manning website.

Go to https://www.manning.com/freebook and follow the instructions to complete your pBook registration.

That's it!
Thanks from Manning!

Angular in Action

JEREMY WILKEN

MANNING
SHELTER ISLAND

For online information and ordering of this and other Manning books, please visit www.manning.com. The publisher offers discounts on this book when ordered in quantity. For more information, please contact

Special Sales Department
Manning Publications Co.
20 Baldwin Road
PO Box 761
Shelter Island, NY 11964
Email: orders@manning.com

Manning Publications Co.
20 Baldwin Road
PO Box 761
Shelter Island, NY 11964

Development editors:	Cynthia Kane, Helen Stergius
Review editor:	Ivan Martinović
Technical development editor:	Alain Couniot
Project editor:	Kevin Sullivan
Copyeditor:	Corbin Collins
Proofreader:	Alyson Brener
Technical proofreader:	Tanya Wilke
Typesetter:	Happenstance Type-O-Rama
Cover designer:	Marija Tudor

ISBN 9781617293313
Printed in the United States
1 2 3 4 5 6 7 8 9 10 - EBM - 23 22 21 20 19 18

To my parents, who gave me great encouragement, support, and latitude to become what I am today.

contents

preface

A major framework for many years, Angular has influenced a generation of web technologies. Even developers who haven't used it have benefitted from its existence, as it helped popularize a number of important concepts and technologies.

Early in its AngularJS days (version 1.x is known as AngularJS), it became perhaps the most popular web application framework of its time. But the 1.x version had limitations, and a number of optimizations were built into the framework. The concept of *two-way databinding* (being able to sync data between the controller and the view automatically), which was touted early on as its best feature, became a performance bottleneck in large applications that abused its utility. To help mitigate this problem, one-way and one-time binding options were introduced to improve performance, but they required developers to opt in. Also, *components* were introduced as a better way to organize and structure applications, but taking advantage of them required refactoring of existing applications.

You could build an amazing and performant application with AngularJS 1.x, but it wasn't always the default mode and required unlearning concepts that were believed to be best practices from earlier releases. Simply put, writing well-designed applications was possible because of workarounds from the original concepts that AngularJS embraced.

Instead of evolving the version 1.x codebase, the decision was made to rewrite it from scratch to implement the lessons learned into the foundations of the next major version. This was a multiyear endeavor that involved both the Angular team at Google and the larger community of early adopters. It was a long journey, and I rode alongside and built applications on top of it during early alpha and beta phases. The final result of that journey was Angular 2.0 (version 2.0 and above is known as just Angular), and its community has grown rapidly since its release.

I started working on *Angular in Action* while Angular was still in early beta for version 2.0. Angular then underwent regular and rapid iterations during the book's writing and development. But today Angular is stable and evolves with a well-defined release cycle for new features and deprecations. The book examples are written to work with Angular 5 and above, and going forward, the GitHub projects will have notes about any required changes to keep up with Angular's evolution.

acknowledgments

I'd like to thank first and foremost my wife, Linda, for her patience and understanding as I wrote this book, largely during the evening and weekend hours. I appreciate your support, and I pledge to make up some of the lost time.

Manning provided a team of professionals dedicated to making this book happen. Dozens of individuals were involved, including my developmental editors Helen Stergius and Cynthia Kane, technical developmental editor Alain Couniot, technical proofreader Tanya Wilke, and review editor Ivan Martinović. Several external reviewers also provided helpful feedback on different stages of the manuscript: Harsh Raval, Kumar Unnikrishnan, Michael A. Angelo, Phily Austria, Radoslaw Pilski, and Tony Brown.

Along with that team were others at Manning who helped manage the cycle of early releases and the final production release, including project editor Kevin Sullivan, copyeditor Corbin Collins, and proofreader Alyson Brener.

A big thank you goes to the Angular team for creating Angular and also for the opportunities they've given me to talk with team members individually. Google also sponsors the Google Developer Experts program, which has a great list of Angular experts who have been helpful and which I'm proud to belong to.

I also want to thank Jason and David Aden for their early contributions and time working on the manuscript with me.

Finally, thank you, the reader, for picking up this book to spend your precious time with me between these pages. If it weren't for you, I wouldn't have a reason to write. I hope to hear from you and see what you build!

about this book

Angular in Action is designed to help you learn how to use Angular in building your own web applications. I've brought the core lessons from my own experiences into this book. I've built a number of large enterprise applications on Angular and many smaller ones as well. I believe similar best practices go into most well-written applications no matter their size, so I share those as well.

My goal is to ensure you have a strong foundation in how Angular works, how it's used to build web applications, and how to then ship those into production. This foundational knowledge will enable you to learn additional concepts more quickly and easily (often by reviewing the documentation or even blog posts).

There are certainly more Angular topics than could be covered in a single book, as Angular is an ambitious and comprehensive set of tools and libraries. I took great care to make this a book that works on multiple levels. You may find some topics to be more advanced than you need right now, but you can always come back to them later. Or you may find that the basics are familiar but the more advanced topics help fill in the gaps.

Who should read this book

Although I believe Angular is accessible for developers, this book is targeted at readers who have the subject knowledge detailed in the following list. Other readers will certainly find value in the content, but may have knowledge gaps that aren't covered specifically:

- *Web applications*—You understand the role of web applications and have a little bit of experience with building them.
- *JavaScript*—You have enough knowledge of JavaScript and its syntax to be able to follow along with the examples.
- *HTML/CSS*—You understand the roles of HTML and CSS, as well as their syntax.

I mention some topics in the book that are important but not part of Angular. You may know nothing about some of these, but the book provides enough cursory knowledge that you should be able to follow along:

- *TypeScript*—Angular is written with TypeScript, and so are all the examples in this book. If you're new to TypeScript, I provide many hints along the way, but I suggest you review the official documentation at www.typescriptlang.org.
- *Reactive programming*—Angular's design often allows and recommends using reactive-style programming, which is usually used in conjunction with the popular RxJS library. There's a lot of great material out there for learning reactive and RxJS, and I share a few links to it in the book.

How this book is organized

This book is divided into themed chapters, beginning with the core details of Angular and expanding into more complex themes. Chapters 1–3 lay the groundwork for understanding what Angular is (and isn't) and discuss its role in building your applications. These chapters also provide a quick but fairly comprehensive tutorial of many of Angular's key features. If you're already familiar with Angular, you may find these sections easy to skim to find new insights.

Chapters 4–5 act like a single unit on the topic of components. Angular (like HTML) is based on the idea of building individual components that can be composed together for more complex interactions. You can't have an Angular application without components, and I cover them in great detail in these chapters so you can focus on other aspects in the remainder of the book.

Chapters 6–9 focus on key topics in building applications. Chapter 6 is all about services and, subsequently, dependency injection. Understanding how to manage your services is key to building a larger Angular application, and often key to using other capabilities as well. Chapter 7 looks closely at the router and how to use it to create simple to complex navigation patterns that are used in many web applications. Chapter 8 shows you how to build your own custom directives and pipes, which become crucial when you expand the size of your application and want to make it easier to maintain. Finally, chapter 9 covers the two different approaches to building forms with Angular, as well as how to create your own custom form controls.

The last two chapters round off your Angular training with a focus on testing in chapter 10 and on building and deploying your application for production in chapter 11. You might build some small hobby websites without testing or production tooling, but Angular provides some great tools that make it easy even for large enterprise applications to use. I suggest you use them too! The brief appendix discusses the transition from AngularJS to Angular (or version 1.x to 2+).

If you're brand new to Angular and want a guided tour, I recommend reading the chapters in order. This approach will give you incremental knowledge to build on as you go, as often a chapter glosses over details that were covered in an earlier one.

If you have some prior experience with Angular or are interested in particular topics, feel free to head straight for those chapters. I believe you can skim early sections that cover familiar material and then look more closely at later parts of a chapter to learn more complex capabilities. As you skim, keep an eye out for diagrams that explain various concepts; they're a great way to quickly validate whether you understand the topic at hand. If there are unfamiliar concepts, you can always refer to other chapters.

Most chapters feature fairly extensive examples. In order to do them properly, you'll have to follow along through the whole chapter. The final versions of the code are provided if you don't want to follow the examples and build the code yourself, but I strongly encourage you to code along. You'll understand the coding and retain the information more effectively that way. If you run into any issues with a chapter example, you can check the GitHub project for any potential code changes that were required after the book's publication (such as if a breaking change has been introduced in Angular). Stack Overflow is also a great place to ask any questions that extend beyond the chapter example code.

About the code

All the code in this book can be downloaded from GitHub at https://github.com/ angular-in-action. (A zip file containing the complete code at time of publication will also be available from the publisher's website at https://www.manning.com/books/ angular-in-action.) Each chapter also provides a link to the specific chapter content, so you don't need to download everything ahead of time.

You'll need to have a recent version of NodeJS installed on your machine. Chapter 1 covers more specific things to install for the Angular CLI. You also need a modern browser—preferably one that has good debugging tools, like Chrome. If you're running an outdated browser (like IE10), the code won't run, so update your browser for compatibility and security.

This book contains many examples of source code, both in numbered listings and inline with normal text. In both cases, source code is formatted in a `fixed-width font like this` to separate it from ordinary text. Sometimes code is also **in bold** to highlight code that has changed from previous steps in the chapter, such as when a new feature adds to an existing line of code.

In many cases, the original source code, has been reformatted; we've added line breaks and reworked indentation to accommodate the available page space in the book. In rare cases, even this was not enough, and listings include line-continuation markers (➥). Additionally, comments in the source code have often been removed from the listings when the code is described in the text. Code annotations accompany many of the listings, highlighting important concepts.

Book forum

Purchase of *Angular in Action* includes free access to a private web forum run by Manning Publications where you can make comments about the book, ask technical questions, and receive help from the author and from other users. To access the forum, go to https://forums.manning.com/forums/angular-in-action. You can also learn more about Manning's forums and the rules of conduct at https://forums.manning.com/forums/about.

Manning's commitment to our readers is to provide a venue where a meaningful dialogue between individual readers and between readers and the author can take place. It is not a commitment to any specific amount of participation on the part of the author, whose contribution to the forum remains voluntary (and unpaid). We suggest you try asking the author some challenging questions lest his interest stray! The forum and the archives of previous discussions will be accessible from the publisher's website as long as the book is in print.

about the author

Jeremy Wilken is a software engineer with a passion for designing applications and technology solutions that focus on improving the lives of users. He is a Google Developer Expert for Web Technologies and Angular as well as the Google Assistant, which is an endorsement from Google as a subject matter expert and community leader in Angular and the web.

Most of his day-to-day work is in building Angular applications, but he also spends a lot of time and energy speaking at events, running workshops and trainings, writing, and helping build community through meetups and conferences. He's worked for companies like eBay, Teradata, and VMware, and has been a consultant for many years.

He lives in Austin, Texas, with his wife and two daughters. Outside of the tech world, he is a certified beer judge (it's a real thing) and brews his own beer.

about the cover illustration

The figure on the cover of *Angular in Action* is captioned "A colonel of the Strelitzes, the old Russian militia and body guard to the czars of Moscovy." The illustration is taken from Thomas Jefferys' *A Collection of the Dresses of Different Nations, Ancient and Modern* (four volumes), London, published between 1757 and 1772. The title page states that these are hand-colored copperplate engravings, heightened with gum arabic.

Thomas Jefferys (1719–1771) was called "Geographer to King George III." He was an English cartographer who was the leading map supplier of his day. He engraved and printed maps for government and other official bodies and produced a wide range of commercial maps and atlases, especially of North America. His work as a map maker sparked an interest in local dress customs of the lands he surveyed and mapped, which are brilliantly displayed in this collection. Fascination with faraway lands and travel for pleasure were relatively new phenomena in the late eighteenth century, and collections such as this one were popular, introducing both the tourist as well as the armchair traveler to the inhabitants of other countries.

The diversity of the drawings in Jefferys' volumes speaks vividly of the uniqueness and individuality of the world's nations some 200 years ago. Dress codes have changed since then, and the diversity by region and country, so rich at the time, has faded away. It's now often hard to tell the inhabitants of one continent from another. Perhaps, trying to view it optimistically, we've traded a cultural and visual diversity for a more varied personal life—or a more varied and interesting intellectual and technical life.

At a time when it's difficult to tell one computer book from another, Manning celebrates the inventiveness and initiative of the computer business with book covers based on the rich diversity of regional life of two centuries ago, brought back to life by Jefferys' pictures.

Angular: a modern web platform

This chapter covers

- Angular as a platform for modern applications

- Key reasons for choosing Angular

- Angular's architecture and how components form the basis of it

- How AngularJS differs from Angular

- ES2015 and TypeScript and how Angular uses them

Angular is a modern web application platform that promises to provide developers with a comprehensive set of tools and capabilities to build large, robust applications. The core value proposition of Angular is to make it possible to build applications that work for nearly any platform—whether mobile, web, or desktop. The Angular team has focused on building much more than a robust application framework; they've also built an entire ecosystem.

All that's a bit of a mouthful, which is partly what makes Angular such an exciting technology to work with. Let's start by taking a closer look at why you would choose Angular for your next project.

1.1   *Why choose Angular?*

Building web applications that can meet the needs of users is not a trivial task. The quality and complexity of applications is ever increasing, and so are users' expectations for quality and capabilities. Angular exists to help developers deliver applications to meet these demands.

If you haven't settled on Angular as a tool of choice yet, let's quickly cover some of the top reasons that you should seriously consider Angular. Some items are covered more in section 1.3, but here are the top highlights in my experience:

- *Inspired by web standards, enhanced by modern capabilities*—Anyone building web applications today knows there are many different ways and ideas about how to design applications. Angular tries to design its framework and the development process around common standards (like leveraging the latest JavaScript language features), using modern capabilities (such as embracing TypeScript for type enforcement).
- *Development tooling included, customizations available*—Angular provides a common developer experience through its CLI tooling (for generating, building, testing, and deploying apps), while making those same tools available to be easily integrated into custom solutions (such as a custom build toolchain) and third-party tools (like different editors or IDEs).
- *Powerful ecosystem with a large community*—There is an ever-growing number of third-party libraries, UI libraries, blog posts, and events. Angular's large and active community provides a great foundation on which to learn and should instill confidence that it will remain a valuable technology.
- *Sponsored by Google, open source community driven*—Google has a team of engineers, managers, and evangelists solely dedicated to bringing Angular to the rest of Google and the entire web community. With thousands of "internal customers" who rely on Angular inside Google, the Angular team uses those experiences to inform future development and receives large volumes of external contributions that together shape Angular's future (you can join in too!).

Angular is much more than just a JavaScript library that powers some of the top websites in the world. I'm passionate about open source communities, and I'm an advocate for people to get engaged in a project as part of their regular routine. Projects in the Angular community are where I put a lot of my energy and contributions, and I invite you to join me. Although I do engage with the Angular project itself, I primarily contribute to projects in the Angular ecosystem, such as Clarity, a UI component library and design language.

You may be a developer trying to figure out whether Angular will meet your needs, or you may be a manager trying to understand the role of the technology, or trying to figure out how to improve your current applications. Regardless of where you're starting from, the Angular ecosystem has a lot to offer.

1.2 What you'll learn

This book is designed to be a comprehensive walk through Angular, but it's also meant to get you informed about various aspects of the ecosystem. The approach is always experiential, where you'll learn about a topic and build it yourself to see the concepts come to life. At the end of this book you should be able to make high-quality Angular applications and have the foundational knowledge and experience on which to build a career and applications.

The key takeaways in this book include the following:

- *How Angular works*—We'll look at some of the key internal concepts that make it such a compelling platform for building your applications. You'll learn the concepts and build examples to illustrate them as part of a functional application.
- *How to build applications*—In most chapters, we'll walk step-by-step through a number of real-life examples. The code examples are comprehensive and focus on a certain set of goals for each chapter.
- *Learn about the ecosystem*—Each example uses some third-party libraries and capabilities. This helps you see more of a realistic development experience and gain a foundation for building your own applications.
- *Get practical insights from my experiences*—In many of the examples and notes about them, I share practical advice from my experience, including suggestions on things to avoid (even if it's perfectly legitimate code) and how to choose between different approaches when they're provided.

You should be equipped to design and build web applications with Angular by the end of the book. If you're not as interested in the technical aspects (perhaps as a manager), you'll still glean a lot of the same lessons to get a solid frame of reference for how Angular works and what it provides for your project.

There are a few things I won't be able to cover in this book, but just because these items aren't specifically discussed, it doesn't mean you can't learn many things related to them. The following are *not* core topics covered in this book:

- *How to write libraries*—This book focuses on how to build applications with Angular, and in many ways building a library has different guidelines and recommendations. That would be another book. But building a library is also difficult if you don't know how to build an application first.
- *Every available API and features*—Many APIs and features aren't covered in this book, mostly because they're rarely used. I believe this book will empower you to build your skills to the level that you can quickly learn these additional features as your project needs require.
- *How to design your app and UX principles*—This is such a large topic that I can't cover it fully. I've tried to show several different ideas and patterns in the chapter examples to give you some ideas, but it's often opinion-based. I hope you'll take time to compare the design of each and know that there can be limitations as well due to these being examples and not actual projects.

Angular is an evolving project, with new features and sometimes deprecation of existing ones. I've taken great care to ensure that the concepts taught are the core ideas that are unlikely to change (though they may be enhanced). If there are any changes that break some of the example code or concepts, please check the GitHub project for each chapter or the book's forums, which should have a list of known changes and errata.

To better understand the impact of Angular in today's web, let's go back a few years to look at the history that brought us here.

1.3   *The journey from AngularJS to Angular*

Web applications came of age around 2009–2010, when the Web 2.0 fad finally gave way to better application approaches and frameworks. The term *web application* also became refined, due perhaps in large part to the standardization of HTML5 and EcmaScript 5 (the basis of JavaScript), and focused primarily on the ability to build robust applications that run almost entirely in the browser.

In 2009, Miško Hevery announced AngularJS, which became one of the most popular frameworks (if not *the* most) for building web applications. The AngularJS project was brought into Google, and version 1.0 was officially launched in October 2010. There were many other viable frameworks, but AngularJS struck a chord with a wide audience of developers.

Angular vs. AngularJS

There has been some confusion about Angular versions. The Angular team has decided to provide guidance and call the first version *AngularJS*. That's the name it was given initially, and it separates it architecturally from later versions. Any release from 1.0 through 2.0 is known as AngularJS.

For versions 2.0 and greater, it's known as just *Angular*. Version 2.0 was a complete rewrite, and all versions after it are planned as incremental changes upon it.

Angular version 2, officially announced in September 2014, was developed over the course of two years (plus some time prior to its announcement). It was released as Angular version 2 in September 2016, with Angular 4 being released in March 2017. The Angular team will continue to provide major releases on a six-month schedule, with a focus on easy upgrades. Depending on when you read this, Angular 6, or even 10, could be the most current release.

But you aren't looking at this book to learn about the past—you're interested in building modern web applications. Perhaps you've built Angular 1 applications, or even started with some of the Angular 2 guides. The focus of this book is on building modern web applications, and Angular provides the platform to elegantly accomplish that.

Throughout the book, I'll mention AngularJS occasionally to draw connections for readers who have experience with it, but when I use *Angular* without a number, I'm always referring to Angular version 2 or greater. Check out https://angular.io (figure 1.1) for more info.

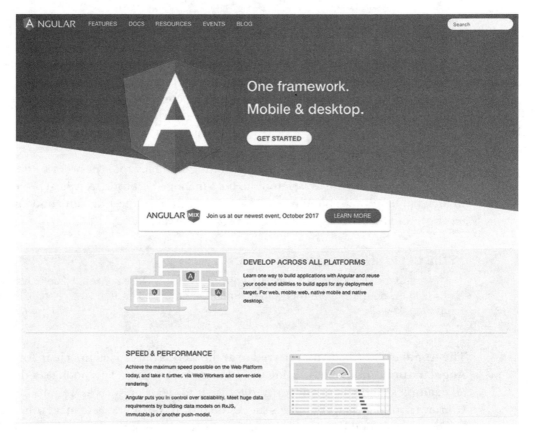

Figure 1.1 The Angular website is a great resource for documentation, events, and everything about Angular.

1.4 *Angular: a platform, not a framework*

There are a few important distinctions between a framework and a platform. A *framework* is usually just the code library used to build an application, whereas a *platform* is more holistic and includes tooling and support beyond a framework. AngularJS was focused solely on building web applications in the browser and was clearly a framework. It had a large ecosystem of third-party modules that could be easily used to add features to your application, but at the heart of it all, it simply built web applications in the browser.

Angular comes with a leaner core library and makes additional features available as separate packages that can be used as needed. It also has many tools that push it beyond a simple framework, including the following:

- Dedicated CLI for application development, testing, and deployment
- Offline rendering capabilities on many back-end server platforms
- Desktop-, mobile-, and browser-based application execution environments

- Comprehensive UI component libraries, such as Material Design

Some of these things existed in some shape with AngularJS, but most were community solutions and were bolted into AngularJS after the fact. In contrast, Angular was developed with these platform features in mind.

These parts are still in refinement and will continue to evolve into more robust options.

1.4.1   Angular CLI

Modern development typically requires setting up many tools in order to start a project, which has given rise to *more* tools to help manage *those* tools. A typical project needs to manage handling a build process (asset optimization), testing (unit and end-to-end testing), and local development support (local server).

> **The CLI is always improving**
>
> The Angular CLI is a wonderful tool that has an ever-growing list of capabilities. Over time, it will likely do many more things than I mention here, and perhaps the capabilities may change as well.

The Angular CLI (often just referred to as the CLI) is the official toolchain for building Angular applications that provide these features and more. This book uses the CLI for all examples, and you're encouraged to use it for your projects as well. You could roll your own build tooling, but that's suggested only if the CLI doesn't meet your needs.

You can install the CLI using npm. It does require that you have a recent version of NodeJS installed to run properly:

```
npm install -g @angular/cli
```

The CLI has a number of features that aid in the development of Angular apps. Here are the primary features:

- *Generates new project scaffolding*—Instead of having to create a new project from an existing project or creating all the files yourself, the CLI will generate a full project with a basic app already started for you.
- *Generates new application pieces*—Need a new component? Easy; it can generate the files for you. It can generate components, services, routes, and pipes, and it also will automatically ensure they are fully wired up in the build process.
- *Manages the entire build toolchain*—Because files need to be processed before being served to the client (such as TypeScript compilation), the CLI will process your source files and build them into an optimized version for development or production.
- *Serves a localhost development server*—The CLI handles the build flow and then starts a server listening on localhost so you can see the results, with a live reload feature.

- *Incorporates code linting and formatting code*—Helps enforce quality code by using the CLI to lint your code for style and semantic errors, and it can also help format your code automatically to the style rules.
- *Supports running unit and e2e tests*—Tests are vital, so the CLI sets up Karma for running your unit tests and works with Protractor to execute your e2e tests. It will automatically pick up and execute new tests as they're generated.

You can add other features and capabilities to the CLI. To see the full list of features, you can run ng help to output the current help documentation. You can also read more about the CLI at https://cli.angular.io.

1.4.2 Server rendering and the compiler

Compiling output in Angular is decoupled from the browser in a way that allows Angular applications to be rendered in different environments, such as a server or desktop app. There are many great side effects of this design pattern, because Angular is much more versatile by being able to render on the client and server, and it opens many different opportunities.

There are two things in play here—first, the decoupled compiler of Angular, and then optional support for universal rendering. It takes a decoupled compiler to enable the universal rendering, because you can implement different rendering patterns depending on the environment.

The compiler in Angular is a very important piece of the puzzle. It's responsible for resolving data bindings, registering event handlers, and rendering out the resulting HTML for components.

The term *server rendering* is about the notion that it shouldn't matter where you run the JavaScript engine that executes Angular code. It should be possible to run Angular universally, such as with browser JavaScript engines, NodeJS, or even less common engines like Java's Nashorn engine. This greatly increases the ways in which Angular can be used.

Why does this matter? Let's explore a few primary use cases:

- *Server rendering for faster loading*—Mobile devices are the primary way to access the internet these days, and mobile connections are frequently slow and unreliable. A server-side rendering option allows you to resolve data bindings and render components on the server so the initial payload sent to the user is pre-initialized. It can also optimize and send the necessary bytes for a quick initial load time and lazy load the other assets as needed.
- *Performance in the browser*—One of the major pain points of JavaScript is that it's single threaded, which means that JavaScript can only handle one instruction at a time. In modern browsers, a newer technology known as web workers allows Angular to push some of the execution of the compiler into another process. This means that a lot more processing can occur, and it allows things like animations and user interactions to be smoother.

- *SEO*—There's a major concern about how heavy JavaScript applications are crawled by search engines. Universal rendering means we can detect crawlers and render the site for them so that content is ready without having to worry if the crawler executes JavaScript (some do, some don't). This will certainly enhance SEO efforts for Angular applications.

- *Multiple platforms*—Many developers want to use other platforms for their back ends, such as .NET or PHP. Angular can be compiled in the platform of choice, assuming there's a supported renderer. Angular will provide support for NodeJS, but the community is actively building and maintaining rendering support for other platforms such as Java and Go.

All of these have been issues for years in building web applications, and Angular provides a comprehensive solution. The great thing is you don't have to do a lot of work to enable these features in your application.

This is an area of evolution at the time of writing, and setting it up correctly is an advanced topic that I can't cover in depth. But the Angular documentation and CLI are being constantly improved to show you how to incorporate these types of benefits easily.

1.4.3   *Mobile and desktop capabilities*

The rendering capabilities enable Angular to work with native mobile and desktop applications. Tools like Cordova have been around for a while; they let you create *hybrid* applications—web applications wrapped up inside some type of native shell. But Angular's rendering design makes it possible to support rendering out to different native platforms entirely.

The major value is that you can share a lot of code between your Angular applications, even if some are designed to build mobile apps and others are web applications. This is particularly valuable in large teams.

The mobile and desktop capabilities of Angular are extensions of the design of the compiler. The following tools are all outside of Angular's core but use the design of Angular to power some powerful design patterns:

- *Ionic (mobile)*—This fantastic and popular hybrid app framework (figure 1.2) for AngularJS has been updated to work with Angular. Millions of mobile apps have been created with Ionic, and it's primarily focused on building hybrid apps. The UI components are all created to run in the browser, but look and feel like native UI components.

- *NativeScript (mobile)*—This is another popular mobile framework that creates native mobile apps. NativeScript implements the native UI components but allows you to write Angular components to describe your application.

- *React Native (mobile, desktop)*—By the name, you'd be correct to assume that React Native is really part of the React framework ecosystem. But with a custom render, it's possible to use the React Native tool to generate native mobile apps.

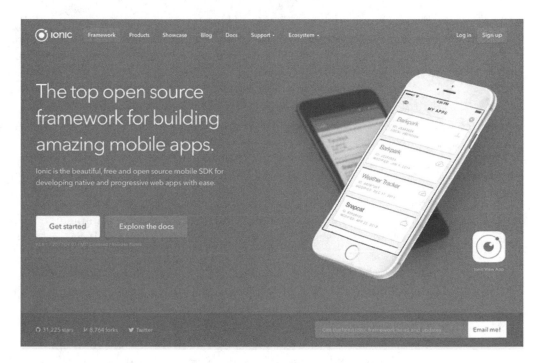

Figure 1.2   Ionic is a popular and powerful mobile framework for Angular.

- *Windows Universal (desktop)*—Windows has support for building native Windows applications using JavaScript. It's possible to use Angular as your application layer but still have to build out a native Windows application.
- *Electron (desktop)*—Based on NodeJS, Electron is a very popular cross-platform application framework. It implements a set of APIs to hook into the native OS, and you can leverage Angular to power the internal logic of your app.
- *Progressive Web Apps (mobile, desktop)*—The capabilities of Progressive Web Apps (PWAs) aren't limited to Angular. They're fundamentally about blurring the line between the web and native. As of this writing, they're in experimental support. This is an exciting potential avenue for building applications of tomorrow.

These different options support the power of the decoupled compiler in Angular. It also means that there will likely be many, many more examples and use cases that allow you to build Angular applications that can run nearly anywhere.

1.4.4   UI libraries

There's an ever-growing catalog of UI libraries built for Angular. They bring different sets of UI components to developers for easy consumption. Rather than having to build your own charts or tabs components, you can use one of the many prebuilt options.

Depending on your team's size and skill sets, implementing your own UI components may be challenging. Making truly reusable and hardened UI components is difficult. These components are rarely what make your application really unique, so it's hard to spend the time (and money) to build them.

These libraries are plentiful. There are so many that I can't cover all the options. You'll notice there's a lot of overlap in the functionalities that each of them provides, so comparing them can be difficult. We'll take a look at some of the most popular options, but I recommend doing additional research before selecting an option:

- *Angular Material (https://github.com/angular/material2)*—Material Design is the official design specification created by Google. It has strong roots in concepts of real-world objects, hence Material in the name. Angular Material is the official UI component library provided by the Angular team and it implements a number of UI components according to the design specification. It has an open source license.

- *Covalent (https://teradata.github.io/covalent)*—This library extends the Angular Material project with a number of additional components and capabilities, but still retains the principles of Material Design. It's a result of work done at Teradata. It has an open source license.

- *Clarity (https://vmware.github.io/clarity)*—This library, shown in figure 1.3, comes from VMware. It's designed as both a library and a design specification for web applications. It contains many components that are specific to Angular but also has some icons and a general CSS framework. It has an open source license.

- *ng-bootstrap (https://ng-bootstrap.github.io)*—Based on the very popular Bootstrap CSS framework, ng-bootstrap implements the components based on the design of Bootstrap. It's built by the same team that created the very popular AngularJS UI Bootstrap project. It has an open source license.

- *Kendo UI (https://www.telerik.com/kendo-angular-ui/)*—From the same company as NativeScript, Kendo UI is a UI library that's been integrated into many different frameworks, but the company is building a set of native Angular UI components that are custom for Angular. It has a commercial license.

- *PrimeNG (www.primefaces.org/primeng/)*—A rich collection of UI components, PrimeNG is developed by PrimeTek and has more than 60 components. It comes with many themes and is designed for mobile and desktops. It has an open source license.

- *Wijmo (http://wijmo.com/angular2/)*—Containing some very complex data grid components, Wijmo implements this set of Angular components without support from other libraries like jQuery. The UI library has a commercial license.

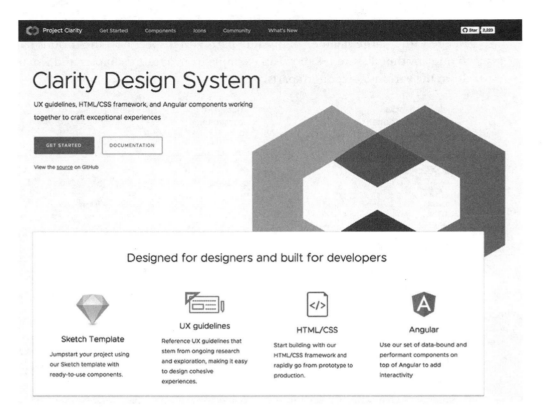

Figure 1.3   Clarity Design System is one of the most popular Angular UI libraries.

- *Ionic (http://ionic.io)*—Primarily for mobile, Ionic is a comprehensive library of components with easy theming, native device integrations, practical services, and its own CLI for app development workflows. The company also provides commercial services for mobile app development. It has an open source license.
- *Fuel-UI (http://fuelinteractive.github.io/fuel-ui/)*—Another Bootstrap CSS framework-based set of components, directives, and pipes by Fuel Travel. It has an open source license.

You're certainly not required to use a UI library, but most developers will find them to be useful. Any reasonable UI library should be fairly well tested, allowing you to focus more on what makes your application unique.

1.5   *Component architecture*

Many modern applications have adopted a component-based approach to developing applications. The intention is to design each piece of your application in a standalone manner that limits the amount of coupling and duplication across various parts of the program. In many ways, a *component* is a way to create custom HTML elements in your application.

The easiest way to think about a component architecture is to look at an example of a page with a large number of discrete parts and inspect how the various parts relate to one another. Figure 1.4 shows an example from a future chapter and visually breaks down the various component parts.

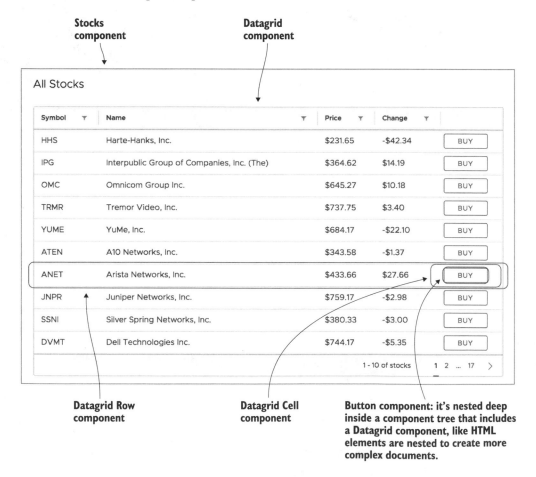

Figure 1.4   Component architecture illustrated by showing how components are nested and combined to create more complex layouts

The figure shows an isolated section from one of the book chapter examples, illustrating that several components combine to create this display. You can see that various parts are independent from the others, but they also work together to create the list of items. There's clearly a hierarchy between them. The list of components on the right shows the parent-to-child relationship each of the components has with the others, and this is essentially how HTML elements work together on the page.

HTML itself is a language of components. Each element has a certain role and functionality, and they're all easily nested to create more complex functionality. They're isolated but still easily manipulated to do whatever is needed at the moment. Some elements work in tandem. For example, INPUTs are used inside of a FORM to describe a set of input controls. Many elements can also emit events when things happen; a FORM can emit an event when the form is submitted, for example. This allows you to wire up additional logic to manipulate HTML elements based on the events that fire—the fundamentals of front-end application development.

Hopefully a component architecture seems fairly approachable and consistent with your current understanding of the web. The intention is to focus on breaking down individual parts of the application (particularly the visual UI elements) into discrete, modular components.

There are many ways to implement a component architecture, as evidenced by the many web application libraries such as React and Ember. Angular has a very obvious component-based architecture (all Angular applications are components). React and Ember also have first-class support for components in their applications. Those with jQuery experience can also imagine that jQuery plugins can be conceptually similar to components, though they're not as consistent or regulated. Even the basic concepts of the Web 2.0 days (think widgets!) are based around building components.

1.5.1 Components' key characteristics

Components have some concepts that drive their design and architecture. This section will explore these concepts in more detail, but also keep an eye open for how Angular applies these concepts to practice throughout the book:

- *Encapsulation*—Keeping component logic in a single place
- *Isolation*—Keeping component internals hidden from external actors
- *Reusability*—Allowing component reuse with minimal effort
- *Evented*—Emitting events during the lifecycle of the component
- *Customizable*—Making it possible to style and extend the component
- *Declarative*—Using a component with simple declarative markup

When we build components, the preceding are the tenets we should consider when designing the best components possible. These concepts have existed in various forms before, but rarely have they all been clearly implemented and standardized into the web platform.

The World Wide Web Consortium (W3C), the primary standards body for the web, is developing an official Web Component specification. Several standards are required in order to implement the full vision of web components:

- Custom elements (encapsulation, declarative, reusability, evented)
- Shadow DOM (isolation, encapsulation, customizable)
- Templates (encapsulation, isolation)
- JavaScript modules (encapsulation, isolation, reusability)

As of this writing, the specification isn't fully adopted in all browsers and possibly never will be. Standards are also subject to change, but it's not crucial that we dive into the specifics of the specification here. The important thing is that these four concepts are central to the idea of components. Let's explore them a little more in detail and see how they enable a component architecture.

CUSTOM ELEMENTS

HTML is the language of the web because it describes the content of a page in a fairly concise set of elements. As a markup language, it's a declarative way to describe your content. *Custom elements* mean being able to extend HTML with our own additional elements, adding to the vocabulary of what is possible. You can read about the official specification at www.w3.org/TR/custom-elements/.

The official specification for custom elements is intended to allow developers to create new HTML elements that essentially blend naturally and natively into the DOM. In other words, using a custom element should be no different from using any other HTML element. For example, imagine you want to create a custom element that implements a tabbing interface. You would likely want to create custom elements like the following code and in figure 1.5:

```
<tabs>
  <tab title="About">
    <h1>This is the about tab</h1>
  </tab>
  <tab title="Profile">
    <h2>This is the profile tab</h2>
  </tab>
  <tab title="Contact Us">
    <form>
      <textarea name="message"></textarea>
      <input type="submit" value="Send">
  </tab>
</tabs>
```

This looks and feels like natural HTML because these would be two custom elements: tabs and tab elements. The real value here is how easy it is to implement tabs. Using jQuery, you would end up creating a lot of div elements, applying a number of custom IDs or classes, and sprinkling some JavaScript on top.

These tabs could also emit events. For example, anytime the active tab changes there could be a tabChange event. Anything in your application could then listen for this event and act accordingly. Each custom element could implement any number of events that seem practical to the lifecycle of the component.

A custom element can also implement its own styling, so the tabs can come by default with a particular look and feel. Anyone using the tabs could write their own CSS to modify it to their particular use case, but custom elements can have a default appearance much like many HTML elements.

Custom elements have a lot of the stuff necessary for building components. In fact, we could stop with custom elements and be fairly happy. It gives us a *declarative* way to create a *reusable* component, which *encapsulates* the internal mechanics of the component away from the rest of the application, but can emit *events* to enable other components to hook into the lifecycle. Angular uses these concepts in its implementation of components.

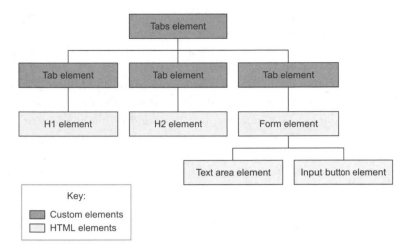

Figure 1.5   Custom elements fit into a normal HTML hierarchy but can implement new behaviors.

Angular provides its own mechanics to create a custom element, which is just an Angular component. Every Angular component is a custom element and fulfills the four tenets (and more) that we expect to get from a custom element.

1.5.2   Shadow DOM

Despite the rather ominous-sounding name, the *Shadow DOM* is really your best friend when it comes to trying to isolate styling behaviors inside of a component. The Shadow DOM is an isolated Document Object Model (DOM) tree that's detached from the typical CSS inheritance, allowing you to create a barrier between markup inside and outside of the Shadow DOM. For example, if you have a button inside of a Shadow DOM and a button outside, any CSS for the button written outside the Shadow DOM won't affect the button inside it. This is important for Angular because it allows us to have better control over how CSS affects the way the components display.

CSS is a powerful language, but most web developers have run into issues where CSS styles have accidentally modified elements other than the intended ones, particularly when adding CSS from external sources. Shadow DOM provides a way to truly encapsulate your component HTML and CSS from other parts of the page, which is known as Light DOM. You can read about the official specification at www.w3.org/TR/shadow-dom.

Developers should be familiar with the standard Light DOM, defining the standard DOM behaviors with regard to element styling and visibility. When you write a CSS rule, the CSS selector is the only way to limit which elements receive that particular styling. Outside of some fairly small, hand-crafted web pages, most CSS is written with some kind of systematic approach to set clear rules about how CSS styles get applied. This gave rise to many of the great CSS grid and component frameworks, such as Bootstrap and Foundation. It also gave us a selection of CSS selector nomenclatures, such as Scalable Modular Architecture for CSS (SMACSS) and Block Element Modifier (BEM). Although we've found ways to manage the Light DOM with these systems, it doesn't change the underlying behavior that someone could still manage to break your whole application by adding a single rule that doesn't adhere to the guidelines.

There's always been pain associated with scaling page styling with CSS due to the greedy nature of CSS selectors always trying to match as many things as possible. In contrast with the Light DOM, the Shadow DOM gives us the ability to denote that a fragment of the DOM be shifted into a new realm that doesn't play with the Light DOM styles.

In many science fiction stories, characters may get caught somehow in a new dimension of reality that is separated from normal reality, and they're usually unable to interact between these realities except through some "bridge" between the realities. Similarly, I like to think of using Shadow DOM as like shifting the current context to a new dimension that has very limited connection to the Light DOM and therefore allows us to write CSS and HTML that gets rendered without having the ability to modify other styles.

Developers can create a new Shadow DOM (known as a *shadow root*) that will carve out an isolated DOM tree that has limited interaction with the Light DOM. You still attach this root inside the DOM tree as a node. The *shadow boundary* is the line between the Light and Shadow DOMs. There are many nuances and features that enable certain forms of styles to target inside or outside of the boundary, but I'll leave those details for you to dive into if they become needed.

In figure 1.6, you can see a simple example where the first line of text output in the middle of the image has the black background and white text, whereas the second line of text (which is inside the shadow root) doesn't.

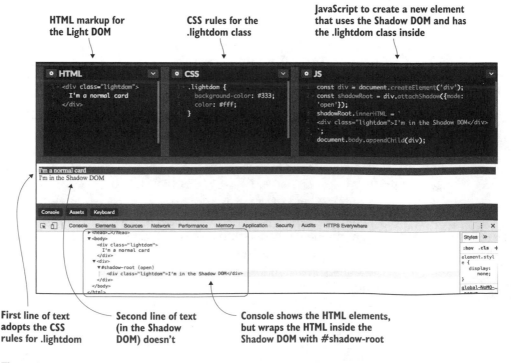

Figure 1.6   Shadow DOM example where the styles from outside the shadow root don't cross the boundary and apply to inner elements

Shadow DOM enables the best form of encapsulation available in the browser for styles and templates. It's able to isolate the internals of a component in such a way that outside styles and scripts won't accidentally attach and modify it. It does provide some customization features that allow you to communicate across the shadow boundary. These are particularly important features when we want to build out complex and reusable components that can be entirely self-contained with styling.

Unfortunately, Shadow DOM support may not be available in all browsers and may require a polyfill. Chapter 4 explores this in more detail, but Angular lets us write components that use either the Shadow DOM, an emulated version of the Shadow DOM, or just the Light DOM.

1.5.3 Templates

Templates are a powerful feature that allow us to create isolated fragments of the DOM to use in our components. Our custom elements need to have some kind of internal structure, and often we'll need to be able to reuse this markup. Ideally this shouldn't clutter the main document, and HTML5 introduces a new `template` tag to help us out. You can read the spec at https://www.w3.org/TR/html5/semantics-scripting.html#the-template-element.

Any markup written inside a template is just a fragment that's not part of the current page unless it's explicitly initialized. In other words, if you were to look at the DOM tree, the content in templates doesn't appear. If your markup has CSS, inline scripts, image elements, or other elements that typically trigger a browser action, those actions won't run until the template is used.

Templates are often used with the Shadow DOM because it allows you to define the template and then inject it into the shadow root. Without templates, the Shadow DOM APIs would require us to inject content node by node. They're also used by Angular as part of the lifecycle of components and the compilation process, allowing Angular to keep isolated, inert copies of the template as data changes and needs to be recompiled.

The role of templates folds in nicely with the overall component architecture and works in tandem with the Shadow DOM and custom elements. They provide a layer of encapsulation that lets you define a template that remains inactive until it's needed and therefore isolates the template from the rest of the application.

1.5.4 JavaScript modules

Neither HTML nor JavaScript has traditionally had a native means to load additional files or assets during the lifecycle of the application. You had to ensure that all the needed files were loaded on page load, or use some workaround that usually relied on making an XHR request or adding a new script tag to the page. Though these approaches worked, they weren't particularly elegant or always easy to use.

Today we have modules and module loaders in JavaScript, which give a native way to load and execute code throughout the entire lifecycle of the app, not just on page load. Previously, developers had to build a bundle of all the assets for the web application ahead of time and deliver the whole package to the user. Modules (figure 1.7) give us a lot of interesting capabilities, many of which are familiar to developers who have worked with other languages with package or module capabilities, like Java, Python, or Go.

API List

TYPE: All	STATUS: All	Q Filter

animations

c AnimationBuilder	**c** AnimationFactory	**I** AnimationEvent
K AUTO_STYLE	**I** AnimateChildOptions	**T** AnimateTimings
I AnimationAnimateChildMetadata	**I** AnimationAnimateMetadata	**I** AnimationAnimateRefMetadata
I AnimationGroupMetadata	**I** AnimationKeyframesSequenceMetadata	**I** AnimationMetadata
E AnimationMetadataType	**I** AnimationOptions	**I** AnimationQueryMetadata
I AnimationQueryOptions	**I** AnimationReferenceMetadata	**I** AnimationSequenceMetadata
I AnimationStaggerMetadata	**I** AnimationStateMetadata	**I** AnimationStyleMetadata
I AnimationTransitionMetadata	**I** AnimationTriggerMetadata	**F** animate
F animateChild	**F** animation	**F** group
F keyframes	**F** query	**F** sequence
F stagger	**F** state	**F** style
F transition	**F** trigger	**F** useAnimation
I AnimationPlayer	**c** NoopAnimationPlayer	

animations/browser

c AnimationDriver

animations/browser/testing

c MockAnimationDriver	**c** MockAnimationPlayer

common/http

c HttpBackend	**c** HttpHandler	**c** HttpClient

Angular API docs have a list of
modules and the various items
that each module includes.

**Figure 1.7   Angular provides modules (like animation) that contain all the services and objects you'll
need to build your applications, but first you'll have to import them.**

Inherently, modules aren't strictly a component technology. Modules are an isolated
piece of JavaScript that can be used to generate a component, create a reusable service,
or do anything else JavaScript can do. They're fundamentally a way to encapsulate application code and choose what's available for the other parts of the application to use.

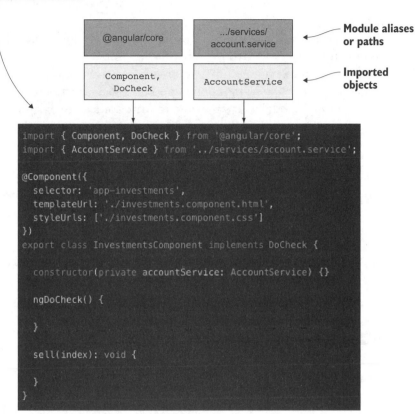

This file imports the Component,
DoCheck, and AccountService
objects from external modules.

Module aliases
or paths

Imported
objects

```
import { Component, DoCheck } from '@angular/core';
import { AccountService } from '../services/account.service';

@Component({
  selector: 'app-investments',
  templateUrl: './investments.component.html',
  styleUrls: ['./investments.component.css']
})
export class InvestmentsComponent implements DoCheck {

  constructor(private accountService: AccountService) {}

  ngDoCheck() {

  }

  sell(index): void {

  }
}
```

Figure 1.8   Loading objects into a file from different modules using imports

In JavaScript, a module is any file of JavaScript code that contains the export keyword. Modules export values that they want to expose to the application and can keep other parts of the internal logic private. Then, in order to use an exported value, you have to first import it from another module (figure 1.8).

In figure 1.8 (a snippet from a later chapter), we're first importing some things from external modules that the rest of the code in this file depends on. The Component and DoCheck objects are being imported from the @angular/core package (which is part of our node modules directory), and AccountService is being imported based on the file path provided.

These modules are powerful because they *encapsulate* the contents of a single Java-Script file into a single coherent whole. They *isolate* the code and allow the developer to conditionally export values to share. They also support *reusability* by defining common mechanics for sharing values in a JavaScript application that previously could only be done by putting values directly on the global scope or by crafting some non-standard service to manage dependency injection, as Angular 1 did.

HTML imports are a similar concept that has been proposed as part of the HTML spec, which would provide similar capabilities. But it's likely that HTML imports won't be adopted, and instead JavaScript modules are used. There are libraries that use HTML imports, such as Polymer, by using a polyfill library.

Angular itself is built entirely around the notion of modules. The source code uses them extensively. When you write your own applications, it's recommended that you also use them. Executing an Angular application is fundamentally loading a module that contains the application bootstrapping logic, which in turn starts to load and trigger additional modules. It's possible to write your Angular applications without modules using ES5 syntax, which is not recommended but discussed next.

1.6   *Modern JavaScript and Angular*

Angular is designed to take advantage of many features that are fairly recent to the web platform. Most of these became part of the JavaScript specification in 2015 with the release of ES2015 (also known as ES6, but I'll refer to its official name ES2015); other features are still in development as of this writing but are likely to be adopted in a future version.

These features are well covered in many places, so I won't go into detail. Though they could be used with AngularJS, Angular was designed to work using these capabilities. I'll cover some of the most important aspects quickly, namely the following:

- Classes
- Decorators
- Modules
- Template literals

Let's look at an example with all these features working together and then review how they're put together. The following listing is a functional but simple Angular component, and you'll get to see many more examples that use the same concepts in more complex ways in this book.

Listing 1.1   Modern JavaScript Syntax

```
import {Component} from '@angular/core';        ◄── Imports the Component object
                                                    from another module

@Component({                                     Uses a decorator to add metadata
  selector: 'my-component',                      to the MyComponent object
  template: `
<div>
  <h4>{{title}}</h4>                             Uses a template literal string
</div>                                           to write inline HTML
`
})
export class MyComponent {
  constructor() {
    this.title = 'My Component';                 Exports the MyComponent object, which
  }                                              was defined as a class
}
```

Let's start from the bottom and go from there. In ES2015, classes were introduced as a new way to define an object, which is in fact a function. Classes are used to create components, directives, pipes, and services, though they can be used in other ways as well. Using the class keyword, the class MyComponent is created and is an object that has a property called title.

Classes are syntactic sugar for creating objects in JavaScript. They don't introduce a new type of inheritance to JavaScript, which is important to remember. Developers familiar with class objects in other languages may accidentally carry over concepts into JavaScript, but in this case the concept of a class doesn't change the way prototypical inheritance works with JavaScript.

Inside of the class there's a special method called constructor(). It's executed immediately when a new copy of the object is created. As long as you name a method constructor(), it will be used during creation.

Classes are also useful because they help ensure that the keyword this references the object itself. The keyword this is a common barrier in JavaScript, and classes help ensure that it behaves more consistently.

The export keyword denotes the file as a module. Any module is isolated into a private space, and unless a value is exported, it won't be available for another file or module to use. This breaks away from the global scope that JavaScript has for values and provides a proper separation between modules. Because the MyComponent class is exported, it can be imported into another module (not shown here).

At the top of the file, the import statement imports the Component value from the angular/core module, which allows it to be used in this module.

Then in the middle we use the @Component decorator, which is a way to add metadata to the class. Decorators always start with the @ symbol, and Angular uses these decorators to understand what type of class has been declared. In this case, it's a component, and Angular will know how to render a component based on this decorator. There are several other ones, such as Injectable and Pipe, and we'll see those in action later.

Finally, the decorator accepts an object that contains the metadata associated with the component itself. In this example, it has two properties for the selector and an inline HTML template. The decorators define what properties can be passed here, but they allow you to customize the way the class is handled by Angular.

1.6.1 Observables

In addition to new syntax, *observables* are a newer pattern for JavaScript applications to manage asynchronous activities. They're also a draft for a feature to be natively implemented in the JavaScript language so it has weight behind the pattern. RxJS is the library we'll use to help us implement observables in our applications.

Promises are another construct to help deal with asynchronous calls, which are useful for making API requests, for example. Promises have a major limitation in that they're only useful for one call cycle. For example, if you wanted to have a promise return a value on an event like a user click, that promise would resolve on the first click. But you might be interested in handling *every* user click action. Normally, you'd use an event listener for this, and that allows you to handle events over time. This is an important distinction: Observables are like event handlers in that they continue to process data over time and allow you to continuously handle that stream of data.

Reactive programming is the higher-level name for what observables provide, which is a pattern for dealing with asynchronous data streams. Many things in a web application are asynchronous data streams, if you think about it. A user typing keystrokes into a form input is really a stream of individual characters. Timers and intervals generate a stream of activity over time. Websockets pass data as a stream over time. It's that simple, but the challenge can be wrapping your mind around it all.

Angular uses observable patterns often, and having a grasp of the fundamentals is useful. During the course of this book, you'll see observables in a number of places, and they all work in the same basic way. We're not going to worry about constructing observables here. Instead we'll just focus on how to use them when they're given to you.

To use observables, you subscribe to the stream of data and pass a function that will run every time there's a new piece of data. We'll see this in action in chapter 2 when we make an HTTP request, but let's look at a quick sample just to see some syntax:

```
this.http.get('/api/user').subscribe(user => {
    // Do something with the user record
}, (error) => {
    // Handle the error
})
```

This snippet is using the HTTP library to make a get request, which returns an observable. Then we subscribe to that observable, and our callback function fires when the data is returned or the error is handled. It's not very different from a promise, except that an observable could continue to send data. Let's take a different example:

```
this.keyboardService.keypress().subscribe(key => {
    // Do something with the key record
}, (error) => {
    // Handle the error
})
```

In this example, imagine keyboardService.keypress() returns an observable, and it emits details about what key was pressed. This is like an event listener, except that it comes in a stream.

Another interesting capability of observables is that they are composable into many combinations. Observables can be combined, flattened into one, filtered, and more. We'll see one example in chapter 9, where we'll combine two observable streams and handle the data they emit in one place. We'll not use many of the more complex features in this book, but you'll likely be interested in how they work, so I recommend the book *RxJS in Action* (www.manning.com/books/rxjs-in-action).

1.7   *TypeScript and Angular*

Angular itself it written with TypeScript, which is a superset of JavaScript that introduces the ability to enforce typing information. It can be used with any version of JavaScript, so you can use it with anything ES3 (that's not a typo) or newer.

The basic value proposition of TypeScript is it can force restrictions on what types of values variables hold. For example, a variable may only hold a number or it may hold an array of strings. JavaScript has types (don't let anyone tell you otherwise!), but variables aren't typed, so you can store any type of value in any variable. This also gave birth to the many types of comparison operators, such as == for loose equality or === for strict equality.

TypeScript can help catch many simple syntax errors before they affect your application. Sometimes you can write valid JavaScript, but the real world shows that valid syntax doesn't always mean valid behavior. Take this example:

```
var bill = 20;
var tip = document.getElementById('tip').value; // Contains '5'
console.log(bill + tip); // 205
```

This snippet shows a simple tip calculator example where you take the value from an input element and add it to the bill to get the total payment amount. The problem here is that the `tip` variable is actually a string (because it's text input). Adding a number and a string together is perhaps one of the most common pitfalls for new JavaScript developers, though it can happen to anyone. If you used TypeScript to enforce types, this code could be written to alert about this common error:

```
var bill: number = 20;
var tip: number = document.getElementById('tip').value; // 5, error!
var total: number = bill + tip; // error!
```

Here we're using TypeScript to declare that all these variables must each hold a number value by using `:number`. This is a simple syntax that sits inside of JavaScript to tell TypeScript what type of value the variable should hold. The `tip` value will error because it's being assigned a string, and then the total value will error because it attempts to add a number and a string type, which results in a string.

This may seem like an obvious error to a seasoned JavaScript developer, but how often do you have new developers work on your code base? How often do you refactor your code? Can you still ensure that your application is passing around the same value types as you continue to maintain the application? Without TypeScript, you're responsible for doing a strict comparator check of every value before it's used.

Many developers wonder why they should bother learning and using TypeScript. Here are the primary reasons to use TypeScript, in my humble opinion:

- *Adds clarity to your code*—Variables that have types are easier to understand, because other developers (or yourself in six months) don't have to think very hard about what the variable should be.

- *Enables a smarter editor*—When you use TypeScript with a supported editor, you'll get automatic IntelliSense support for your code. As you write, the editor can suggest known variables or functions and tell you what type of value it expects.
- *Catches errors before you run code*—TypeScript will catch syntax errors before you run the code in the browser, helping to reduce the feedback loop when you write invalid code.
- *Entirely optional*—You can use types when you want, and optionally leave them out where it doesn't matter.

I hope you're sold on the value of TypeScript. If not, I hope you'll give it a closer look during the course of the book. This book uses it in examples to help provide more clarity and to help further demonstrate the power of TypeScript. I'll try to provide additional insight into TypeScript features and functionality as we use features in the examples, but you can always learn all there is to know at www.typescriptlang.org/docs/tutorial.html.

Even if you choose not to use TypeScript for type enforcement in your application, you can use TypeScript to compile your application. Because the Angular CLI already uses TypeScript internally, you may be using it without even knowing. If you decide to build your own build tooling, TypeScript is still a worthwhile compiler option.

If you're wondering whether using TypeScript in your Angular application is required, the answer is technically no. There are ways to write your application in vanilla JavaScript and avoid TypeScript, to a certain degree. But it's intentionally not documented because there are simply too many features of Angular that don't work unless you use TypeScript. If you're afraid it will be hard to learn, don't be. It's straightforward, and in several places throughout the book I'll explain some nuances of TypeScript that you may not have seen before.

Summary

This chapter introduced you to Angular as a development platform, not just an application framework. There are so many features and capabilities with Angular. Here's a quick summary:

- Angular is a platform, with many key elements such as tooling, UI libraries, and testing built in or easily incorporated into your application projects.
- Applications are essentially combinations of components. These components build upon the core principles of encapsulation, isolation, and reusability, which should have events, be customizable, and be declarative.
- ES6 and TypeScript provide a lot of the underpinnings for Angular's architecture and syntax, making it a powerful framework without having to build a lot of custom language capabilities.

Building your first Angular app

This chapter covers

- Angular components and how they form a basis for your app

- Defining a number of types of components, using decorators

- Learning how services can be used to share data across your app

- Setting up routing to display different pages

You're going to build an entire Angular app in this chapter, starting from scratch, while learning about the primary concepts of Angular. You'll see some TypeScript features in action, as well as new and upcoming features of JavaScript.

This project will remain focused and simple, yet still be representative of many of the features you'll use in a typical app. The app you'll create is a stock tracking app, with data coming from Yahoo! Finance. It will be able to fetch current stock prices, add or remove stocks from a list, and adapt a visual display based on the current day's gains or losses.

In this chapter, we'll build this app piece by piece. We'll focus on getting through the example application with enough detail to understand the various pieces and complexity in this chapter:

- *Bootstrapping the app*—To start the app, we'll use the *bootstrap* feature to kick things off once they're loaded. This happens once during the app lifecycle, and we'll bootstrap the App component.
- *Creating components*—Angular is all about *components*, and we'll create several components for different purposes. We'll learn about how they're built and how they nest to create complex applications.
- *Creating services and using HttpClient*—For code reuse, we'll encapsulate some logic that helps manage the list of stocks into a *service* and also uses the HttpClient service from Angular to load stock quote data.
- *Using pipes and directives in templates*—Using *pipes*, we can transform data from one format into another during display, such as formatting a timestamp into a local date format. *Directives* are useful tools to modify the behavior of DOM elements inside a template, such as the ability to repeat pieces or conditionally show elements.
- *Setting up routing*—Most applications need the ability to allow users to navigate around the application, and by using the *router* we can see how to route between different components.

Using a limited amount of code, you'll be able to create a robust application that does a number of complex tasks. Subsequent chapters focus on each of the individual features in detail for a more complete picture of everything Angular has to offer.

You should be familiar with ES2015 and the newer capabilities of the JavaScript language. I won't be going into detail about the newer language constructs, such as imports or classes. I recommend spending some time reading at the Mozilla Developer Network (https://developer.mozilla.org/en-US/docs/Web/JavaScript) for more details, or pick up a book.

2.1 Previewing the chapter project

When we are done, the app should appear as you see in figures 2.1 and 2.2. We'll walk through the various pieces briefly before we build them so you'll see how they all come together.

First, there's an API that loads current stock price data from Yahoo! Finance; it's deployed on Heroku and isn't covered in this chapter, but you can view the code for the API at https://github.com/angular-in-action/api. It's a standard REST API and doesn't require authentication. We'll create a service to help us access and load data from the API.

When the app loads, it shows the dashboard page (figure 2.1) with a list of cards. Each card contains a single stock, the current price, and the day's change in price (as a currency value and as a percentage). The background of the cards will be red for negative change, green for a positive change, or gray for no change. Each of these cards is an instance of a component that takes the stock data and determines how to render the card.

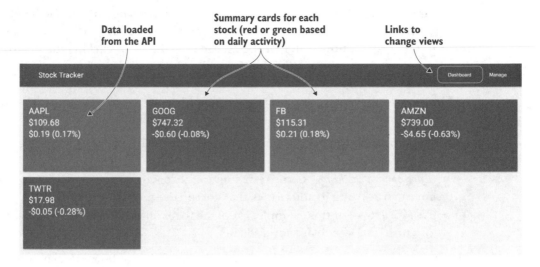

Figure 2.1 The dashboard page for the stock tracking app with links and summary cards

Lastly, the top navbar has two links, to the dashboard and manage views, which allow for general navigation between the views. We'll use the Angular Router to set up these routes and manage how the browser determines which to display.

When you click the Manage link in the navbar, you'll see the manage page (figure 2.2) with a list of the stocks. Here you can remove any of the stocks by clicking the Remove button. You can also add new stocks by typing the stock symbol into the text area and pressing the Enter key.

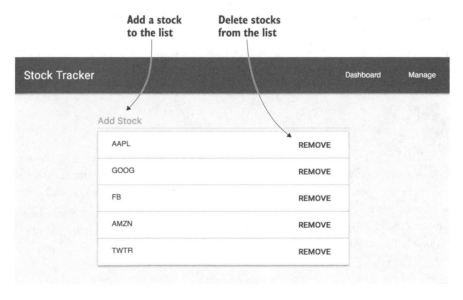

Figure 2.2 The manage page for the stock tracking app with the form to change the list of symbols to display

This page is a single component, but contains a form that's updated immediately upon changes input by the user. The list can be extended by putting a new stock symbol in the input field and hitting Enter, or the list can be reduced by clicking the Remove button. In both cases, the list of symbols is immediately changed, and if you go back to the dashboard you'll see the updated list appear.

This project has a few limitations you should be aware of. To keep the example focused and simple, there are a few details that aren't included in the app:

- *No persistence*—Anytime you refresh the app in the browser, the list of stocks resets to the default list.
- *Lack of error checking*—Some situations can throw an error or cause strange behavior, such as trying to add a stock that doesn't exist.
- *No unit tests*—For this example, I kept the focus on the code and intentionally left out unit tests, which are covered later.

This example is intended to provide you with an overview of how Angular apps can be built—not to provide a bulletproof app. I provide you a number of interesting challenges you can attempt near the end of the chapter, and there are many possible features that can be imagined.

2.2   *Setting up the project*

We'll build this example from scratch using the Angular CLI. If you ever need to look at the code for this project, it can be found on GitHub at https://github.com/angular-in-action/stocks, and each step is tagged so you can follow along using Git, or you can copy the contents from the chapter as it appears.

If you haven't set up the Angular CLI, please go back to chapter 1 and set it up. We're using the CLI version 1.5 in this book, so if you're using an older version you'll want to upgrade.

In the terminal, start from a directory that you want to generate a new project folder inside. Then you can run the following command to generate a new project, and then start the development server:

```
ng new stocks
cd stocks
ng serve
```

This will take a few moments as the CLI installs a number of packages from npm, and this depends greatly on the speed of your network and how busy the registry is. Once it has completed, you can use your browser to view the app at http://localhost:4200. You should see a simple page that says something about being a new Angular app, as shown in figure 2.3. The default content of a new project changes over time, so don't worry if it looks a little different.

Welcome to app!

Here are some links to help you start:

- Tour of Heroes
- CLI Documentation
- Angular blog

Figure 2.3   The CLI generates a blank app with some default content.

If you see a similar screen, then everything should be set up and ready to go. It's not the most exciting-looking example, but it sets up a few things for you automatically. We're now going to take a tour of what has been generated and how it works to display this simple message.

> **Keeping examples up-to-date with Angular releases**
>
> Because the book was developed to run against Angular 5 versions of code, there may be changes that happen in future versions that could cause an example in this book to fail. Don't worry—you can always visit the chapter project's GitHub page to see any notes that are added to discuss possible changes or errata, as well as view the book forum on Manning's website.

2.3   *The basic app scaffolding*

The CLI generated a new project that contains a lot of files. We'll look at the most important ones for the moment and learn more about the rest over time. It's important to note that the CLI generates files in a specific way, and making changes to file locations or names may cause the CLI to fail. For now, I recommend leaving files where they are until you're more comfortable or unless you plan to build your own tooling later. Over time, the exact files and filenames that are generated by the CLI may change, so if you have any issues, look at the CLI changelog and documentation.

The project contains several directories and files. The primary files are listed in table 2.1, along with their general roles in the application. Most of these are configuration for various aspects of the development, such as linting rules, unit test configuration, and CLI configuration.

Table 2.1   Top-level contents of the project generated by the CLI and their roles

Asset	Role
e2e	End-to-end testing folder, contains a basic stub test
node_modules	Standard NPM modules directory, no code should be placed here
src	Source directory for the application
.editorconfig	Editor configuration defaults
.angular-cli.json	Configuration file for the CLI about this project
karma.conf.js	Karma configuration file for unit test runner
package.json	Standard NPM package manifest file
protractor.conf.js	Protractor configuration file for e2e test runner
README.md	Standard readme file, contains starter information
tsconfig.json	Default configuration file for TypeScript compiler
tslint.json	TSLint configuration file for TypeScript linting rules

In this chapter, you'll only modify files that exist inside the src directory, which contains all the application code. Table 2.2 contains a listing of all the assets generated inside src. This may seem like a lot of files, but they each play a role, and if you aren't sure what one does, leave it alone for now.

Table 2.2   Contents of the src directory and their roles

Asset	Role
app	Contains the primary App component and module
assets	Empty directory to store static assets like images
environments	Environment configurations to allow you to build for different targets, like dev or production
favicon.ico	Image displayed as browser favorite icon
index.html	Root HTML file for the application
main.ts	Entry point for the web application code
polyfills.ts	Imports some common polyfills required to run Angular properly on some browsers
styles.css	Global stylesheet
test.ts	Unit test entry point, not part of application
tsconfig.app.json	TypeScript compiler configuration for apps

Table 2.2 Contents of the src directory and their roles *(continued)*

Asset	Role
tsconfig.spec.json	TypeScript compiler configuration for unit tests
typings.d.ts	Typings configuration

Now that you have a general idea of what was generated, we're going to inspect a few of the key files that comprise the application logic. The next section takes a closer look at how Angular renders the contents of the app directory into the output that you view on the screen.

2.4 How Angular renders the base application

Before we start to build our application, you need to understand how this base scaffolding works and what we'll need to add. This is a whirlwind tour to get you up and running as fast as possible, so expect more depth and nuance later in the book. In chapter 3, we'll spend more time on these topics to get a deeper understanding of how everything is constructed.

Angular requires at least one component and one module. A *component* is the basic building block of Angular applications and acts much like any other HTML element. A *module* is a way for Angular to organize different parts of the application into a single unit that Angular can understand. You might think of components as LEGO® bricks, which can be many different shapes, sizes, and colors, and modules would be the packaging the LEGOs come in. Components are for functionality and structure, whereas modules are for packaging and distribution.

2.4.1 App component

We're going to start by looking at the src/app/app.component.ts file. This contains what's called the *App component*, which is the root of the application. In LEGO® terms, you could picture this component as the big green platform you use to start building from. The following listing shows the code for the component. Again, the exact code may change over time, so don't worry if it's slightly different—it will have the same basic requirements.

Listing 2.1 Generated App component (src/app/app.component.ts)

```
import { Component } from '@angular/core';          ◄──── Import the component annotation

@Component({
  selector: 'app-root',
  templateUrl: './app.component.html',              Define the component
  styleUrls: ['./app.component.css']                and its properties
})
export class AppComponent {
  title = 'app works!';                             Create the component controller,
}                                                   with a single property
```

That listing might contain some unfamiliar syntax if you're new to TypeScript, so let's take a closer look at each section of the code. First, you import the `Component` annotation. It's used to decorate the App component by adding details that are related to the component but aren't part of its controller logic, which is the `AppComponent` class. Angular looks at these annotations and uses them with the `AppComponent` controller class to create the component at runtime.

The `@Component` annotation declares that this class is a component by accepting an object. It has a selector property that declares the HTML selector of the component. That means the component is used in the template by adding an HTML tag `<app-root>` `</app-root>`.

The `templateUrl` property declares a link to a template containing an HTML template. Likewise, the `styleUrls` property contains an array of links to any CSS files that should be loaded for this component. The `@Component` annotation can have more properties, and you'll see a few more in action in this chapter.

Finally, you see that the `AppComponent` class has a single property called `title`. The value is what you should see rendered in the browser, so this is the source of the value that ultimately appears. Angular relies greatly on ES2015 classes to create objects, and almost all entities in Angular are created with classes and annotations.

Now let's look at the markup associated with the App component by opening src/app/app.component.html, shown here:

```
<h1>
  {{title}}
</h1>
```

As you can see, this is just a simple header tag, but there's the `title` property defined between double curly braces. This is a common convention for how to bind a value into a template (perhaps you're familiar with *Mustache templates*), and it means Angular will replace `{{title}}` with the value of the `title` property from the component. This is called *interpolation* and is frequently used to display data in a template.

We've looked at the App component, but now we need to look at the App module to see how things get wired up and rendered with Angular.

2.4.2   App module

The App module is the packaging that helps tell Angular what's available to render. Just as most food items have packaging that describes the various ingredients inside and other important values, a module describes the various dependencies that are needed to render the module.

There's at least one module in an application, but it's possible to create multiple modules for different reasons (covered later). In this case, it's the App component from earlier plus additional capabilities that are needed in most applications (such as routing, forms, and HttpClient).

The CLI generated the module for us, so we can look at it in src/app/app.module.ts, as shown in the following listing. Once again, this may change over time, but the structure and purpose remain.

Listing 2.2   App module (src/app/app.module.ts)

Providers are any services used in the app.

```
import { BrowserModule } from '@angular/platform-browser';      Imports Angular
import { NgModule } from '@angular/core';                       dependencies needed

import { AppComponent } from './app.component';    ◄────── Imports the App component

@NgModule({   ◄──────────── Uses the NgModule annotation to define a module by passing an object
  declarations: [
    AppComponent          Declarations are to list any components
  ],                      and directives used in the app.
  imports: [
    BrowserModule,        Imports are other modules that
  ],                      are used in the app.
  providers: [],                                 Bootstrap declares which component to use
  bootstrap: [AppComponent]   ◄──────────────┘  as the first to bootstrap the application.
})
export class AppModule { }    ◄──┐ Exports an empty class, which gets annotated
                                 │ with configuration from NgModule
```

Just like a component, a module is an object with an decorator. The object here is called `AppModule`, and `NgModule` is the decorator. The first block is to import any Angular dependencies that are common to most apps and the App component.

The `NgModule` decorator takes an object with a few different properties. The `declarations` property is to provide a list of any components and directives to make available to the entire application.

The `imports` property is an array of other modules upon which this module depends—in this case, the Browser module (a collection of required capabilities). If you ever include other modules, such as third-party modules or ones you've created, they also need to be listed here.

The next property is the `providers` property, which is empty by default. Any services that are created are to be listed here, and we'll see how to do this shortly.

Lastly, the `bootstrap` property defines which components to bootstrap at runtime. Typically, this will be the same App component, and the CLI already set it up for us. The `bootstrap` property should match the component that you bootstrap in the next section.

We've written code that creates a configuration for Angular to look at and understand how to render. The last step to look at is the code that gets executed at launch, which is called *bootstrapping*.

2.4.3   Bootstrapping the app

The application must be bootstrapped at runtime to start the process of rendering. So far, we've only declared code, but now we'll see how it gets executed. The CLI takes care of wiring up the build tooling, which is based on webpack.

Start by taking a look at the .angular-cli.json file. You'll see an array of apps, and one of the properties is the `main` property. By default, it points to the src/app/main.ts file. This means that when the application gets built, it will automatically call the contents of the main.ts file as the first set of instructions.

The role of main.ts is to bootstrap the Angular application. The contents of the main.ts file are included in the following listing, and contain only a few basic instructions.

Listing 2.3 The main file that is called on launch (src/app/main.ts)

Imports dependencies
```
import { platformBrowserDynamic } from '@angular/platform-browser-dynamic';
import { enableProdMode } from '@angular/core';
import { environment } from './environments/environment';
import { AppModule } from './app/';

if (environment.production) {
  enableProdMode();
}
```
If production is enabled, turn off Angular developer mode.

```
platformBrowserDynamic().bootstrapModule(AppModule);
```
Bootstraps the App module

The first section imports some dependencies, particularly platformBrowserDynamic and AppModule. The name is a bit long, but the platformBrowserDynamic object is used to tell Angular which module is being loading, and in this case that's the AppModule from earlier. I cover the rendering of modules later in the book, but for now it's important to understand that this is the point where the code begins to execute.

There's one last piece to review by looking at the index.html file. If you remember from the App component code, there was a selector of app-root used to identify the component in markup. You should see the following in the src/index.html file:

```
<body>
  <app-root></app-root>
</body>
```

Once the app is bootstrapped (by the code from listing 2.3), Angular will look for the app-root element and replace it with the rendered component. That's what you end up seeing in the screen from figure 2.1, but while it's loading everything, you'll see a "Loading ..." message. It can take a moment for all the assets to load and initialize before the component renders. This is known as *Just in Time* compilation (JiT), meaning that everything is loaded and rendered on demand in the browser. JiT is only meant for development, and may be removed in future releases.

I'd like to add a couple of small touches that will help us style the rest of the application, by adding some basic CSS and markup. First we need to add two link tags to our src/index.html:

```
<link rel="stylesheet" href="//storage.googleapis.com/code.getmdl.io/1.0.1/
    material.indigo-orange.min.css">
<link rel="stylesheet" href="//fonts.googleapis.com/
    icon?family=Material+Icons">
```

This will load some font icons and the global styles for the application, which are based on the Material Design Lite project. This is one way you can load external references to style libraries or other assets.

We'd like to give our application some global styles. Add the following to the src/ styles.css file—it will give the application a light gray background:

```
body {
  background: #f3f3f3;
}
```

Lastly we want to set up some base markup to structure our application. Let's replace the content of the src/app/app.component.html file with the markup in the following listing.

Listing 2.4   Base markup scaffolding (src/app/app.component.html)

```
<div class="mdl-layout mdl-js-layout mdl-layout--fixed-header">
  <header class="mdl-layout__header">
    <div class="mdl-layout__header-row">
      <span class="mdl-layout-title">Stock Tracker</span>
      <div class="mdl-layout-spacer"></div>
      <nav class="mdl-navigation mdl-layout--large-screen-only">
        <a class="mdl-navigation__link">Dashboard</a>
        <a class="mdl-navigation__link">Manage</a>
      </nav>
    </div>
  </header>
  <main class="mdl-layout__content" style="padding: 20px;">

  </main>
</div>
```

This markup is based around the Material Design Lite design style for how to create a basic toolbar and main body. The toolbar has the title and two links (which are currently inactive), and should appear like figure 2.4.

Figure 2.4   Modified base scaffolding to have Material Design Lite markup

All right, we've created the base app scaffolding using the CLI, seen the App component, App module, and bootstrap logic, and found the markup that renders out the component. Congratulations, you've made your first Angular app! Okay, I know it isn't that impressive—yet—but this is the fundamental part of every Angular app. For the rest of the chapter, we'll take this basic application and build it up to the full stock tracking example. To get started, you'll learn about creating an Angular service that loads data from an API.

2.5   *Building services*

Services are objects that abstract some common logic that you plan to reuse in multiple places. They can do about anything you need them to do, because they're objects. Using ES2015 modules, these classes are exported, and so any component can import them as necessary. They could also have functions or even static values, like a string or number, as a way to share data between various parts of your application.

Another way to think of services is as sharable objects that any part of your app can import as needed. They're able to abstract some logic or data (such as the logic necessary to load some data from a source), so it's easy to use inside of any component.

Although services will often help manage data, they're not restricted to any particular job. The intention of a service is to enable reuse of code. A service might be a set of common methods that need to be shared. You could have various "helper methods" that you don't want to write over and over, such as utilities to parse data formats or authentication logic that needs to be run in multiple places.

In the app, you'll want to have a list of the stocks for both the dashboard and manage pages to use. This is a perfect scenario of when to use a service to help manage the data and share it across different components.

The CLI gives us a nice way to create a service that has the scaffolding we need to get started. It will generate a simple service and a test stub for that service, as well. To generate a service, you run the following:

```
ng generate service services/stocks
```

The CLI will generate the files in the src/app/services directory. It contains the most basic service, which does nothing. Let's go ahead and fill in the code for the entire service and go over how it works. You'll end up supplementing what was generated with the code from the following listing. The Stocks service will have an array that contains a list of the stock symbols and expose a set of methods to retrieve or modify the list of stocks.

Listing 2.5   Stocks service (src/app/services/stocks.service.ts)

```
import { Injectable } from '@angular/core';          Imports dependencies
import { HttpClient } from '@angular/common/http';

let stocks: Array<string> = ['AAPL', 'GOOG', 'FB', 'AMZN', 'TWTR'];
let service: string = 'https://angular2-in-action-api.herokuapp.com';

export interface StockInterface {
  symbol: string;
  lastTradePriceOnly: number;      Defines and exports the TypeScript
  change: number;                  interface for a stock object
  changeInPercent: number;
}

@Injectable()          Annotates with Injectable to
                       wire up dependency injection
export class StocksService {          Defines class and exports it

  constructor(private http: HttpClient) {}          Constructor method to inject
                                                    HttpClient service into class
                                                    http property
```

Declares a stock array and API variables

```
get() {
  return stocks.slice();
}
```
Method to get the stocks

```
add(stock) {
  stocks.push(stock);
  return this.get();
}
```
Method to add a new stock to list

```
remove(stock) {
  stocks.splice(stocks.indexOf(stock), 1);
  return this.get();
}
```
Method to remove a stock from list

```
load(symbols) {
  if (symbols) {
    return this.http.get<Array<StockInterface>>(service + '/stocks/
  snapshot?symbols=' + symbols.join());
  }
 }
}
```
Method to call HttpClient service to load stock values from API

The service first needs to import its dependencies; one is the decorator for a service, and the other is the HttpClient service. Then it declares two variables; one is to track the list of stock symbols, and the other is the API endpoint URL.

Then the StockInterface interface is defined and exported for other components to use. This provides a TypeScript definition of what a stock object should contain, which is used by TypeScript to ensure the use of the data remains consistent. We'll use this later to ensure that we're typing our stock objects correctly when they're used.

The StocksService class is exported and is decorated by the Injectable decorator. The decorator is used to set up the proper wiring for Angular to know how to use it elsewhere, so if you forget to include the decorator, the class might not be injectable into your application.

In the constructor method, the HttpClient service is injected using the TypeScript technique of declaring a private variable called http and then giving it a type of HttpClient. Angular can inspect the type definition and determine how to inject the requested object into the class. If you're new to TypeScript, keep in mind that anytime you see a colon after a variable declaration, you're defining the object type that should be assigned to that variable.

The service contains four methods. The get() method is a simple method that returns the current value of the stocks array, but it always returns a copy instead of the direct value. This is done to encapsulate the stock values and prevent them from being directly modified. The add() method adds a new item to the stocks array and returns the newly modified value. The remove() method will drop an item from the stocks array.

Finally, the load() method makes a call to the HttpClient service to load the data for current stock price values. The HttpClient service is called and returns an observable, which is a construct for handling asynchronous events, such as data from an API call. We've covered observables briefly in chapter 1 and will see them more in other chapters, but this is your first glimpse of them in action.

There is a little feature of the HttpClient that appears as part of the get() method and is put between two angle brackets:

```
this.http.get<Array<StockInterface>>(...
```

This is known as a *type variable*, which is a feature of TypeScript that allows you to tell the http.get() method what type of object it should expect, and in this case it will expect to get an array of objects that conform to the StockInterface (our stock objects). This is optional, but it's very helpful to alert the compiler if you try to access properties that don't exist.

There's one more step we have to do, because the CLI doesn't automatically register the service with the App module, and we need to register HttpClient with the application as well. Open the src/app/app.module.ts file and near the top add these two imports:

```
import { HttpClientModule } from '@angular/common/http';
import { StocksService } from './services/stocks.service';
```

This will import the Stocks service and HttpClientModule into the file, but we need to register the HttpClientModule with the application. Find the imports section as defined in the NgModule, and update it like you see here to include the HttpClientModule:

```
imports: [
  BrowserModule,
  HttpClientModule
],
```

Now we need to register the new StocksService with the providers property to inform Angular that it should be made available for the module to use:

```
providers: [StocksService],
```

Your service is wired up and ready to consume, but we haven't used it yet anywhere in our application. The next section looks at how to consume it.

This service is not too complex. It's mostly designed to abstract the modification of the array so it's not directly modified and load the data from the API. While the application runs, the stocks array can be modified, and changes are reflected in both the dashboard and manage components, as you'll see shortly. Because it's exported, it's easily imported when needed.

Now you'll create a component that uses some default directives and allow configurable properties to modify the component's display.

2.6   *Creating your first component*

You've already seen a basic component (the App component). Now you'll build a more complex component that uses some directives and pipes and has a property. We're going to create a component that displays a basic summary card of the stock price information.

This component will only receive data to display from its parent component and modify its own display based on that input value. For example, a parent component will pass along the current data for a particular stock, and the Summary component will use the daily change to determine whether the background should be green or red based on whether the stock went up or down.

The key goals of this component are to do the following:

- Accept stock data and display it
- Change background color depending on the day's activity (green for increase, red for decrease)
- Format values for proper display, such as currency or percentage values

Figure 2.5 shows the component in place, and we'll even wire it up to load the data from the API. Eventually, we'll instantiate multiple copies of this component to display a card for each of the stocks.

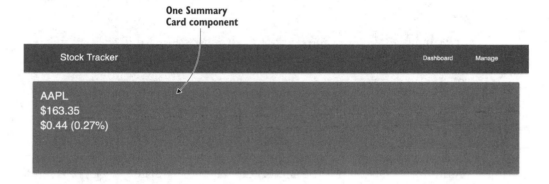

Figure 2.5 Single Summary component displaying stock data

Obviously, when you run this the stock values will change based on the latest data, but you can see the card displaying the current data. Let's dig into building this card and then we'll walk through the individual parts of how it results in this output.

Go back to the terminal and run the following:

```
ng generate component components/summary
```

The CLI will generate a new component inside the src/app/components/summary directory. We had to create the src/app/components directory first, because the CLI doesn't make new folders for you automatically if they're missing. This helps organize the components into a single directory, though you could choose to generate them elsewhere.

Now the contents of the component are pretty similar to how the App component appeared originally. It contains an empty CSS file, basic HTML template, test stub, and empty class already initialized with the component annotation.

We'll start by setting up the template for our component and then we'll create the controller to manage it. Open the src/app/components/summary/summary.component.html file and replace the contents with what you see in the following listing.

Listing 2.6   Summary component template

Uses NgClass directive to help toggle background color

Displays last price and formats it as currency

Displays the symbol value and converts to uppercase

Displays the day's change as currency and as percent

```
<div class="mdl-card stock-card mdl-shadow--2dp" [ngClass]="{increase:
    isPositive(), decrease: isNegative()}" style="width: 100%;">
  <span>
    <div class="mdl-card__title">
      <h4 style="color: #fff; margin: 0">
        {{stock?.symbol?.toUpperCase()}}<br />
        {{stock?.lastTradePriceOnly | currency:'USD':'symbol':'.2'}}<br />

        {{stock?.change | currency:'USD':'symbol':'.2'}} ({{stock?.
        changeInPercent | percent:'.2'}})
      </h4>
    </div>
  </span>
</div>
```

The template contains some markup to structure the card like a material design card. If we look at the first line, we see this snippet as an attribute on the div element:

```
[ngClass]="{increase: isPositive(), decrease: isNegative()}"
```

This is a special kind of attribute called a directive. *Directives* allow you to modify the behavior and display of DOM elements in a template. Think of them as attributes on HTML elements that cause the element to change its behavior, such as the disabled attribute that disables an HTML input element. Directives make it possible to add some conditional logic or otherwise modify the way the template behaves or is rendered.

The NgClass directive is able to add or remove CSS classes to and from the element. It's assigned a value, which is an object that contains properties that are the CSS class names, and those properties map to a method on the controller (to be written). If the method returns true, it will add the class; if false, it will be removed. In this snippet, the card will get the increase CSS class when it's positive, or the decrease CSS class when it's negative, for the day's trading.

Angular has a few directives built in, and you'll see a couple more in this chapter. Directives usually take an expression (like our object in this example), which is evaluated by Angular and passed to the directive. The expression might evaluate to a Boolean or other primitive value or resolve to a function call that would be run to return a value before the directive runs. Based on the value of the expression, the directive might do different things, such as show or hide whether the expression is true or false.

We saw an example of interpolation earlier, but we now have a more complex example that displays the symbol of the stock. The controller is expected to have a property called stock, which is an object with various values:

```
{{stock?.symbol?.toUpperCase()}}
```

The double curly braces syntax is the way to display some value in the page. This is called *interpolation*, if you'll recall from earlier, though this is a bit more complex. The content between the braces is called an *Angular expression* and is evaluated against the controller (like the directive), meaning that it will try to find a property on the controller to display. If it fails, normally it will throw an error, but the safe navigation operator ?. will silently fail and not display anything if the property is missing.

This block will display the stock symbol, but as uppercase. Most JavaScript expressions are valid Angular expressions, though some things are different, such as the safe navigation operator. The ability to call prototype methods like toUpperCase() remains, and that's how it's able to render the text as uppercase.

The next interpolation shows the last trade price and adds another feature called *pipes*, which are added directly into the expression to format the output. The interpolation expression is extended with a pipe symbol, |, and then a pipe is named and optionally configured with values separated with the colon : symbol. The price value comes back as a normal float (like 111.8), which is not the same format as currency, which should appear like $111.80:

```
{{stock?.lastTradePriceOnly | currency:'USD':'symbol':'.2'}}
```

Pipes only modify the data before it is displayed, and do not change the value in the controller. In this code, the double curly braces indicate that you want to bind the data stored in the stock.lastTradePriceOnly property to display it. The data is piped through the Currency pipe, which converts the value into a financial figure based on a USD figure, and rounds to two decimal points. Now let's look at the next line:

```
{{stock?.change | currency:'USD':'symbol':'.2'}} ({{stock?.changeInPercent |
    percent:'.2'}})
```

The next line also has two different interpolation bindings with a Currency or Percentage pipe. The first will convert to the same currency format, but the second will take a percentage as a decimal, such as 0.06, and turn it into 6%. The Angular documentation can detail all the options available and how to use them for each pipe.

This template doesn't work in isolation; it requires a controller to wire up the data and the methods. Let's open the src/app/components/summary/summary.component.ts file and replace the code, as you see in the following listing.

Listing 2.7 Summary component controller

```
import { Component, Input } from '@angular/core';    ◄— Imports the dependencies

@Component({
  selector: 'summary',
  styleUrls: ['./summary.component.css'],      Declares the component metadata
  templateUrl: './summary.component.html'
})
export class SummaryComponent {    ◄— Exports the Summary component class
```

```
@Input() stock: any;        ◄── Declares a property that is an input value

  isNegative() {
    return (this.stock && this.stock.change < 0);     Method to check if stock is negative
  }

  isPositive() {
    return (this.stock && this.stock.change > 0);     Method to check if stock is positive
  }
}
```

This controller imports dependencies, which is almost always the first block of any file written in TypeScript. The component metadata describes the selector, linked styles, and linked template files that comprise the component. We'll add some CSS to the styles in a moment.

The summary controller class starts with a property called `stock`, which is preceded with the `Input` annotation. This indicates that this property is to be provided to the component by a parent component passing it to the summary. Properties are bound to an element using an attribute, as you can see here—this example will set the value of `stockData` of the parent component in the `stock` property of the Summary component:

```
<summary [stock]="stockData"></summary>
```

Because input is passed through a binding attribute, it will evaluate the expression and pass it into that property for the Summary component to consume. Angular expressions behave the same anytime there's a binding. They try to find a corresponding value in the controller to bind to the property.

Lastly, there are the two methods for checking whether the stock value is positive or negative. The stock could also be neutral, so that's the default state, and only if the stock changes will one of the methods return `true`. These methods are used by the NgClass directive to determine whether it should add a particular CSS class, as described earlier in the template.

The final piece we want to add are the CSS classes themselves. Angular has some interesting ways to encapsulate CSS styles so they only apply to a single component. We'll dig into the specifics later, but open the src/app/components/summary/summary.component.css file and add the styles, as shown in the following listing.

Listing 2.8   Summary component CSS styles

```
:host .stock-card {              ◄──────────  Uses the :host CSS selector to narrow the specificity
  background: #333333;                        of the selector and set default background
}
:host .stock-card.increase {     ◄──  increase class defines the
  background: #558B2F;                background as green
  color: #fff;
}
:host .stock-card.decrease {     ◄──  decrease class defines the
  background: #C62828;                background as red
  color: #fff;
}
```

This is typical CSS, though you may not have seen or used the `:host` selector in the past. Because components need to be as self-contained as possible, they rely on the Shadow DOM concepts discussed in chapter 1. When Angular renders this component, it will modify the output to ensure that the CSS selector is unique and doesn't accidentally interfere with other elements on the page. This behavior is configurable, but that will be covered later.

The host selector is a way to specify that you want the styles to apply to the element that hosts the element, so in this case it will look at the Summary component element itself rather than the contents inside it. The primary purpose of the CSS here is to establish the Summary component background color.

We've walked through the Summary component generation and built out a functional component. Let's quickly use it to get a glimpse of how it behaves.

Look at the src/app/app.module.ts file and you'll see that the CLI already modified the module to include the Summary component in the App module. There's nothing to do here, but I wanted to point it out.

Now look at src/app/app.component.ts and update it to the contents of the following listing. This will include the Stocks service and use it to store the stock data onto a property. We'll then use this to display the summary card.

Listing 2.9   App component controller

```
import { Component } from '@angular/core';
import { StocksService, StockInterface } from './services/stocks.service';   ◀──
```
Imports the StockInterface

```
@Component({
  selector: 'app-root',
  templateUrl: './app.component.html',
  styleUrls: ['./app.component.css']
})
export class AppComponent {
  stocks: Array<StockInterface>;   ◀── Declares a property of an array of stocks

  constructor(service: StocksService) {
    service.load(['AAPL']).subscribe(stocks => {
      this.stocks = stocks;   ◀──────────
    });
  }
}
```
When the data loads, it will store it on the stocks property.

Here we store the loaded stock data onto a property called `stocks`. We also provide some typing information, which is imported from our Stocks service, so that TypeScript knows what kind of value to expect. Finally, instead of logging the data to the console, we store it on the `stocks` property.

Now we'll need to update the src/app/app.component.html file to use the Summary component. Here is the snippet you need to update from the template:

```
<main class="mdl-layout__content" style="padding: 20px;" *ngIf="stocks">
  <summary [stock]="stocks[0]"></summary>
</main>
```

The first line added `*ngIf="stocks"`, which is a directive that will only render the contents inside the element when the expression is true. In this case, it won't render the Summary component until the stock data has been loaded.

The middle line shows the instantiation of a single Summary component, and the first value of the `stocks` array is bound into the `stock` property. The data returns as an array, so we're directly accessing the first value. Recall the input value we declared in the Summary component, which is also named `stock`.

Once you save this and run the app, it should finally display a single summary card with the current stock data for Apple's stock. We've made our first component and displayed it inside our application!

Next you'll create another component and use it together with the Summary component to create the dashboard that displays the list of stocks and their current statuses.

2.7   *Components that use components and services*

We're ready to combine the previously created Summary component and Stocks service into a working Dashboard component. This component will comprise one entire page of the application, as you see in figure 2.6. This component will manage the loading of the data using the Stocks service and then display each stock using a copy of the Summary component.

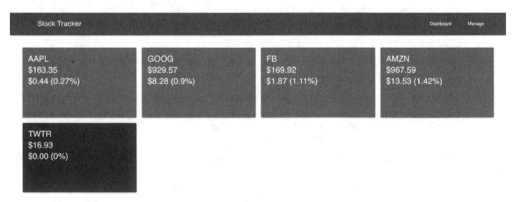

Figure 2.6   Dashboard component wired up with loading data and showing five Summary component instances

We'll see how to properly orchestrate a complete view, rather than our isolated examples so far. To get started, we can use the CLI again to generate another component:

```
ng generate component components/dashboard
```

This will output new files into the src/app/components/dashboard directory for the HTML, CSS, controller, and unit test. It also adds the component to the App module to be immediately consumable. Let's reset our working project to display this new component by modifying the src/app/app.component.html file with the content here:

```
<main class="mdl-layout__content" style="padding: 20px;">
  <dashboard></dashboard>
</main>
```

This should display the default component message in the application, since that's the default code generated by the CLI. We also need to remove some logic from the App component controller; it should now appear as you see here. This removes the imports and loading of stock data in the App component itself, and we'll put it instead into the dashboard in a moment. Replace the contents of src/app/app.component.ts with the following:

```
import { Component } from '@angular/core';

@Component({
  selector: 'app-root',
  templateUrl: './app.component.html',
  styleUrls: ['./app.component.css']
})
export class AppComponent {}
```

Great! We've now cleaned up the App component and are ready to start building out the dashboard. Our first order of business is to set up the dashboard controller. Its job is to use the Stocks service to load data and make it available for the component to consume.

Open the controller at src/app/components/dashboard/dashboard.component.ts and replace it with the code in the following listing.

Listing 2.10   Dashboard controller

```
import { Component, OnInit } from '@angular/core';              Imports
import { StocksService, StockInterface } from '../../services/stocks.   dependencies
    service';

@Component({
  selector: 'dashboard',
  templateUrl: './dashboard.component.html',        Exports the component
  styleUrls: ['./dashboard.component.css']          class, but also
})                                                  implements the OnInit
export class DashboardComponent implements OnInit {  interface
  stocks: Array<StockInterface>;
  symbols: Array<string>;    ◄── Declares a property for holding an array of stock symbols

  constructor(private service: StocksService) {     Gets the stock symbols from the service
    this.symbols = service.get();                   when the component is first constructed
  }

  ngOnInit() {                                      Implements the ngOnInit
    this.service.load(this.symbols)                 method and calls the service
      .subscribe(stocks => this.stocks = stocks);   to load stock data over Http
  }
}
```
Declares a property for holding an array of stocks

The controller starts by importing the Component annotation and the OnInit interface. If you haven't implemented an interface before, an interface is a means to enforce that a class contains a required method—in this case, the method named ngOnInit.

Leveraging TypeScript's capabilities for enforcing code typings and interfaces is helpful as projects get larger.

The DashboardComponent class is the component controller, and it declares that it must implement the requirements of OnInit. If it doesn't, TypeScript will fail to compile the code and throw an error. It then has two properties: an array of stocks and an array of strings that represent the stock symbols to display. Initially they're empty arrays, so we'll need to get them loaded for the component to render.

The constructor method runs as soon as the component is created. It will import the Stocks service onto the service property and then request the current list of stock symbols from it. This works because this is a synchronous action that loads a value directly from memory.

But we don't load data from the service in the constructor for a number of reasons. We'll dig into the complexities later in the book, but the primary reason is due to the way that components are rendered. The constructor fires early in the rendering of a component, which means that often, values are not yet ready to be consumed. Components expose a number of lifecycle hooks that allow you to execute commands at various stages of rendering, giving you greater control over when things occur.

In our code, we use the ngOnInit lifecycle hook to call the service to load the stock data. It uses the list of stock symbols that was loaded in the constructor. We then subscribe to wait for the results to return and store them in the stocks property. This uses the observable approach to handling asynchronous requests. We'll look at observables in depth later as well. Here we are using them because the HttpClient returns an observable for us to receive the response. This is exposed as a stream of data, even though it is a single event.

Now we need to complete the component by adding the template. Open the src/app/components/dashboard/dashboard.component.html file and replace it with the contents of the following listing.

Listing 2.11 Dashboard component template

```
<div class="mdl-grid">
  <div class="mdl-cell mdl-cell--12-col" *ngIf="!stocks" style="text-align:
    center;">
    Loading
  </div>
  <div class="mdl-cell mdl-cell--3-col" *ngFor="let stock of stocks">
    <summary [stock]="stock"></summary>
  </div>
</div>
```

Use NgIf to show a loading message until stocks have loaded.

Use NgFor to loop over each stock.

Instantiate a Summary component for each stock and pass that stock data.

The template has some classes to use the Material Design Lite UI framework for a grid structure. The template contains another NgIf attribute to show a loading message while the data is loaded, like we used earlier. Once the stock data has returned from the API, the loading message will be hidden.

Then we see another element that has a new directive, NgFor. Like NgIf, it starts with an *, and the expression is similar to what you would use in a traditional JavaScript for loop. The expression contains let stock of stocks, which means that it will loop over each of the items in the stocks array and expose a local variable by the name of stock. Again, this is the same kind of behavior that you would see in a JavaScript for loop, but applied in the context of HTML elements.

NgFor will then create an instance of the Summary component for each of the stock items. It binds the stock data into the component. Each copy of the Summary component is distinct from the others, and they don't directly share data.

You've now completed the dashboard view, which uses a service and another component to render the experience. When you run the application now, you should see the five default stocks appearing as separate cards in the page. The grid layout should lay them out in four columns.

Next you'll build a new component that has a form that manages the list of stock symbols to use when displaying the stocks.

2.8 Components with forms and events

We want to manage the stocks that are displayed, so we'll need to add another component that has a form to edit the list of stocks (figure 2.7). This form will allow users to input new stock symbols to add to the list and will have a list of the current stocks with a button that will remove a stock from the list. This list of stocks is shared throughout the entire application, so any changes will replicate elsewhere.

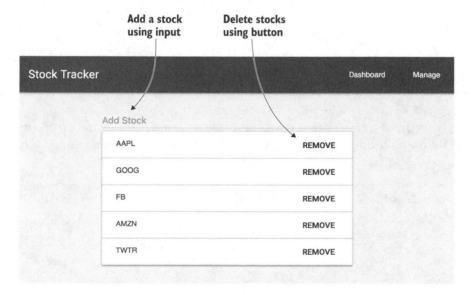

Figure 2.7 Manage component with a form to add an item and buttons to remove existing stocks

Forms are essential in applications, and Angular comes with built-in support for building complex forms with many features. Forms in Angular are comprised of any number of *controls*, which are the various types of inputs and fields the form may contain (such as a text input, a checkbox, or some custom element).

Let's start by generating a new component for the manage view. Using the CLI, run the following command, and remember, this will also automatically register the component with the App module so it's ready to consume:

```
ng generate component components/manage
```

Now update the src/app/app.component.html file and change the content of the main element, as you see in the following code, so the Manage component will display in the application. Then when you run the application, it will display the default message you see with any new component:

```
<main class="mdl-layout__content" style="padding: 20px;">
  <manage></manage>
</main>
```

We also need to add the `FormsModule` to our application, because we are going to use the form features that aren't automatically included by Angular. Open up the src/app/app.module.ts file and add a new import:

```
import { FormsModule } from '@angular/forms';
```

Then update the imports definition of the module to declare the `FormsModule` like you see here:

```
imports: [
  BrowserModule,
  HttpClientModule,
  FormsModule,
],
```

Let's start making our Manage component by updating the controller with some logic. In figure 2.7, you'll see we need to load the list of symbols stored in memory. There will also need to be two methods: one to handle the removal of a stock and another to add a new stock symbol to the list.

Open src/app/components/manage/manage.component.ts and update it to match the following listing. This will comprise the additional methods and setup required for this view.

Listing 2.12   Manage component controller

```
import { Component } from '@angular/core';          Imports
                                                    dependencies
import { StocksService } from '../../services/stocks.service';

@Component({
  selector: 'manage',
  templateUrl: './manage.component.html',           Declares component metadata
  styleUrls: ['./manage.component.css']
})
export class ManageComponent {          Defines class and two properties
  symbols: Array<string>;               for storing the array of symbols
                                        and a string for input
```

```
stock: string;

constructor(private service: StocksService) {
  this.symbols = service.get();
}

add() {
  this.symbols = this.service.add(this.stock.toUpperCase());
  this.stock = '';
}

remove(symbol) {
  this.symbols = this.service.remove(symbol);
}
}
```

Gets the current list of symbols during class instantiation

Method to add a new stock to the list

Method to remove a stock symbol from the list

As usual, we start by importing dependencies for the component. Then the component metadata is declared using the @Component annotation. The class object is then declared, which contains two properties: the first is the array of symbols that's retrieved from the Stocks service, and the second is a property to hold the value of the input. We'll see how the stock property is linked to the input field in the template, but this is where it's first defined.

The constructor uses the service to get the array of stock symbols and store it on the symbols property. This doesn't require the OnInit lifecycle hook, because it's a synchronous request to get data that exists in memory.

Then we have the two methods to add or remove the symbols from the list. The service always returns a copy of the stocks symbol array, so we have to use the service methods to manage the list (which is encapsulated inside the service and isn't directly modifiable). The add method will add a new item to the list of symbols, and then store the modified list onto the symbols list. Conversely, the remove method will remove the item from the array and refresh the symbols list in the controller.

This controller satisfies our needs for handling the actions of the form, but now we need to create the template to display the form and its contents. Open src/app/components/manage/manage.component.html and add the contents from the following listing.

Listing 2.13 Manage component template

Two-way binding for the symbol input box

```
<div class="mdl-grid">
  <div class="mdl-cell mdl-cell--4-col"></div>
  <div class="mdl-cell mdl-cell--4-col">
    <form style="margin-bottom: 5px;" (submit)="add()">
      <input name="stock" [(ngModel)]="stock" class="mdl-textfield__input"
  type="text" placeholder="Add Stock" />
    </form>
    <table class="mdl-data-table mdl-data-table--selectable mdl-shadow--2dp"
    style="width: 100%;">
      <tbody>
        <tr *ngFor="let symbol of symbols">
```

Binds the submit event to call the add method

Loops over symbols list with NgFor

Displays the ——▶
symbol

```
                <td class="mdl-data-table__cell--non-numeric">{{symbol}}</td>
                <td style="padding-top: 6px;">
                    <button class="mdl-button" (click)="remove(symbol)">
        Remove</button>                ◀——  Binds the click event on the button
                </td>                          to call the remove method
              </tr>
            </tbody>
          </table>
        </div>
        <div class="mdl-cell mdl-cell--4-col"></div>
      </div>
```

In this template there's a decent amount of markup only for the grid layout. Any class that starts with mdl- is part of the styles provided by Material Design Lite's grid and UI library.

The first interesting section is the form, which has a new type of attribute we haven't seen before. The (submit)="add()" attribute is a way to add an event listener, known as an *event binding*. When the form is submitted (which is done by pressing Enter), it will call the add method. Any attribute that's surrounded by parentheses is an event binding, and the name of the event should match the event without the *on* (onsubmit is submit).

The form contains a single input element, which has another new type of attribute. The [(ngModel)]="stock" attribute is a two-way binding that will sync the value of the input and the value of the property in the controller anytime it changes from either location. This way, as the user types into the text field, the value will be immediately available for the controller to consume. When the user hits Enter, the submit event fires and will use the value of the stock property when adding the new symbol. I cover form concepts in greater detail later, but this is your first preview of how a simple form is constructed.

The next section loops over the list of symbols using NgFor. I covered how this works earlier, so I won't go into detail. For each symbol, it will create a local variable called symbol, create a new table row that binds the value, and a button that's for removing the item.

The remove button contains another event binding, this one to handle the click event. The (click)="remove(symbol)" attribute adds an event listener to the click event and will call the remove method in the controller, passing along the symbol. Because there are multiple instances of the button, each one passes along the local variable to know which symbol to remove.

The last task is to add routing to the application to activate routes for the two views to act like two different pages.

2.9   *Application routing*

The final piece of the application is the *routing*, which configures the different pages that the application can render. Most applications need some form of routing so it can display the correct part of the application at the expected time. Angular has a router that works well with the Angular architecture by mapping components to routes.

The router works by declaring an outlet in the template, which is the place in the template that the final rendered component will be displayed. Think of the outlet as the default placeholder for the content, and until the content is ready to be displayed, it will be empty.

To set up our routes, we'll link the Manage and Dashboard components to two routes. We'll handle the configuration ourselves, because the CLI doesn't support setting up routes in this particular release. To begin, create a new file at src/app/app.routes.ts and fill it with the code from the following listing.

Listing 2.14   App routing configuration

```
import { Routes, RouterModule } from '@angular/router';        ◄─── Imports router dependencies

import { DashboardComponent } from './components/dashboard/dashboard.
    component';
import { ManageComponent } from './components/manage/manage.component';

                                                              Imports App components
                                                              that are linked to a route

const routes: Routes = [
  {
    path: '',
    component: DashboardComponent
  },                                    Defines a route configuration array
  {
    path: 'manage',
    component: ManageComponent
  }
];

export const AppRoutes = RouterModule.forRoot(routes);    ◄─── Exports the routes for use
```

This file's main purpose is to configure the routes for the application, and we start by importing the RouterModule and the Route type definition. The RouterModule is used to activate the router and accepts the routes configuration when it's initialized. We also import the two routable components, the Dashboard and Manage components, so we can reference them properly in our routes configuration.

The routes are defined as an array of objects that have at least one property—in this case two, for a URL path and a component. For the first route, there's no path, so it acts as the application index (which will be http://localhost:4200) and links to the Dashboard component. The second route provides a URL path of manage (which will be http://localhost:4200/manage) and links to the Manage component. This is the most likely type of routing that you'll do with Angular, though there are many ways to configure and nest routes.

Finally, we create a new value AppRoutes, which is assigned to the result of RouterModule.forRoot(routes). We'll dig further into how the forRoot method behaves later, but it's a way to pass configuration to the module. In this case, we're passing the array of routes. We export this so we can import it into our App module and register it.

Open the src/app/app.module.ts file and add a new line at the end of the imports that imports the AppRoutes object you created in the previous file:

```
import { AppRoutes } from './app.routes';
```

Now update the `imports` property of your module to include the `AppRoutes` object. This will register the Router module and our configuration with our application:

```
imports: [
  BrowserModule,
  HttpClientModule,
  FormsModule,
  AppRoutes
],
```

The final step is to declare a place for the router to render, and update the links to use the router to navigate. Open the src/app/app.component.html file one last time and make a few modifications. First you'll change the contents of the main element to have a different element, the router outlet:

```
<main class="mdl-layout__content" style="padding: 20px;">
  <router-outlet></router-outlet>
</main>
```

This declares the specific location in the application that the router should render the component. It's the same place that we've put our components while building them, so it should make sense that this is the best place.

Then we need to update the links to use a new directive that will set up the navigation between routes. The RouterLink directive binds to an array of paths that are used to build a URL:

```
<nav class="mdl-navigation mdl-layout--large-screen-only">
  <a class="mdl-navigation__link" [routerLink]="['/']">Dashboard</a>
  <a class="mdl-navigation__link" [routerLink]="['/manage']">Manage</a>
</nav>
```

The directive parses the array and tries to match to a known route. Once it matches a route, it will add an `href` to the anchor tag that correctly links to that route.

The router is capable of more advanced configuration, such as nested routes, accepting parameters, and having multiple outlets. I cover the router in more detail in chapter 7.

Now your project is complete, and you can reload the application in the browser to see it running, as previewed earlier. Congratulations! You've got a working Angular app running, and now you can try to make it do some more things.

Summary

Congratulations on making it through a functional Angular app! We went through a lot of Angular features quickly, but you should now have an understanding of how various parts are assembled into an app. Here is a quick recap of the primary takeaways:

- Angular apps are components that contain a tree of components. The root app is bootstrapped on page load to initialize the application.
- A component is an ES6 class with an `@Component` annotation that adds metadata to the class for Angular to properly render it.

- Services are also ES6 modules and should be designed for portability. Any ES6 class could be used, even if it isn't specifically meant for Angular.
- Directives are attributes that modify the template in some way, such as NgIf, which conditionally shows or hides the DOM element based on the value of an expression.
- Angular has built-in form support that includes the ability to automatically validate, group, and bind data with any form control, as well as use events.
- Routing in Angular is based around paths mapping to a component. Routes will render a single component, and that component will also be able to render any additional components it needs.

App essentials

This chapter covers the essentials of Angular applications so that you can understand how everything fits together. It will be a good reference for the fundamentals.

It is focused on concepts, and there are no coding projects. You may be eager to jump into coding, and I certainly understand that. I recommend you take the time to read this chapter in its entirety, but you can also start by skimming the first couple paragraphs of each section.

While in college, I studied abroad in Germany and was fortunate enough to do some traveling. I took a number of tours, but two I remember well were a tour of some salt mines in southern Germany and a tour of the Uffizi Museum in Florence, Italy. I learned a lot of interesting facts about salt mines, but I had no real background in mining. On the other hand, I had been taking an art history class, which made the experience of the Uffizi Museum far more satisfying.

I hope you went through chapter 2, which provides a hands-on tour of Angular, because I'll use it as a reference as we talk about application essentials. It probably felt a bit like the salt mine tour, where you ran through it quickly and saw some interesting things. Now I'm going to fill in the backstory to give you a more complete picture of Angular so you can have your own Uffizi experience.

Chapter 2 may have seemed fairly easy, or it might have been a challenge to keep everything straight. As with most technologies, there are a lot of potential things to learn, but most aren't the things you'll use on a regular basis. I've had my moments of clarity and confusion with Angular, and most often the problem is that I was fixating on too many things at once instead of focusing on the core problem and building up from there.

Based on that experience, I'm going to walk you through key aspects of the chapter 2 app in greater detail and talk about the core concepts in play. I'll layer on a few more concepts that will ultimately give you a more holistic picture of your Angular application and how it's rendered to the screen.

Figure 3.1 shows the stock application from chapter 2. If you want to see the example in action again, go to https://angular-in-action.github.io/stocks/. You probably recall some of the things used to generate this application, which include several components, a service, directives, and more. Let's look at these entities in Angular and better understand their roles.

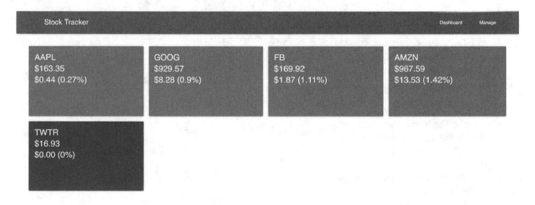

Figure 3.1 Stock app from chapter 2, which we'll use to describe Angular concepts in more detail

3.1 Entities in Angular

Angular has several top-level types of entities, all of which you saw in chapter 2. But we didn't give them a lot of attention in the context of how they are bundled and rendered into the application.

These different entities have specific roles and capabilities, and you'll be using them in various combinations to create your application. Here is a quick overview of the types:

- *Modules*—Objects that help you to organize dependencies into discrete units
- *Components*—New elements that will compose the majority of your application's structure and logic
- *Directives*—Objects that modify elements to give them new capabilities or change behaviors
- *Pipes*—Functions that format data before it's rendered
- *Services*—Reusable objects that fill niche roles such as data access or helper utilities

For the most part, everything you write in Angular will fall into one of these five types (okay, I'm sure there are some exceptions). Looking at our stock application from chapter 2, we can see how these different entities came into play. Figure 3.2 outlines the basic relationship of the entities and how they ultimately fit together.

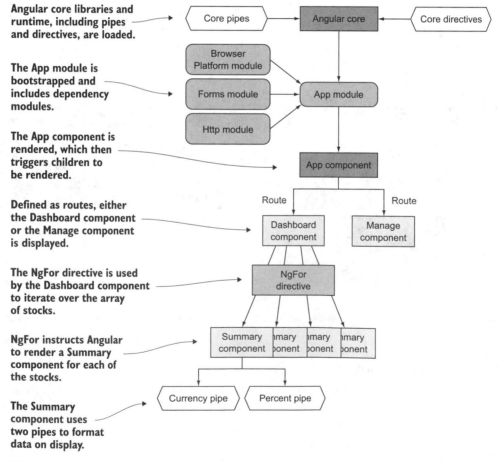

Figure 3.2   The entities and how they are leveraged during the application execution

As you can see, all these entities are ultimately merged into one application and are what generate the resulting user experience. I'll refer to these types of entities often, so let's dive a little deeper into each one.

3.1.1 Modules

Modules are buckets for storing related entities for easy reuse and distribution. Angular itself is composed of several modules, and any external libraries that you consume will also be packaged as modules.

There are two kinds of modules in Angular, and we need to clarify the difference. There are JavaScript modules (specifically modules added to the language in ES2015, and not other module systems like CommonJS and AMD), and then there are Angular modules.

JavaScript modules are language constructs and are a way to separate code into different files that can be loaded as needed. We leverage JavaScript modules heavily in our code, but they are not Angular modules. Every TypeScript file we wrote in chapter 2 was a JavaScript module because it either imported or exported some values.

Whereas JavaScript modules are language constructs, Angular modules are logical constructs used for organizing similar groups of entities (such as all things needed for the router) and are used by Angular to understand what needs to be loaded as well as what dependencies exist. Recall from chapter 2 that your application has an App module that holds a reference to all the application logic for Angular to render. There must always be an App module, but there will likely be additional modules in your application—either official Angular modules, third-party ones, or other ones you may create.

A module is declared by creating a class and decorating it with the @NgModule decorator. The following listing shows the module we created for the chapter 2 stocks example.

Listing 3.1 App module from chapter 2

```
@NgModule({          ◄──── Decorates using @NgModule
  declarations: [
    AppComponent,          Defines array of components
    SummaryComponent       and directives
  ],
  imports: [
    BrowserModule,         Defines array of
    FormsModule,           modules to import
    HttpModule
  ],                                              Defines array of
  providers: [StocksService],   ◄───────────     services to load
  bootstrap: [AppComponent]  ◄─────────────────
})                                                 Defines array of components
export class AppModule { }   ◄──── App module class   to bootstrap on startup
```

This module declaration was generated by the CLI for us (though we could have written it ourselves), and it provides key pieces of information to Angular so it can understand how to render and load the application. The @NgModule decorator contains the metadata for the App module, and the empty class acts as the vessel for storing the data.

The `declarations` array contains a list of all components and directives that the application's main module wants to make available to the entire application. Likewise, the `providers` array contains a list of all of the services that you want to make available to the whole application.

The `imports` array contains a list of the other modules that this module depends upon. If you're having trouble with another module not loading, this is the first place to check to see if it's being registered with Angular.

To start rendering, Angular also needs to know what component(s) to render on the screen, and it looks at the `bootstrap` array for this list. Almost always, this will only contain one component, but in some rare cases you may need to render multiple components on load.

There are a few additional properties you don't see listed here, but they're less commonly used. I'll cover them as they become relevant for our use cases.

3.1.2   Components

Understanding components is vital to understanding Angular, as understanding words is vital to language. We'll be focusing on the role and design of components in this section before we dive into the technical implementation details.

A *component* is an encapsulated element that maintains its own internal logic for how it desires to render some output, such as our Summary component from chapter 2. In HTML, a select element can be considered a component. Using Angular, we create our own HTML elements using components, though they are more than that. Components can have any number of capabilities or properties that you define.

As a review, here are the key principles of a component discussed in chapter 1, where we saw some of the web technologies that make it possible to build components. These principles focus on the way that components are best designed and how they behave in Angular:

- *Encapsulation*—Keep component logic isolated
- *Isolation*—Keep component internals hidden
- *Reusability*—Allow component reuse with minimal effort
- *Event-based*—Emit events during the lifecycle of the component
- *Customizable*—Possible to style and extend the component
- *Declarative*—Component used with simple declarative markup

Components may not implement all of these principles, but they should certainly be a guidepost for your thinking. It also helps to keep track of how components relate to one another—you can nest multiple components together to compose a more complex interaction.

Let's take an example of a login form using only HTML elements. You start any form with the `form` element that wraps the entire form structure. This gives context to the rest of the elements inside the form, but it doesn't provide any UI elements for the user to interact with. For that, we'd need to use a text input for the username, a password input for the password, and some kind of button to trigger the form action. In figure 3.3 we have a basic example of a form from Facebook™ that contains these elements.

Figure 3.3 Login form on Facebook that has several nested elements to produce a single form

Form events are provided access to the values of the inputs inside the form. This is like the Angular notion of data binding, where values from one element are connected to another. Then the form has a submit button, which when clicked triggers the submit event for the form.

This should be pretty standard HTML, but now let's look at a combination of Angular components in a similar arrangement. In chapter 2, we had a Dashboard component that contained multiple instances of the Summary component. In figure 3.4, I've outlined the two types of components.

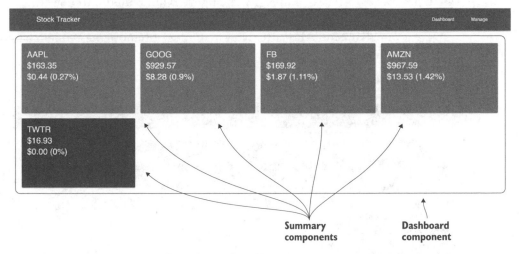

Figure 3.4 Nested components from chapter 2 dashboard screen

The Dashboard component holds the data for all the stocks and binds that information into the individual Summary components. Each Summary component uses the provided stock data to display itself. Any changes in the dashboard data will cause the child Summary components to be updated.

The basic interaction of components is to push data down from parent components, usually through binding, and back up, usually through events. There are other ways for components to communicate (something I cover in more detail later), but much of your time working with Angular will be composing trees of components into a meaningful interface.

3.1.3 Directives

Angular favors putting logic and capabilities straight into the HTML markup of the application, and directives are a powerful tool to teach HTML elements new skills.

You likely have used jQuery plugins in the past to enhance existing elements with new behaviors. There are endless plugins to turn regular elements into slideshows, tabs, and other things. The way these plugins work is that they take an existing element and apply new capabilities, such as making an image open up in a modal window.

Similarly, directives can take a normal element and give it additional capabilities that don't exist naturally. Imagine you're building a form in which it's important that the user doesn't accidentally click any links to navigate away. You could create a directive that can disable links depending on whether the user has started to use the form or if they've completed it, and internally it would modify the anchor link to disable the `href` and therefore the clickability of the link.

Let's look back to chapter 2 again and see how we used different directives to give regular elements new skills. Figure 3.5 shows the directives used on the dashboard view, which has NgFor, NgClass, and NgIf. The figure is annotated with how these directives changed the element behavior.

Here is one that adds a directive that will render or remove the element based on the value inside the attribute value (known as an expression):

```
<div *ngIf="!stocks">
```

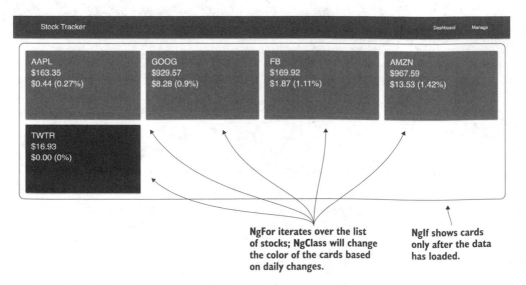

Figure 3.5   Directives used in chapter 2 stock application

The *ngIf is the directive, which is applied as an attribute to the element, and it will evaluate the value it's assigned to (more on this later in section 3.6). In this case, if the expression is truthy, it will render the element—otherwise it will remove it from the DOM. NgIf gives an element the ability to conditionally render or be removed, which is possibly the most common use of JavaScript on the web.

There are three categories of directives: attribute directives, structural directives, and components. We already talked about components, and it should make sense how a component adds new capabilities to HTML, making it also a directive. But components are special because they're the only type of directive with a template, and therefore I suggest thinking of them as their own type of entity.

Attribute directives are like our earlier example, where they modify the appearance or behavior of an element. The NgClass directive is one such example provided by Angular out of the box, which we saw in chapter 2. There are a number of built-in attribute directives, so you won't necessarily have to build many of your own. Typically, they work by changing the various properties of the element they are associated with, such as the NgClass directive changing the list of classes attached. Most directives are attribute directives.

On the other hand, structural directives modify the DOM tree based on some conditions. In chapter 2 we also saw NgIf as a way to conditionally display a DOM element, and NgFor as a way to iterate over a list of items and display them. There are fewer of these types of directives built into Angular because they're versatile. They work by adding or removing DOM elements to or from the page.

We used three directives in chapter 2, as outlined in figure 3.5. NgIf was used to hide the cards list until the data had loaded. NgFor was used to loop over each stock and create N number of copies. Then NgClass was used to change the card background, depending on the positive or negative change for the stock price. But we didn't go into detail about some of the other directives.

The primary default directives provided by Angular consist of the following (there are also some provided by the Forms and Router modules):

- *NgClass*—Conditionally apply a class to an element
- *NgStyle*—Conditionally apply a set of styles to an element
- *NgIf*—Conditionally insert or remove an element from the DOM
- *NgFor*—Iterate over a collection of items
- *NgSwitch*—Conditionally display an item from a set of options

Without directives in the stock application, we would have to write JavaScript that would dynamically create multiple summary cards, and that gets harder to manage over time. Directives make life much easier because they modify an element to give it a new capability, without having to use JavaScript to reach into the template and modify it on the fly. We don't have to use something like jQuery to modify the DOM and put our logic in an external, dissociated location.

3.1.4   *Pipes*

Often you want to display data in a different format than the format it's stored in. Typically, you want to have a date stored as a timestamp value, but that's not particularly user-friendly. Using pipes, we can transform the data in the view during rendering without changing the underlying data value.

Pipes are added into template expressions using the pipe character (|). For example, you could have an expression that looks like this:

```
{{user.registered_date | date:'shortDate'}}
```

The expression on the left side remains the same as we've seen throughout the chapter, but the addition of the pipe on the right side then applies a transformation to the value of the expression. In this case, it will use the Date pipe to format the user's registration date. It also takes an option; a colon (:) denotes that the following value is passed to the pipe as a configuration option. In this example, you're passing a configuration option that formats the date according to the format of 'shortDate', which I'll cover shortly.

In the stock app, we used the Currency and Percent pipes to display content. Figure 3.6 points out the pipes used.

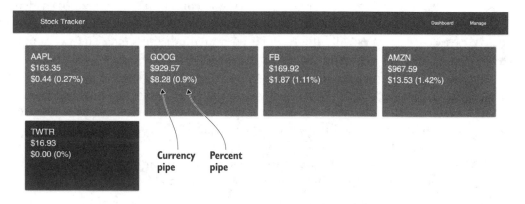

Figure 3.6   Pipes used by the stock application

Angular comes with a set of default pipes that cover a number of common use cases. The default pipes are always available and don't need to be injected or imported, so we can use them in our templates. Pipes are used by adding the pipe character and the name of the pipe.

Using a pipe changes the way the data is rendered, but it doesn't change the value of the property. It creates a copy of the output, modifies it, and displays the resulting value. For example, the price for the FB stock is stored as a number, but when rendered, a copy of that value is converted to a string and formatted as a currency.

I like to create my own pipes to handle formatting whenever possible. This helps because the logic is easy to reuse and keeps code out of the component controller.

Anytime you're doing any kind of formatting of data, you should consider whether it can be a pipe. You'll likely only create a handful of pipes, because they tend to be reusable and easily shared.

3.1.5 Services

The last primary entity type is services, which are a way to reuse functional pieces of JavaScript logic across your application. Developers often need to write some code that does repetitive tasks, and we don't want it to be duplicated all around. Sometimes these services are a gateway to access data (such as we built in chapter 2), and other times they're more like helper functions, like custom sorting algorithms. I'll talk more in depth in section 3.4 about dependency injection to explain how these services are made available and shared.

Angular provides a number of services out of the box, and many third-party modules will also expose services. In chapter 2, we built a service that also used the Angular Http service to request data—we created a wrapper around the Angular service to make it easier for us to use in our application. Let's take another look at this code snippet in the following listing, though it has been simplified to highlight the use of the HttpClient service.

> **Listing 3.2   Stock service, simplified**

```
import { Injectable } from '@angular/core';        Imports dependencies
import { HttpClient } from '@angular/common/http';

let service: string = 'https://angular2-in-action-api.herokuapp.com';

@Injectable()
export class StocksService {
                                                    Injects the HttpClient
  constructor(private http: HttpClient) {}   ◄──── service into the controller

  load(symbols) {
    if (symbols) {
      return this.http.get(service + '/stocks/snapshot?symbols=' +
      symbols.join());
    }
  }
}
```

The load() method returns an
Http service call to load data.

In this example, I've removed some of the extra code that isn't related to using the HttpClient service. First HttpClient is imported to the file and then it's injected into the StocksService through the controller. These are the steps to make a service consumable by your objects in Angular. For example, the same two steps would apply if this were a component controller.

The load() method uses the HttpClient service to make a GET request, but it constructs the proper URL to call, making it easier to consume elsewhere in the application. Services are ideal for placing this type of logic that simplifies the usage of code and makes it possible to reuse.

Services are also the ideal place for data access, and component controllers aren't. The principle of separation of concerns applies in Angular, and keeping individual entities focused on a single set of tasks is important for maintainability and testability. Make services that do one thing well.

I often write services for anything that isn't inherently linked to the component controller, or that can be easily abstracted externally to the component. Sometimes I may only use a service in one place, but it helps better organize logic and intent for my code as well as help focus the testing. If at any point in the future I need to reuse that service, it's ready to go. I find it's easier to write another service than it is to over-engineer an existing service.

Now that we have a grasp of the primary entities in Angular, we can talk about how they all get combined during the rendering of the application.

3.2   *How Angular begins to render an app*

The Angular CLI generates a fairly simple app that displays a single message on the screen, as we saw in chapter 2. A number of things come together to make that simple message appear, and though we quickly covered how the app runs, we need to spend more time and dig into the details.

In Angular, the CLI generates a fairly lightweight app. It could be slightly smaller, but it's easiest to consider the generated app as the base for future development, and I'll often refer to it as the *base app*. We'll focus on the app that's generated when you run `ng new app-name`.

Angular has an app bootstrapping mechanism that kicks off the rendering. Figure 3.7 shows the primary entities involved in the bootstrapping process and rendering of the content that gets displayed based on the base app.

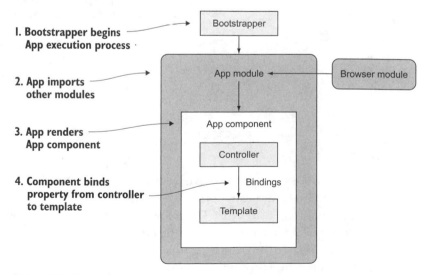

Figure 3.7   **How Angular renders the base app into the browser**

Immediately upon loading the page, the bootstrapper is called to begin Angular execution. You may be asking yourself, how does the bootstrap begin? The CLI uses webpack to build, and it compiles all the JavaScript and adds it as script tags to the bottom of the index.html on build. (You can learn more about webpack at https://webpack .github.io/ if you're curious about the way it compiles.) This is when it will run the code to begin your app.

Now that Angular has started, it loads your App module and reads through any additional dependencies that need to be loaded and bootstrapped. In the base app, the Browser module is loaded into the application before further execution happens.

Then Angular renders the App component, which is the root element of your application. As this App component renders, any child components are also rendered as part of the component tree. This is like the DOM tree, except any special Angular template syntax has to be rendered by Angular. As it renders, it will also resolve bindings and set up event listeners for anything that declares it. Once this has been completed, the full application should be rendered out and available for the user to begin interacting with.

The lifecycle of the application continues as the user begins to use the application, and the application will begin to react. As a user navigates around, the components on the screen will be removed, and new components will get loaded and rendered. The cycle of reacting to the user and rendering the component tree continues until the application is closed.

Figure 3.7 doesn't look closely at how a tree of components becomes the application, which we'll see in more detail in chapter 4.

3.3 *Types of compilers*

Angular provides two types of compilers, called the Just-in-Time (JiT) compiler and the Ahead-of-Time (AoT) compiler. The primary difference is the tooling and timing for the compiler, and that can change the way your application behaves and how it's served to the user.

With JiT compilation, it means that the compiling of the application happens in the browser only after the assets have all been loaded. That means there will be a lag between initially loading the page and being able to see the content. You saw that in the chapter 2 example, because there is a fairly basic "loading" message displayed until everything is ready and the compiler has run.

AoT, on the other hand, is a way to render the content before sending it to the browser. This means the user will be sent exactly what's needed to display the content without any kind of loading message once the application assets have loaded.

The other big difference is that with JiT, the application must also load the compiler library before the application can execute, whereas the AoT version is able to drop this payload from being sent, causing a faster load experience.

With AoT, we have the ability to perform a number of interesting optimizations, because the application is compiled before serving. The other possibility it provides is server-side rendering for applications, which can be useful for pre-rendering applications with user-specific data.

You should work to ensure your applications compile with the AoT compiler, because anytime you build your application for production it will use the AoT compiler. It is possible that in future releases of Angular, the JiT compiler may be removed entirely once AoT compilation is fast enough for development.

We'll use JiT for all development in this book because it's much faster to render and preview the application. We'll also cover how to set up AoT compilation and reap the benefits when we build the application for production purposes.

3.4   *Dependency injection*

All but the most basic code relies on using objects from other parts of the application. The problem is that the larger your code base becomes, the harder it is to ensure that individual parts are encapsulated while still being easy to access. Therefore, many programming languages or frameworks have some mechanism to facilitate tracking and sharing objects.

There are many approaches to structuring your code in a way that allows you to easily share objects. *Dependency injection* (DI) is a pattern for obtaining objects that uses a registry to maintain a list of available objects and a service that allows you to request the object you need. Rather than having to pass around objects, you can ask for what you need when you need it.

You may be wondering how this is different from using JavaScript module imports and exports. Why do we need another method to pass code around when JavaScript now has modules? Dependency injection shouldn't be confused with JavaScript module imports. There is a need for Angular to be able to keep track of what parts of the application need a particular service. JavaScript has no awareness of how dependencies are linked together, which can be useful information in understanding how to best assemble dependencies. Also, injecting a dependency with Angular will resolve any additional dependencies.

There are a few key pieces to the DI system. The first is the *injector*. This is the service that Angular provides for requesting and registering dependencies. The injector is often at work behind the scenes, but occasionally is used directly. Most of the time, you'll invoke the injector by declaring a type annotation on the property. You may recall from chapter 2 how we injected the HttpClient service like this:

```
constructor(private http: HttpClient) {}
```

Because we declare the type as `HttpClient` (which is a known service in Angular), the application will use the injector to ensure that the `http` property contains an instance of the HttpClient service. This seems like magic, but it's merely a way to alias the dependency you would like to request without directly calling the injector API.

The second part of DI is *providers*. Providers are responsible for creating the instance of the object requested. The injector knows the list of available providers, and based on the name (which above is HttpClient), it calls a factory function from the provider and returns the requested object.

Anything that has been registered with an NgModule's `providers` array is available to be injected in your application code. You can inject anywhere, but I prefer to use the TypeScript approach, as we saw earlier, where the constructor properties are annotated with the specific type of service to inject. Alternatively, you could use the `@Inject` decorator to inject the Http service, like this:

```
constructor(private @Inject(HttpClient) http) {}
```

This decorator wires up the dependency injection the same way as the TypeScript typing information. Either way you'll get the same result.

Providers don't have to be exposed to the root module and instead can be made visible only to a particular component or component tree. We'll look at how this works in more detail in chapter 6, but for now know that there's a lot of power that can be harnessed with DI.

Let's now take a look at how Angular knows about changes in the application and how that results in re-rendering the application.

3.5 Change detection

Simply put, *change detection* is the mechanism for keeping data and the rendered views in sync with one another. Changes always come down from the model into the view, and Angular employs a unidirectional propagation of changes from parents down to children. This helps ensure that if a parent changes, any children are also checked, due to potential linked data.

Angular will run a change detection process to check whether values have changed since the last time the process ran. JavaScript has no guaranteed way to notify about any change to an object, so Angular runs this process instead. It may sound heavy to be running these checks, but there are a number of optimizations that allow this to occur in a few milliseconds.

To make this happen, Angular creates a special class, known as a *change detector*, when it renders a component. This class is in charge of keeping track of the state of the component data and detecting whether any values have changed between the times the change detection ran.

When a value change is detected in a component, it will update the component and potentially any child components as well. Also, because Angular applications are component trees, Angular can determine which components might be impacted by the change and limit the work involved.

Angular has two ways for changes to be triggered. The Default mode will traverse the entire tree looking for changes with each change detection process. The OnPush mode tells Angular that the component only cares about changes to any values that are input into the component from its parent, and gives Angular the ability to skip checking the component during change detection if it already knows the parent hasn't changed.

Change detection is triggered by either events, receiving HTTP responses, or timers/intervals. The best way to think of it is that anytime something asynchronous occurs, the change detection process begins to determine what may have changed, because synchronous calls are already handled during the normal rendering flow of Angular. Think of it like this: You can turn on your car, but until you put it in gear, push the pedal, or brake, the vehicle is in an idle state, waiting for the driver to give it something to do.

If we go back to how the component trees are designed, you'll remember how the tree pushes data down to children and events bubble data up. Change detection is the mechanism that allows components to be updated when data changes in a parent component, and ensure views and data are in sync.

3.6 *Template expressions and bindings*

A component always has a template, and therefore it's a logical place to start our deep dive into how templates shape the behavior of your application. Unlike many other approaches to building web applications, Angular allows the placement of logic and customization directly into the template, which allows for more declarative templates. This may feel a bit strange to you at first, but I have found it to be an elegant way to design applications. There are certainly some pitfalls that may arise, but keep an open mind and see how it can be embraced with Angular. Sometimes people think this is mixing presentation and business logic, which is true to some degree, but it allows us to write much cleaner code.

A template by itself is regular HTML, but with a few Angular capabilities that HTML markup takes on a whole new life. A template can leverage values stored in the controller inside the template logic. We saw a few templates in chapter 2, and they demonstrated several concepts:

- *Interpolation*—Displaying content in the page
- *Attribute and property bindings*—Linking data from the component controller into attributes or properties of other elements
- *Event bindings*—Adding event listeners to elements
- *Directives*—Modifying the behavior or adding additional structure to elements
- *Pipes*—Formatting data before it's displayed on the page

Throughout the template you'll see template *expressions*. These are like normal JavaScript expressions (any statements you could conclude with a semicolon), and all values resolve against the component controller. There are some additional features and limitations that template expressions have when compared to expressions in JavaScript:

- They're unable to reach globals, such as `console` or `window`.
- They can't be used to assign values to variables (except in events).
- They can't use the `new`, `++`, `--`, `|`, and `&` operators.
- They provide new operators: `|` for pipes and the Elvis operator `?.` for allowing null properties.

Template expressions are used in three places: for interpolation, property bindings, and event bindings. Interpolation bindings, like the examples we've seen so far in this section, are shorthand for property bindings.

Let's imagine we have a controller, and it has a `user` property and a `save` method. In the page, we'd want to display the user's name and profile image and have a form so they could update their details. The basics would look something like figure 3.8. We'll use this example to discover how data flows from the controller into a template, or how events flow up from the template to the controller.

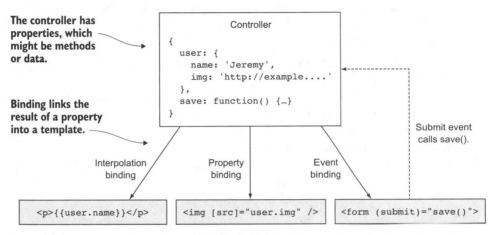

Figure 3.8 How a controller binds data into a template for interpolation, property, and event bindings, each using a different syntax

Bindings are the conduit for data or methods to be used from a controller in the template; they allow data in the controller to flow into the template, or events to call from the template back into the controller.

Let's go through a bit more detail on bindings and template capabilities Angular provides, and then we'll see how they get applied to our chapter example.

3.6.1 Interpolation

Interpolation is probably the most used type of template syntax in Angular. We used it several times in chapter 2, but didn't dig deeper into how it works. Interpolation resolves a binding and displays the resulting value as a string in the page.

The binding works by taking an expression, evaluating it, and replacing the binding with the result. This is similar to how a spreadsheet can take a formula (such as adding the values of a column of cells), calculate the resulting value (by resolving the formula against the data stored in the spreadsheet), and then display the value in that cell (in place of the formula). Here is our interpolation example:

```
<p>{{user.name}}</p>
```

Interpolations always use the {{value}} syntax to bind data into the template. It's a familiar pattern for anyone who has used mustache templates, as anything between the double curly braces is evaluated to render some text. Here are some additional valid interpolation expressions that bind values into the view:

```
<!-- 1. Calculates the value of two numbers, adds to 30 -->
{{10 + 20}}
<!-- 2. Outputs a string "Just a simple string" -->
{{'Just a simple string'}}
<!-- 3. Binds into an attribute value, to link to profile -->
<a href="/users/{{user.user_id}}">View Profile</a>
<!-- 4. Outputs first and last name -->
{{user.first_name}} {{user.last_name}}
<!-- 5. Calls a method in the controller that should return a string -->
{{getName()}}
```

The first two expressions evaluate simple values. Most of the time, though, you'll be referencing a value from the component to display or evaluate, as you see in the five examples in the preceding code. These expressions are evaluated within the context of the component, meaning your component controller should have a property called user and a getName() method. The expression context is how the view resolves what a particular value refers to, so {{user.name}} is resolved based on the user.name property from the controller, as demonstrated in figure 3.8.

Next we'll take a look at property bindings and how they're used to modify properties of elements that we want to make dynamic in some way.

3.6.2 Property bindings

In addition to interpolation, another binding type is *property bindings*, which allow you to bind values to properties of an element to modify their behavior or appearance. This can include properties such as class, disabled, href, or textContent. Property bindings also allow you to bind to custom component properties (called *inputs*—covered in much greater detail in chapter 4). For example, if you load a record from the database that contains a URL to an image, you can bind that URL into an img element to display that image:

```
<img [src]="user.img" />
```

In fact, interpolation is shorthand for binding to the textContent property of an element. They can both accomplish the same thing in many situations, so you can choose to use whichever feels most natural.

The syntax for property bindings is to put the property onto the element wrapped in brackets ([]). The name should match the property, usually in camel case, like textContent. We can rewrite the interpolation template to use property bindings like this:

```
<p [textContent]="user.name"></p>
```

Interpolation is a shortcut for a property binding to the textContent property of an element.

As with interpolation, the bindings are evaluated in the component context, so the binding will reference properties of the controller. Here you have the [src]="user.img" property binding, which does the same thing as src="{{user.img}}". Both will evaluate the expression to bind the value to the image src property, but the syntax is different. Property bindings don't use the curly braces and evaluate everything inside the quotes as the expression. I almost always use property bindings over interpolation when binding data into properties.

To restate: interpolation is a shortcut for a property binding to the textContent property of an element. We could rewrite our interpolation example like this:

```
<p [textContent]="user.name"></p>
```

This results in the same output of rendering the user's name in this case, but doing it this way isn't common because it makes it harder to create longer text strings. Also, most developers will find the interpolation version to be more readable and concise. This might give you a new appreciation for how interpolation works, because under the hood, interpolation evaluates its own binding this way.

Using the [] syntax binds to an element's property, not the attribute. This is an important distinction, because properties are the DOM element's property. That makes it possible to use any valid HTML element property (such as the img src property). Instead of binding the data to the attribute, you're binding data directly to the element property, which is quite efficient.

Note that sometimes properties are in camel case even if the HTML attribute isn't. For example, the rowspan attribute for table cell elements is exposed as the rowSpan property for the element. If you did interpolation, you could use rowspan="{{rows}}"; if you did property binding, you would have to use [rowSpan]="rows". I know it can be a little confusing, so when you're debugging bindings, be sure to check that the names match.

3.6.3 Special property bindings

There are a couple of special property bindings for setting a class and style property for an element. They are both different from many properties that you typically bind to, because these properties contain a list of classes or styles, instead of setting a single property, and Angular has a special syntax for setting these properties.

The class property on an element is a DOMTokenList, which is a fancy array. You can do [class]="getClass()" and it will set a string of class or classes, but this will mess with any of the classes on the element if they're already set. Often you'll want to toggle a single class, which you can do by using a [class.className] syntax in the property. It will see the class. prefix for the property binding and know you are binding a particular class called className. Let's see an example and how it is rendered:

```
<!-- isActive() returns true or false in order to set active class -->
<h1 class="leading" [class.active]="isActive()">Title</h1>
<!-- Renders to the following -->
<h1 class="leading accent">Title</h1>
```

The class binding syntax is useful for targeting specific classes to be added or removed from an element. It also only adds to the existing classes instead of replacing them entirely, like if you use [class]="getClass()".

Likewise, the `style` property is a `CSSStyleDeclaration` object, which is a special object that holds all the CSS properties. Angular has the same type of syntax for style binding to set individual style properties. Using `[style.styleName]` you can set the value of any valid CSS style. For example

```
<!-- getColor() returns a valid color -->
<h1 [style.color]="getColor()">Title</h1>
<h1 [style.line-height.em]="'2'">Title</h1>
<!-- Renders to the following -->
<h1 style="color: blue;">Title</h1>
<h1 style="line-height: 2em;">Title</h1>
```

Any valid CSS property can be used here, and it will render the binding as a `style` value directly on the element. Did you notice the second example has a third item, `.em`? For properties that accept units, you can use this syntax to declare the unit for the value that is returned by the expression. You can also leave it off and have the expression return the unit.

I find these special bindings to be most useful in simple or edge cases where I need to make a simple change. I usually use NgClass or NgStyle, because if you're trying to change multiple classes or style rules on the same element, this syntax becomes cumbersome.

3.6.4   *Attribute bindings*

Some element properties can't be directly bound, because some HTML elements have attributes that aren't also made available as properties of the element. The `aria` (accessibility) attributes are one such example of an attribute that doesn't get added as a property to the element.

You can always inspect an element in the developer tools to see the available properties. That's the fastest way to verify if you can bind to a particular attribute or not. Once you've verified that the attribute isn't exposed as a property, you have an alternative syntax that Angular supports to bind to those attributes.

`aria` attributes are used to indicate information to assistive devices about elements, such as `aria-required`, which marks an input as required for submission. Normally, you'd use an attribute like this:

```
<input id="username" type="text" aria-required="true" />
```

Imagine that this field might not always be required, because your form may require giving a username or an email, depending on the situation. If you try to do `aria-required="{{isRequired()}}"` or `[aria-required]="isRequired()"`, you'll get a template parsing error. Because this attribute isn't a property, it can't be directly bound to.

The workaround is using the special attribute binding syntax, which looks like a property binding, except you put the name of the attribute in the brackets with the prefix `attr.`, like this:

```
<input id="username" type="text" [attr.aria-required]="isRequired()" />
```

Angular will now bind to the attribute and not the nonexistent property. There aren't many attributes that aren't also properties, but if you come across a template parse error that your binding isn't a known native property, you're probably binding to one of these attributes.

There aren't too many situations where you'll need to use attribute bindings, but it's likely that you'll need them occasionally.

3.6.5   Event bindings

So far, all data has flowed from the component into the template elements. That's great for displaying data, but we need some way for the elements in our template to bind back into the component. The good news is that JavaScript has a great mechanism built in to pass data back up, by using *events*.

When people use applications, they generate all kinds of events as they interact with them. Any time they move the mouse, click, type, or touch the screen, they generate events in JavaScript. You've probably written event listeners before, and we'll use Angular's event bindings to do the same thing. You can also create your own events and fire them as needed.

First let's take some general use cases to understand the use cases for event bindings. When a user is logging into your app, they fill in their login credentials and submit the form (usually by hitting Enter or clicking a button). The event is the *form submit*, and you then want that event to trigger some behavior in your component. Traditionally, you would create an event listener that listens to the form submit event, but with Angular we can create a binding that will call a method on the component controller to handle the event (figure 3.9).

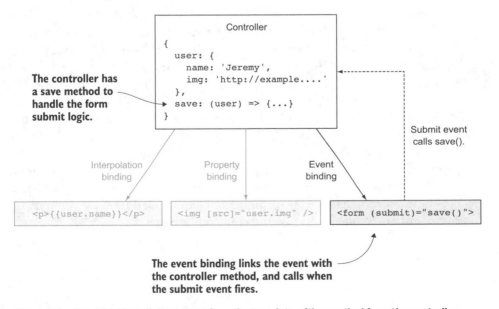

Figure 3.9   Event bindings link an event from the template with a method from the controller.

The syntax for event bindings uses parentheses () to bind to a known event. You will use the name of the event inside the parentheses, without the *on* part of the name. For an example form submit event, you would write it like this:

```
<form (submit)="save()">...</form>
```

This will create an event listener on the form that will call the save() method in the component controller when the form is submitted. The context is important because the event binding only binds up to the current component, but you can trigger events and those will bubble up to parent elements and components if they're listening. If you need a reference of available standard events in HTML, https://developer.mozilla .org/en-US/docs/Web/Events is an excellent reference. Chapter 4 goes into more depth about events.

Components and directives can emit their own events, and you can listen to those events. Chapter 4 looks at how to do this in detail, but let's also look at an example from chapter 2. In the manage view, we had a form that let you add a new stock. Here's the form again:

```
<form style="margin-bottom: 5px;" (submit)="add()">
  <input name="stock" [(ngModel)]="stock" class="mdl-textfield__input"
     type="text" placeholder="Add Stock" />
</form>
```

There are two parts: the form element that has the submit event binding and the input that holds the data the user inputs via the keyboard. When the user hits the Enter key, the form submit event fires, calling the add() method in the controller. The method looks at the value from the input box and adds the stock to the list. This was all triggered by the submit event.

We also see a special binding syntax here: the two-way binding approach. It uses both the property and event binding syntax together, which Angular likes to call *banana in a box* (it does kind of look like that if you type [()] and use your imagination). Those familiar with AngularJS will be familiar with how it allows you to sync the value of a binding as it changes in either the template or the controller. It does this by doing a regular property binding and setting up an event binding for you behind the scenes. You can only use NgModel with form elements, but you can use two-way binding syntax on properties. Generally, you will want to limit the use of this two-way binding for when it's absolutely needed.

Event bindings are important to the way components and templates communicate, as well as to how components can communicate with one another. The syntax and concepts of event bindings are fairly simple, but can be used in more complex orchestrations to enhance communication between components.

Summary

We've covered a lot of ground with Angular essentials in this chapter. This chapter should act as a helpful reference for the remainder of the book. The primary take-aways are as follows:

- An Angular application is a tree of components, and there is always a root application component.
- The various entity types (modules, components, directives, pipes, services) each have a specific role and purpose.
- Angular has two types of compilers, Ahead-of-Time (AoT) and Just-in-Time (JiT), to give you different ways to render the application.
- Dependency injection is fundamental for Angular to track all the objects in the application and make them available when they're requested.
- Change detection keeps the components in sync with the model data as asynchronous changes occur from user input or other events.
- Templates contain several types of bindings: interpolation for displaying data, property bindings for modifying the element's properties, attribute bindings for modifying non-property values of an element, and event bindings for handling events.

Component basics

This chapter covers

- The basics of components and their role

- The `@Component` decorator and its most important properties

- Rendering a component

- Passing data into and out of a component using inputs and outputs

- Customizing components with templates and styling

- Injecting content into a component using projection

Components are so central to how Angular applications are structured that almost every feature is somehow linked to them. It's impossible to make an Angular application without a component, after all. This means being able to harness the capabilities of components is vital to any developer. They are so important, I've dedicated the next chapter to additional, more advanced topics involving components.

You saw a couple of components in action in the chapter 2 examples, but in this chapter we'll start with the basics of components to ensure that you have a clear overview of how they're declared and designed. We'll then look at some of the additional capabilities of components that you'll use most frequently.

A component includes a template, which is the HTML markup used to describe its visual layout and behavior. We'll look at how to make the most of these templates, understand how they're rendered, and give them individual stylings.

A component also creates a view, which is the rendered result of a component that the user can interact with and is comprised of rendering the component template. Templates may include references to other components, which will trigger them to also be rendered as part of the rendering of the parent component. As discussed in chapter 3, an Angular application is a tree of components that all start with the App component.

During this chapter, we'll build a realistic-looking dashboard that contains several components, and we'll use mock data to simplify the implementation and focus purely on the components themselves. Let's set up the example.

4.1 Setting up the chapter example

We'll be making a tree of components in this chapter, and the components will have various means by which they communicate and share information. In addition to the App component, we'll create seven (yes, seven) other components. You can see the visual output of the application in figure 4.1, where each type of component is identified.

As you can see, this is a fictional dashboard for a data center, which shows two clusters (with three nodes each) at the bottom and the combined metrics of CPU and memory usage. All the data is generated randomly every 15 seconds, but it will also change color from green to red as usage reaches higher than desired levels. There is also a Reload button at the top right that will generate a new set of data so you can see the components update their behaviors.

Because an Angular application is a tree of components, we can visualize the relationships of the components, as you see in figure 4.2. This is important to consider because although components are declared independently from one another, they build upon one another to create the overall application and experience for users.

This tree shows the relationship between the components, where a line points to a child component. Two components in this tree have dotted lines to them—they're dynamically created in the page on demand and aren't always present. The Nodes Detail component has six dotted lines, because any of the Nodes Row components can trigger it to display.

We'll look at parts of the component tree again later to see how the various components communicate. The way the HTML elements are nested is directly related to the way Angular will instantiate and render them, so it should be fairly natural for anyone who writes HTML to understand how this tree is built.

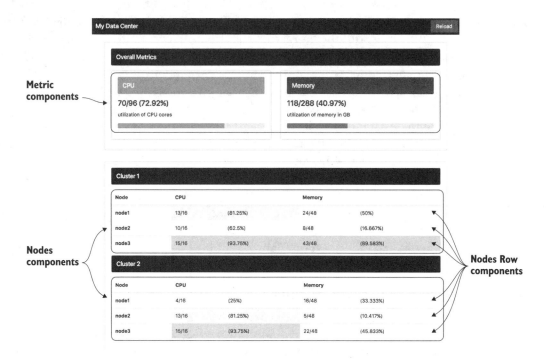

Figure 4.1   The completed application with the three component types noted

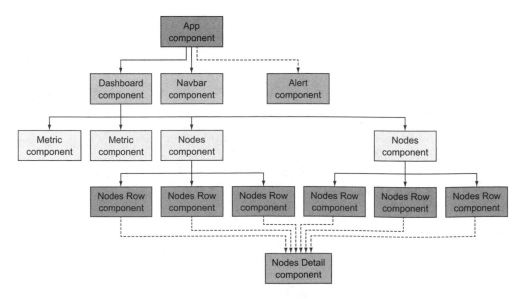

Figure 4.2   Component tree showing relationships between instances of each component

4.1.1   Getting the code

To get started, we're going to get the code from GitHub so we can get the correct setup ready. You can clone the repo using `git` by running the following command:

```
git clone -b start https://github.com/angular-in-action/datacenter.git
```

Alternatively, you can download it from https://github.com/angular-in-action/data-center/archive/start.zip.

Open the directory and make sure you run `npm install` to get all the dependencies. This may take a moment, but then you should be able to view the app by running `ng serve`.

This chapter will use the ng-bootstrap project, which can be found at https://ng-bootstrap.github.io. This is an implementation of the popular Bootstrap CSS and component framework with Angular. We'll use only a small portion of the available UI library, but it's a popular option and will give you insight into how it could be used for your own projects.

We already have a rudimentary Navbar component that displays the top menu. When you view the app running, the result should be a gray navbar sticking to the top of the page like you see in figure 4.3.

Figure 4.3   Navbar for the application with Reload button

That gets us to the point where we have a basic functioning app with one component displaying. Let's step back and talk a little bit about the lifecycle and role of components in our application before we build our next step.

4.2   Composition and lifecycle of a component

Components have a lifecycle that begins with their initial instantiation, and continues with their rendering until they're destroyed and removed from the application. Before we can understand the lifecycle, we should look more closely at what goes into a component.

The composition of components is important to master over time to create more complex and efficient Angular applications. I have seen large, real-world Angular applications with hundreds to thousands of components, and the quality of those applications is largely a byproduct of how well the components are designed.

Components have several distinct parts that are combined to create the resulting UI that the user can interact with, displayed in figure 4.4.

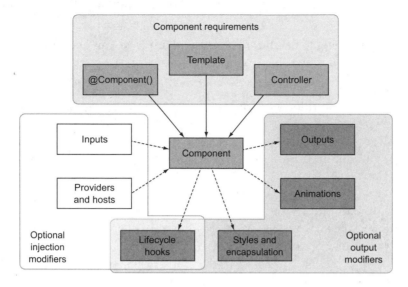

Figure 4.4   Concepts that compose and influence a component's behavior

When we generate a component with the CLI, it creates a set of files that contain assets that are combined during rendering. Here's a list of the primary things that compose a component:

- *Component Metadata Decorator*—All components must be annotated with the @Component() decorator to properly register the component with Angular. The metadata contains numerous properties to help modify the way the component behaves or is rendered.

- *Controller*—The controller is the class that is decorated with @Component(), and it contains all the properties and methods for the component. Most of the logic exists in the controller.

- *Template*—A component isn't a component without a template. The markup for a component defines the layout and content of the UI that a user can see, and the rendered version of the template will look at the values from the controller to bind any data.

These three pieces must exist for any component to be valid. Additionally, there are some optional capabilities that can ride alongside components to enhance them in certain situations. The first two are concepts that inject values into the component, and the rest are concepts that modify the resulting component behavior, appearance, or interaction with other components:

- *Providers and hosts*—Services can be injected directly into a component if they're not already provided at the root module level. You also have some control over how these services are discovered and where they are made available.

- *Inputs*—Components can accept data being passed to them using the component inputs, which make it possible for a parent component to bind data directly into a child component, which is a way to pass data down the component tree.
- *Styles and encapsulation*—Optionally, components can include a set of CSS styles that are meant to apply only to the component. This provides a layer of encapsulation for the design of components, because component styles don't have to be injected globally. Components can configure the way that styles are injected and encapsulated into the application.
- *Animations*—Angular provides an animation library that makes it easy to style component transitions and animations that plug into the template, and can define keyframes or animation states to toggle between.
- *Outputs*—Outputs are properties that are linked to events that can be used to listen for data changes or other events that a parent component might be interested in, and can also be used to share data up the component tree.
- *Lifecycle hooks*—During the rendering and lifecycle of a component, you can use various hooks to trigger application logic to execute. For example, you can run initialization logic once during the instantiation of the component and tear down logic during the destruction. You can also use these hooks to bring data into the component, so lifecycle hooks work well with both inputs and outputs.

There are a few more capabilities that aren't covered here, but you can always find them in the documentation, and we will use them in situations that call for them. You can find details by reviewing the additional @Component decorator properties in the documentation at https://angular.io/api/core/Component.

Now that you know what comprises a component, we can more easily look at the lifecycle of a component and see how they're rendered on the screen.

4.2.1 Component lifecycle

Components have a lifecycle from creation to removal, and understanding that flow will help you design quality components. There can be slight variances in how a component's lifecycle behaves depending on the build tooling used, but in most cases that tooling will be the Angular CLI.

> **A word about build tooling**
>
> The Angular CLI isn't the only way to build your Angular applications—you could roll your own build tooling. In addition, there's more than one module loader that you could use with Angular (such as webpack or SystemJS). This means not all applications are built the same.
>
> All the concepts in this book assume you'll use the Angular CLI's approach for building the application. If you do your own tooling, you may change the way your application works to some degree.

In figure 4.5, you see the primary phases that happen during a component's lifecycle. The first major action is that a component is registered with the App module. This usually happens because we declare a component as part of the NgModule metadata and occurs during application bootstrap, but components could also be registered dynamically on the fly later while the application is running. When the component is registered, it creates a component factory class and stores it for later use.

Then, during the application lifecycle, something will request the component. This is typically because the component was found in a template and the compiler needs the component, but sometimes components are also requested manually. At this point, an instance of the component needs to be loaded. There is a registry of components that belong to the module, and Angular will look up the component in question and retrieve its component factory, which is generated during the compilation using the CLI before the app is run. This special class knows how to instantiate a new instance of the component.

As the component is instantiated, the metadata is read and the constructor method is fired. Any construction logic will run early in the component's life, and you should be careful not to put anything that might depend on child components being available, because the template won't have been parsed yet.

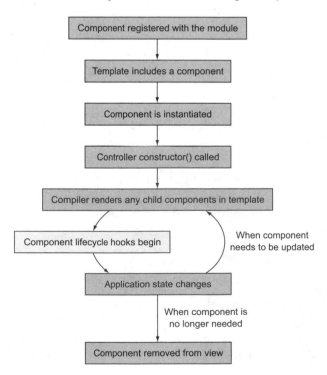

Figure 4.5   Component lifecycle while the application is running

The component metadata will then be fully processed by Angular, including the parsing of the component template, styles, and bindings. If the template contains any child components, those will kick off the same lifecycle for those components as well, but they won't block this component from continuing to render.

At this point, we've initialized the component, and a cycle begins where the child components become fully rendered, application state changes, and components are updated. During this cycle, lifecycle hooks will fire to alert you to important times when you'll know it's safe to do certain actions. For example, there's a lifecycle hook that lets you know when any of the inputs have changed; another lets you know when all the child components have fully resolved (in case you have logic that depends on them to run).

At some point, the component may no longer be needed in the application. At that point, Angular will destroy the component (and all of its children). Any new instances will need to be recreated from the component factory class, as we saw earlier.

4.2.2 Lifecycle hooks

During the application rendering process and reaction to user inputs, various hooks can be used to run code at various checkpoints. These hooks are useful when you need to know that certain conditions are true before executing the code, such as ensuring that child components have been initialized, or when changes are detected.

In chapter 2, we saw the `OnInit` lifecycle hook in action. It runs early in the cycle but after all bindings have been resolved, so it's safer to know that all data is available for the component.

Angular will only run a lifecycle hook if it's defined in the component. Lifecycle hooks aren't like event listeners—they're special methods with specific names that are called during the component's lifecycle if they're defined.

The lifecycle hooks are all named as you see in table 4.1, but when you implement the hook in your controllers, you prefix it with `ng` as well. `OnInit` needs to be implemented as the `ngOnInit()` method.

Table 4.1   List of lifecycle hooks and their roles

Lifecycle hook	Role
OnChanges	Fires any time the input bindings have changed. It will give you an object (`SimpleChange`) that includes the current and previous values so you can inspect what's changed. This is most useful to read changes in binding values.
OnInit	This runs once after the component has fully initialized (though not necessarily when all child components are ready), which is after the first `OnChanges` hook. This is the best place to do any initialization code, such as loading data from APIs.
OnDestroy	Before a component is completely removed, the `OnDestroy` hook allows you to run some logic. This is most useful if you need to stop listening for incoming data or clear a timer.

Table 4.1   List of lifecycle hooks and their roles *(continued)*

Lifecycle hook	Role
DoCheck	Any time that change detection runs to determine whether the application needs to be updated, the DoCheck lifecycle hook lets you implement your own type of change detection.
AfterContentInit	When any content children have been fully initialized, this hook will allow you to do any initial work necessary to finish setting up the content children components, such as if you need to verify whether content passed in was valid or not.
AfterContentChecked	Every time that Angular checks the content children, this can run so you can implement additional change detection logic.
AfterViewInit	This hook lets you run logic after all View Children have been initially rendered. This lets you know when the whole component tree has fully initialized and can be manipulated.
AfterViewChecked	When Angular checks the component view and any View Children have been checked, you can implement additional logic to determine whether changes occurred.

The OnInit, OnChanges, and OnDestroy hooks are the most commonly used lifecycle hooks. The DoCheck, AfterContentChecked, and AfterViewChecked hooks are most useful to keep track of logic that needs to run during any change detection process, and respond if necessary. The OnInit, AfterContentInit, and AfterViewInit hooks are primarily useful to run logic during the component's initial rendering to set it up, and each one ensures a different level of component integrity (such as it's ready or if the child components are also ready).

You may be wondering about the differences between a Content Child and View Child. Let's briefly talk about how components are nested and how that impacts the rendering of a component.

4.2.3   *Nesting components*

Because Angular is a tree of components, you'll be nesting components inside one another. There are two ways to nest components and they're named differently based on how they're rendered. Take a look again at the chapter example in figure 4.1, and you'll see how components are nested inside one another to create a more complex interface.

Most often, components are nested by being declared in the template of another component. Any component that's nested inside another's template is called a *View Child*, so named because the template represents the view of the component and therefore is a child inside that view. A View Child is declared inside the component template.

Occasionally a component accepts content to be inserted into its template, and this is known as a *Content Child*, so named because these components are inserted as content inside the component rather than being directly declared in the template. A Content Child is declared between the opening and closing tags when a component is used.

Let's take an example to be sure we can see the difference. Imagine we have a UserProfile component with the following template:

```
<user-avatar [avatar]="avatar"></user-avatar>
<ng-content></ng-content>
```

The first line is using a component, UserAvatar, which is a View Child. Notice how it's declared in the template of the component. Then there's this NgContent element—which I cover in more detail later, but suffice it to say it's a place to render additional content. Any component passed in through NgContent would be considered a Content Child. When we use the UserProfile component, its use would look something like this:

```
<user-profile [avatar]="user.avatar">
  <user-details [user]="user"></user-details>
</user-profile>
```

When we use the UserProfile component, we're passing another component, UserDetails, into the component by declaring it between the opening and closing tags. This is how a Content Child is passed into a component and then is put where the NgContent element sits in the UserProfile component.

In our example here, we had two nested components, UserAvatar as a View Child and UserDetails as a Content Child. The distinction is where they're declared and has nothing to do with the component design themselves.

Generally, the code of a single component should focus on its own business and not have to worry a lot about child components (of either type). But there are some use cases where you'll build a component that needs to distinguish between these types of components and its children. The concern is always making components too coupled, but sometimes it's unavoidable or even desirable (such as a Tabs and Tab component working together to make a tabbed interface), so this distinction can be important.

Now that we've covered a lot of the high-level concepts behind components, we can get back to our example. The next step is to create our second component and get some data generated to display.

4.3 Types of components

Fundamentally there's only one type of component, but I like to think about components as four categories, based on their roles. All components are declared and function in fundamentally the same way, but they can be instantiated differently, may or may not contain state, or have coupling to other aspects of the application that make them distinct from other components.

I think these classifications are useful to describe the roles of components and give general guidance about how they should be designed. This shouldn't be considered a rigid set of rules to follow—you'll certainly build components that don't fit perfectly into these guidelines, and that's perfectly acceptable. Keep these ideas in the back of your mind, and I believe they will be helpful. Here are the four roles of components, and the names I've given them:

- *App component*—This is the root app component, and you only get one of these per application.
- *Display component*—This is a stateless component that reflects the values passed into it, making it highly reusable.
- *Data component*—This is a component that helps get data into the application by loading it from external sources.
- *Route component*—When using the router, each route will render a component, and this makes the component intrinsically linked to the route.

Angular doesn't provide a standard nomenclature like this for various roles of components, so you won't be able to go searching for related content based on these names. The real value is in understanding that it's typically best to give your components specific roles instead of trying to make them do too many things. Let's take a closer look at these different roles and why they're designated as separate groups.

APP COMPONENT

The App component is a special case component. As you know, every Angular application starts by rendering a component, and if you used the CLI it will be the AppComponent (but could be named anything if you changed it).

Here are the guidelines I recommend for your App component:

- *Keep it simple*—If possible, don't put any logic into the component. Think of it more like a container. It's easier to reuse and optimize the rest of your components if the App component doesn't have complex behaviors they depend upon.
- *Use for application layout scaffolding*—The template is the primary part of the component, and you'll see later in this chapter how we create the primary application layout in this component.
- *Avoid loading data*—Usually you will avoid loading data in this component, because I like to load data closer to the component that uses that data. You might load some global data (perhaps something like a user session), though that could also be done separately. On less complex applications, you might load data because it's more complicated to abstract it on smaller applications.

In my opinion, the best rule is to keep the App component as simple as possible. Typically, I have only a template and an empty controller. The intention is to avoid doing too much "global"-type logic and configuration in the app controller to increase the modularity of your other components and keep the logic inside components that need it.

DISPLAY COMPONENT

The Display component role is likely to be the most common one that you create or consume as you build your Angular expertise. These are components that generally are useful for rendering out content and are typically given the necessary data to display. Most third-party components will be in this role because it's the most decoupled type of component.

Here are the primary guidelines I suggest for a Display component:

- *Decouple*—Ensure that the component has no real coupling to other components, except that data may be passed into it as an input when requested.
- *Make it only as flexible as necessary*—Avoid making these components overly complex and adding a lot of configuration and options out of the box. Over time, you might enhance them, but I find it's best to start simple and add later.
- *Don't load data*—Always accept data through an input binding instead of loading data dynamically through HTTP or through a service.
- *Have a clean API*—Accept input bindings to obtain data into the component and emit events for any actions that need to be pushed back up to other components.
- *Optionally use a service for configuration*—Sometimes you may need to provide configuration defaults, and instead of having to declare the preferences with every use of the component, you can use a service that sets application defaults.

Sometimes it may feel like overkill to make your components more isolated and specific for displaying output. The more encapsulated and isolated the component is, the easier it will be to reuse.

I often find that when I start to refactor some code, I begin by identifying individual aspects of my code that could be standalone display components. I might notice a lot of repeated snippets of code that mostly have the same capabilities and refactor them into a single component.

It's also common for these components to have a template and little to no logic in the controller. That's perfectly acceptable, because it allows you to easily reuse a template snippet across your application.

DATA COMPONENT

The Data component oversees loading or managing data. Most applications need data from some external source (HTTP or user input), and it's best to contain that inside a Data component versus a Display component. I find that most developers build these first and eventually start to abstract out pieces into either route or display component types.

Data components are primarily about handling, retrieving, or accepting data. Typically, they rely on a service to handle the loading of data, as we saw in chapter 2. Here are some considerations for a Data component:

- *Use appropriate lifecycle hooks*—To do the initial data loading, always leverage the best lifecycle hook for when to trigger the loading or persistence of data. We'll look at this more later in this chapter.
- *Don't worry about reusability*—These components are not likely to be reused because they have a special role to manage data, which is difficult to decouple.
- *Set up display components*—Think about how this component can load data needed by other display components and handle any data from user interactions.
- *Isolate business logic inside*—This can be a great place to store your application business logic, because anytime you manage data, you're likely dealing with a specialized implementation that works for a specific use case.

I try to limit the number of components that deal with data so I can avoid making too many specialized components. Each application is different, and perhaps you also leverage a nice UI library and don't need to make many of your own display components, so it's possible that the code you write for an application may be weighted toward data components (while the overall application will still have a lot of display components provided by the third-party module).

ROUTE COMPONENT

The Route component is any component that's linked directly to a route. These components aren't very reusable and are typically created specifically for a specific route in an application.

These components also often follow the principles of a Data component because routes often require loading more data for the new view. The reason I distinguish between them is that a single route could render out multiple data components, such as in a dashboard that has several components loading metric information.

A route component should primarily follow these guidelines:

- *Template scaffolding for the route*—The route will render this component, so this is the most logical place to put the template that's associated with the route.
- *Load data or rely on data components*—Depending on the complexity of your route, the route component may load data for the route or rely on one or more data components to do that for it. If you're unsure, I'd suggest loading data initially in the Route component and decoupling as your view gets more complex.
- *Handles route parameters*—As you navigate, there are likely to be router parameters (such as the ID of the content item being viewed), and this is the best place to handle those parameters, which often determine what content to load from the back end.

Every route that you can navigate to is linked to a component, so the number of route components you create is directly linked to the number of routes you add into your application. You could route to the same component for different routes, but that isn't common.

4.4 *Creating a Data component*

We're going to start by making a component that will help us manage data. This is a dashboard for a data center, so the data it provides is largely numeric values of various metrics that are important to determine the health of the data center. We'll create a component, aptly named the Dashboard component, which will host our data and display it in the app.

We'll have the raw data print to the screen for the moment until we create other components. At the end of this section your app should look like figure 4.6.

Figure 4.6 App with Dashboard component that generates a random data set and is displaying it raw

Start by generating a new component using the CLI. Then we'll add the logic into the controller and see a few lifecycle hooks in action. This will be a good example of a Data component because it will handle the data for the entire application and not deal too much with the display of content:

```
ng generate component dashboard
```

Now open the src/app/dashboard/dashboard.component.ts file and replace its contents with what you see in the following listing.

Listing 4.1 Dashboard component controller

```
import { Component, OnInit, OnDestroy } from '@angular/core';

interface Metric {
  used: number,
  available: number        Declares the interfaces for a
};                         Metric and Node data type
interface Node {
  name: string,
  cpu: Metric,
  mem: Metric
};

@Component({
  selector: 'app-dashboard',
  templateUrl: './dashboard.component.html',
  styleUrls: ['./dashboard.component.css']    Creates controller class; declare must
})                                            implement OnInit and OnDestroy
export class DashboardComponent implements OnInit, OnDestroy {
  cpu: Metric;
  mem: Metric;
  cluster1: Node[];        Defines properties and
  cluster2: Node[];        grants them types
  interval: any;
```

```
ngOnInit(): void {
  this.generateData();

  this.interval = setInterval(() => {
    this.generateData();
  }, 15000);
}

ngOnDestroy(): void {
  clearInterval(this.interval);
}

generateData(): void {
  this.cluster1 = [];
  this.cluster2 = [];
  this.cpu = { used: 0, available: 0 };
  this.mem = { used: 0, available: 0 };
  for (let i = 1; i < 4; i++) this.cluster1.push(this.randomNode(i));
  for (let i = 4; i < 7; i++) this.cluster2.push(this.randomNode(i));
}

private randomNode(i): Node {
  let node = {
    name: 'node' + i,
    cpu: { available: 16, used: this.randomInteger(0, 16) },
    mem: { available: 48, used: this.randomInteger(0, 48) }
  };
  this.cpu.used += node.cpu.used;
  this.cpu.available += node.cpu.available;
  this.mem.used += node.mem.used;
  this.mem.available += node.mem.available;

  return node;
}

private randomInteger(min: number = 0, max: number = 100): number {
  return Math.floor(Math.random() * max) + 1;
}
}
```

Implements the NgOnInit lifecycle hook to initialize the data, and sets up interval

Clears the interval using NgOnDestroy to free up memory

We start by importing the `OnInit` and `OnDestroy` interfaces, which we use when we create our controller to add better intelligence to the TypeScript compiler about what constitutes a valid controller implementation. In this case, `OnInit` and `OnDestroy` are interfaces that tell TypeScript that it must implement the `ngOnInit` and `ngOnDestroy` methods, respectively.

For additional clarity, the `Metric` and `Node` interfaces describe the structures we're using for our data. It's optional, but I recommend leveraging interfaces for proper enforcement of code and because interfaces help over time with maintaining code. The component has five properties, four of which contain values for our dashboard and the last of which is used to maintain a reference to the interval so it can be cleared later.

Then we use the NgOnInit lifecycle hook to generate the data, and also set up the interval that will generate a new data set every 15 seconds. The NgOnDestroy lifecycle hook is also used then to clear the interval when the Dashboard component is removed from the application. Anytime you use an interval, you'll want to be sure to clear the interval if you no longer need it, or you'll create a memory leak over time because the interval would continue to exist even after navigating to another page.

The rest of the code is a set of methods used to generate the data, which I won't go over in detail. It will generate memory and CPU metrics for six nodes across two clusters and aggregate the total utilization metrics as well. How this data is leveraged will be more obvious as we build the next few components.

Now in the component template, which is found in the file src/app/dashboard/dashboard.component.html, let's bind the raw data to the screen so we can see it as it's generated. Replace the contents of that file with this single interpolation binding that will bind the data for one of the clusters:

```
<p>{{cluster1 | json}}</p>
```

We haven't added the dashboard to our application yet, so open up src/app/app.component.html and add the dashboard to the bottom of the template like so. It should look like what you saw in figure 4.3 earlier in this section:

```
<app-navbar></app-navbar>
<app-dashboard></app-dashboard>
```

That's it for the Dashboard component—for the moment. We'll add more to the Dashboard later in this chapter as we build more components to handle the displaying of the data, starting with the next component, which will display the CPU and memory metrics and will accept data through an input.

4.5 Using inputs with components

When you create your own components, you can define properties that can accept input through property bindings. Any default HTML element properties can also be bound to a component, but you can define additional properties that the component can use to manage its lifecycle or display.

We saw this in chapter 2, and the following is a snippet we used to bind stock data into the Summary component. You see the brackets around the stock attribute to indicate that the value is binding to the data found in the stock property:

```
<summary [stock]="stock"></summary>
```

By default, all properties of a component aren't immediately bind-able, as you saw earlier. They must be declared as an input to allow the property to be bound. One reason is that we want encapsulation of our components, and it's best not to automatically expose all properties. Another reason is that Angular needs to know which properties exist so it can properly handle the wiring of values into a component.

In our application, we want to display some metric data of the entire data center. This is shown in figure 4.7, which is the result of the work we'll do in this section. The role of these components is to display the CPU and Memory metric information of the entire data center. Because the only difference between these components is the data, we'll make it reusable, using inputs to pass data into the component.

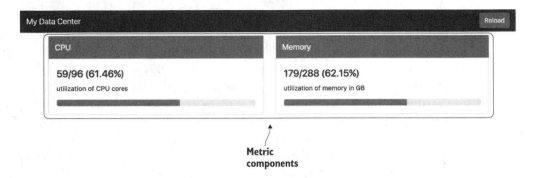

Figure 4.7   **Adding the metric components to the app that share the same display with different data**

4.5.1   *Input basics*

Let's build our component that has an input and see it in action before we dig into it further. Use the CLI to generate a new component like you see here:

```
ng generate component metric
```

We'll start by looking at the component controller, so open the src/app/metric/metric.component.ts file and update it with what you see in the following listing.

Listing 4.2   Metric component controller

```
import { Component, Input } from '@angular/core';          ◄──── Imports the Input
                                                                  decorator
@Component({
  selector: 'app-metric',
  templateUrl: './metric.component.html',
  styleUrls: ['./metric.component.css']
})
export class MetricComponent {
  @Input() title: string = '';
  @Input() description: string = '';          Declares properties with Input decorator
  @Input('used') value: number = 0;           and default values
  @Input('available') max: number = 100;

  isDanger() {
    return this.value / this.max > 0.7;       Method to check if utilization exceeds 70%
  }
}
```

The Metric component first imports the Input decorator, which is used to decorate any property that you want to define as an input. In this case, we have four inputs declared, which means that all the properties of this component are made available for binding. Then we implement a simple method called isDanger() that will tell us whether the utilization is above 70% or not, so we can display the metric in a different way.

The first two properties are the title and description. The Input decorator sits in front and will make each of the properties available for binding based on the name of the property. Though I've declared a typing for each of the properties, it's important to note that they don't verify that the input matches that type at runtime. You'll still need to sanitize the inputs or handle invalid values.

The last two properties pass an optional value into the Input decorator, which is a way to change the name of the property that's used in the binding from the name used internally for the component. That allows us to alias the used attribute to the value property, and the available attribute to the max property. When you bind to the Metric component, you'll use the binding like [used]="node.used", but inside the component it will use the property value.

You may hear some refer to the *component API*, and what they're talking about is the component inputs. Because this is the primary way for passing data into a component, it's much like a contract for how to consume the component in your application. Being able to rename the input can be beneficial for code clarity because it allows you to expose bindings differently from the internal implementation. But I recommend making the names consistent for simplicity and debugging.

I also recommend that you ensure that your input bindings and property names are as clear as possible. Making your property names short to save characters is rarely worth it, because developers no longer know what that property is about without digging deeper into the code.

As you build more components and work on larger projects, you'll likely start to create components that are reused across projects and applications. This is a core principle of Angular as well—to enable easy reuse of components.

Now let's set up the Metric component template, and we'll even use the ng-bootstrap Progress Bar component as an example of how to consume another component that has inputs. Open the src/app/metric/metric.component.html file and update it to the contents of the following listing.

Listing 4.3 Metric component template

```
                                                    Uses NgClass to conditionally set
<div class="card card-block">                       the navbar color
  <div class="card-body">
    <nav class="navbar navbar-dark bg-primary mb-1" [ngClass]="{'bg-danger':
     isDanger(), 'bg-success': !isDanger()}">  ◄
      <h1 class="navbar-brand mb-0">{{title}}</h1>  ◄——— Binds the title to
    </nav>                                                the page
    <h4 class="card-title">{{value}}/{{max}} ({{value / max |
     percent:'1.0-2'}})</h4>
    <p class="card-text">
      {{description}}  ◄——— Binds the description
    </p>
    <ngb-progressbar [value]="value" [max]="max" [type]="isDanger() ?
     'danger' : 'success'"></ngb-progressbar>  ◄
  </div>                                         Uses Ng-bootstrap Progress Bar and
</div>                                           binds values into the component
```

Displays the value and max properties
and calculates the percentage with pipe

This template uses a lot of the template syntax capabilities of Angular in a short amount of space. First, we're using the bootstrap CSS styling to create a card layout for the Metric component, so the card classes are from bootstrap.

All the bindings in this template will resolve to the four input properties that were defined in the controller, but notice that we're using the property names and not any alias names passed to the Input.

The nav element is used to create the top header bar that contains the title. Using NgClass, it will either apply the bg-danger or bg-success class based on how much of the overall value has been utilized.

There are a few basic interpolation bindings, such as the title, value, max, and description. We also have an example of a more complex interpolation expression that divides the value by max and formats it as a percentage.

Finally, we have a sample of using the ng-bootstrap Progress Bar component. Based on the documentation for the progress bar, it accepts the three bindings we declared to give it the bindings for value, max, and type. value and max are numbers, and type is the bootstrap class (such as danger or success) to use for coloring the bar.

The Progress Bar is a great example of a well-designed component. It has a clear set of input properties. It doesn't require a lot of effort to consume and internalizes much of the logic.

Because we added the ng-bootstrap module to our App module earlier, all the components provided by ng-bootstrap are available without having to make any special requests for them. Most third-party library experiences will be similar, and once you've added the third-party module to your app, your application can easily consume the values made available by the third party.

Let's get this Metric component on the screen. Open up the src/app/dashboard/dashboard.component.html file and replace its contents with the code in the following listing. Remember, the Dashboard component contains the data that's now able to be bound into the component.

Listing 4.4   Using the metric components

```
<div class="container mt-2">
  <div class="card card-block">
    <nav class="navbar navbar-dark bg-inverse mb-1">
      <h1 class="navbar-brand mb-0">Overall Metrics</h1>
    </nav>
    <div class="row">
      <app-metric class="col-sm-6"
        [used]="cpu.used"
        [available]="cpu.available"          Metric component
        [title]="'CPU'"                      for CPU
        [description]="'utilization of CPU cores'">
      </app-metric>
```

```
    <app-metric class="col-sm-6"
      [used]="mem.used"
      [available]="mem.available"
      [title]="'Memory'"
      [description]="'utilization of memory in GB'">
    </app-metric>
  </div>
 </div>
</div>
```

Metric component for Memory

Here we define a bit of markup for the bootstrap styling to create a new container and card block for display purposes. The really meaningful part is the use of the Metric component. Notice we're still able to apply a class to the element because it's treated like a regular HTML element when rendered.

Each of the four properties we defined in our component is listed as an attribute with the binding syntax of brackets around it. Remember, this is the syntax to tell Angular to evaluate the expression against the parent component (the Dashboard component) and return its value to the child component (the Metric component). Because they were marked as inputs, we can bind values to those properties that aren't standard HTML properties. For the used and available properties, we bind to the corresponding properties on the cpu and mem controller values. Then for the title and description, we provide a string literal, because they're evaluated as an expression.

Did you notice how this component is more generic? It accepts the four inputs that it needs to display, which even includes some text. We can easily use the same component more than once and have it display for each metric uniquely. This is usually preferred over making a lot of components that do nearly the same task.

4.5.2 *Intercepting inputs*

We're currently blindly accepting whatever values are passed into the component and using them without any kind of validation. It's easy to forget to validate or sanitize data inputs, especially when you're building the component tree and are confident about the types of data that are being passed along.

The problem is as applications grow or as components get reused in new ways, it becomes harder to keep track of the inputs. It's also good practice to try and validate inputs when possible to harden your components.

For instance, if we changed the value of a binding to a Metric component to give it the wrong type, the Metric component would have some issues. Try it out yourself. Change [used]="cpu.used" to [used]="'fail'". This changes the binding to pass a string instead of a number. The Metric component will throw an error because eventually it will try to divide the string and a number, which isn't valid.

I like to use a method to intercept inputs that need validation by using getter and setter methods. This is a feature that has been in JavaScript for a while, but I haven't seen it widely used until more recently.

The main idea here is that instead of having a property to bind to directly, you bind the input to the setter method, which stores the real value on a private property so you can protect it from direct access. The setter method is also where you can run any validation logic. Then you use the getter method to return the value of the private property anytime it's requested.

Let's modify our Metric component to use this approach to validate input values and protect our template from division errors with values that aren't numbers. Open the src/app/metric/metric.component.ts file and change the class to what you see in the following listing.

Listing 4.5   Metric component intercepting inputs

```
export class MetricComponent {
  @Input() title: string;
  @Input() description: string;
  private _value: number = 0;          Private properties for storing the
  private _max: number = 100;          validated values

  @Input('used')
  set value(value: number) {
    if (isNaN(value)) value = 0;       Setter method for value with Input
    this._value = value;               decorator
  }

  get value(): number { return this._value; }    ← Getter method for value to
                                                     return private property

  @Input('available')
  set max(max: number) {
    if (isNaN(max)) max = 100;         Setter method for max with Input
    this._max = max;                   decorator
  }

  get max(): number { return this._max; }     ← Getter method for max to
                                                 return private property

  isDanger() {
    return this.value / this.max > 0.7;
  }
}
```

If you haven't used a getter or setter method before, they're functions that are proceeded by the get or set keyword. The name of the method has to match the name of the property, so in this example get value(){} will be called anytime something requests the this.value property. Likewise, anytime something stores a new value to this.value, it will call the setvalue(value){} method and pass the value that was stored.

We started by creating two new private properties, _value and _max. With the private keyword, TypeScript will ensure they're not directly exposed in the controller so they can't be mutated outside of this controller. The underscore before the name is a common convention to notify developers that a property is considered private.

We implement the value setter method and also decorate it with the Input decorator. This registers a normal input property, but, instead, when the binding into the component happens, it will pass through this function. The function does a check to ensure that the value is a number—if not, it sets it to 0 and stores that value on the _value property. Then we implement the getter method to retrieve the _value property. We do the same basic thing for the max property, but set the default to 100 if the input is invalid.

We've now guarded our inputs against invalid values, but there are other scenarios where you may want to intercept values. You may want to format some values before they're used, such as ensuring that words are capitalized.

The main problem with this approach is that every time you read the property using a getter method, it will run the logic inside the getter method. This probably isn't a big deal in most cases, such as if you're only returning a private property as we're doing here, but if you have more complex logic, the functions might take a toll on rendering speed. Also, don't do any mutation in the getter function! Doing so will cause unexpected behaviors because you can't be sure how many times the getter function will be called.

There's one more way that we'll intercept and modify inputs as they come into the component, but we'll first take a look at how to project content inside your components.

4.6 *Content projection*

Imagine that you created a Card component and you wanted the card content area to be flexible to accept any kind of markup that a developer needed to insert. We can accomplish this using *content projection*, which allows us to declare the place to insert external content into our component.

Content projection is a concept Angular implements that comes from web components. If we think about the role of display components, the need to accept markup to display inside the component is fairly common. Tabs, cards, navbars, modals, dialogs, sidebars—the list goes on for types of UI elements that could accept a generic set of markups to display within the component.

Because we want to create reusable display components, content projection is a key capability that we'll need to use. The good news is that it's fairly simple to implement, so let's go ahead and see it in action.

We're going to build two components that help us create a table to display each of the nodes in a cluster of servers. If you think about it, a table already uses content projection because you create a table and then nest rows inside the headers, and then inside the rows you insert the cells. See figure 4.8.

Using the CLI, generate two new components, one for the Nodes component and another for the Nodes Row component:

```
ng generate component nodes
ng generate component nodes-row
```

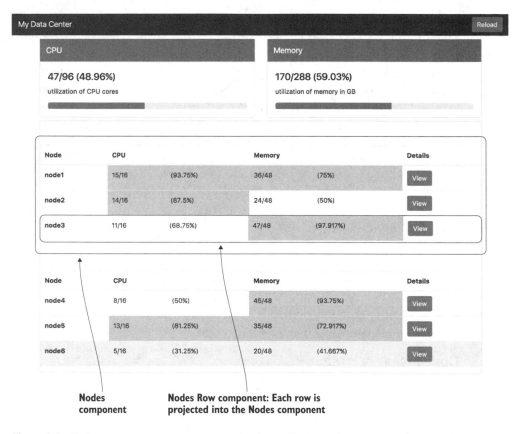

Figure 4.8   Nodes component uses content projection to display nodes row components

We'll start by getting the Nodes component up and running, and we're only going to start with the template. The controller is empty, and for this use case we don't need any controller logic to use content projection. Open src/app/nodes/nodes.component. html and replace its contents with the following listing.

Listing 4.6   Nodes component template

```
<thead>
  <tr>
    <th>Node</th>
    <th [colSpan]="2">CPU</th>
    <th [colSpan]="2">Memory</th>
    <th>Details</th>
  </tr>
</thead>
<ng-content></ng-content>
```

Use of binding to a non-standard property name

Use of Ng-content element to mark insertion point

You can see this template has the markup for a table header. I want to point out the use of property binding to a non-standard name; in this case the attribute is colspan, but the property on the element is colSpan. The only benefit to using the binding here is that normally you need to bind to an expression instead of a static value, so you wouldn't do this.

The really interesting aspect is the NgContent element, which tells Angular that this component has an insertion point for content. When someone uses this element and they nest additional markup inside the element, it will be placed where the NgContent element currently sits. That allows you to choose exactly where the content is inserted (hence the name *insertion point*).

We'll get to see how this works shortly, but we want to make one small change to the component decorator. Open the src/app/nodes/nodes.component.ts file and change the selector to the following:

```
selector: '[app-nodes]',
```

We've changed the selector here to say that it will look for the attribute `app-nodes` instead of an element called `app-nodes`. The selector can take any valid CSS selector. In this case, we use the attribute CSS selector to target an element with the `app-nodes` attribute. We do this so we can apply this component onto another element.

The Nodes component creates our table header, and now we need to create a component that handles displaying the individual rows of content. Open the src/app/nodes-row/nodes-row.component.html file and replace its content with the code found in the following listing.

Listing 4.7 Nodes Row component template

```
<th scope="row">{{node.name}}</th>
<td [class.table-danger]="isDanger('cpu')">        ◄——— Use of special class binding
  {{node.cpu.used}}/{{node.cpu.available}}
</td>
<td [class.table-danger]="isDanger('cpu')">        ⎤  Binding that divides values
  ({{node.cpu.used / node.cpu.available | percent}})  ◄—⎦  and formats as percent
</td>
<td [class.table-danger]="isDanger('mem')">
  {{node.mem.used}}/{{node.mem.available}}
</td>
<td [class.table-danger]="isDanger('mem')">
  ({{node.mem.used / node.mem.available | percent}})
</td>
<td><button class="btn btn-secondary">View</button></td>
```

The template consists of a set of table cells that display various data. The data cells use the special `class` binding to conditionally apply the `table-danger` CSS class to a cell if the value is over the 70% threshold. It also contains a binding that divides the values to produce a percentage of utilization, and uses the Percent pipe to format the value.

Now hopefully you're thinking that the component must receive the node object via an input because, as we already discussed, the Dashboard component holds all the data. For that to work, we need to set up our component controller properly and also implement the `isDanger()` method that is called in this template. To do that, open the src/app/nodes-row/nodes-row.component.ts file and replace its contents with what you see in the following listing.

Listing 4.8   Nodes Row component controller

```
import { Component, Input } from '@angular/core';

@Component({
  selector: '[app-nodes-row]',                    ◄──────  Updates the selector to also use the
  templateUrl: './nodes-row.component.html',               attribute app-nodes-row
  styleUrls: ['./nodes-row.component.css']
})
export class NodesRowComponent {
  @Input() node: any;    ◄──────────────────── Declares the node property as an input

  isDanger(prop) {
    return this.node[prop].used / this.node[prop].available > 0.7;
  }
}
```

Implements the method to check if the
value exceeds 70% utilization

We want to use the attribute selector for this component as well, so update the selector
accordingly. Then we set up the `node` property as an input so that we can bind values
into this component, and implement the `isDanger()` method to calculate whether the
usage exceeds the 70% threshold we've set.

This component doesn't have any content insertion, because it only describes a table
row. But because we'll use it more than once, it was prudent to abstract it into its own
component. This makes it a perfect example of a Display component that modifies its
own display based on the data that's provided as an input.

Now we can see these two components in action. Open the src/app/dashboard/
dashboard.component.html file and add the code in the following listing to the bottom
of the template (don't remove anything—add it).

Listing 4.9   Dashboard using the Nodes and Nodes Row components

```
<div class="container mt-2">
  <div class="card card-block">
    <div class="card-body">
      <nav class="navbar navbar-dark bg-inverse mb-1">
        <h1 class="navbar-brand mb-0">Cluster 1</h1>
      </nav>
      <table app-nodes class="table table-hover">      ◄──── Implements the Nodes
        <tr app-nodes-row *ngFor="let node of cluster1" [node]="node"></tr>
      </table>                                                 component using an
      <nav class="navbar navbar-dark bg-inverse mb-1">         attribute on the table
        <h1 class="navbar-brand mb-0">Cluster 2</h1>           element
      </nav>
      <table app-nodes class="table table-hover">
        <tr app-nodes-row *ngFor="let node of cluster2" [node]="node"></tr>
      </table>
    </div>
  </div>
</div>
```

Implements the Nodes Row component on the table row,
iterates over the nodes, and binds the node

The dashboard now implements another section that contains the two cluster tables. Because we used the attribute selector for the Nodes component on the table element, it will apply the component template inside the table. That will insert the table head elements that are in the Nodes component template, but it also contains the NgContent insertion point.

The table has a child element, the table row element, and the Nodes Row component is applied to that row. It also has ngFor to loop over all the nodes in a given cluster, so there will be three instances of it created per table. Finally, the table row also has a binding to capture the specific node value. The table rows show several distinct Angular capabilities working together to easily iterate over a list and display a table row that is abstracted into a component.

We've injected content into one place, but what if we want to have multiple insertion points? We can do that too by naming our insertion points. To demonstrate, let's replace the way we bind the title and description of the Metric component with child elements.

Open src/app/metric/metric.component.html and update it to reflect the code in the following listing. We can use multiple NgContent elements by adding an attribute that has a CSS selector to use for targeting.

Listing 4.10 Metric component template with content projection

```
<div class="card card-block">
  <div class="card-body">
    <nav class="navbar navbar-dark bg-primary mb-1" [ngClass]="{'bg-danger':
     isDanger(), 'bg-success': !isDanger()}">
      <h1 class="navbar-brand mb-0"><ng-content select="metric-title"></ng-
       content></h1>
    </nav>
    <h4 class="card-title">{{value}}/{{max}} ({{value / max |
     percent:'1.0-2'}})</h4>
    <p class="card-text">
      <ng-content select="metric-description"></ng-content>
    </p>
    <ngb-progressbar [value]="value" [max]="max" [type]="isDanger() ?
     'danger' : 'success'"></ngb-progressbar>
  </div>
</div>
```

Replaces the interpolation with a named NgContent element →

We've replaced the interpolation bindings with an NgContent element, and in both cases it has a select attribute. This is a CSS selector that Angular will look for while rendering to determine what content to insert where. In this case, we're expecting to have two elements, metric-title and metric-description.

That means the Metric component needs to have two child elements by those names to properly display that content, but if it's missing, it will be blank. You could use other CSS selectors, and it would locate the elements based on those selectors, such as a class name or attribute.

We should also remove the title and description inputs from the component, so open src/app/metric/metric.component.ts and remove these two lines:

```
@Input() title: string;
@Input() description: string;
```

Now we need to update our Dashboard component to use these new elements instead of binding directly to properties, because it will throw errors after removing them from the Metric component. Open src/app/dashboard/dashboard.component.html and modify the section, as you see in the following listing.

Listing 4.11 Projecting metric information into the component

Provides the title as an element instead of binding

```
<div class="container mt-2">
  <div class="row">
    <app-metric class="col-sm-6" [used]="cpu.used" [available]="cpu.
     available">
      <metric-title>CPU</metric-title>
      <metric-description>utilization of CPU cores</metric-description>
    </app-metric>
    <app-metric class="col-sm-6" [used]="mem.used" [available]="mem.
     available">
      <metric-title>Memory</metric-title>
      <metric-description>utilization of memory in GB</metric-description>
    </app-metric>
  </div>
</div>
```

Provides the description as an element instead of binding

As you can see here, we've replaced the `title` and `description` bindings with custom elements by the names we declared in our NgContent select attribute. The resulting UI appears the same, but it does put the elements in the insertion points as they are, so you could have nested more markup inside of the elements.

Now if you run the code, you'll get a compilation error from Angular. It will try to parse these new elements, recognize that they're not registered components, and throw an error. We can fix that by setting some configuration in the App module that tells Angular not to get upset about finding an element it doesn't understand.

Open the src/app/app.module.ts file and make two small changes. The first is to import the `NO_ERRORS_SCHEMA` object from @angular/core:

```
import { NgModule, NO_ERRORS_SCHEMA } from '@angular/core';
```

Then you'll add a new property to the NgModule definition called `schemas`. Add it after the `bootstrap` property, as you see here:

```
  bootstrap: [AppComponent],
  schemas: [NO_ERRORS_SCHEMA]
})
```

Angular will now disable throwing errors on unknown elements and allow you to create content insertion points based on element names. Alternatively, you could have used other CSS selectors for a class or attribute and it wouldn't have required this schema fix. I find elements to be more accessible and clearer in many cases, so I still recommend doing this. You only lose the error handling of unknown component names, which usually helps to catch typos in your markup.

Content projection is powerful and quite useful for components that fit the role of display components. As you saw, you can use named or unnamed content insertion points to include markup provided into your component template, all by using the NgContent element.

That wraps up the first chapter about components, and in the next chapter we'll dig into more advanced topics, like how to optimize change detection and watch for changes in our inputs.

Summary

In this first chapter on components, you've learned a lot about the foundations of components and many useful ways they can be constructed for different purposes. Components are the building blocks of any Angular application, and every other feature of Angular stems from them in some way. We've covered

- Components are self-contained elements that include a component class, a template implemented in HTML, and associated CSS that styles the component.
- Components can play various roles inside an application. The roles are what I call app, display, data, and routing components. Although they're not hard-and-fast rules, it's best to design your components to tackle a single set of tasks to keep them focused.
- The @Component decorator has a number of configuration capabilities, and though you won't likely use them all in the same component, you'll certainly need to harness most of them at some point.
- I talked about how to pass data into a component using input properties defined using the Input decorator or the inputs property. You also saw that input properties aren't available in the component class's constructor method, but are available in the NgOnInit component lifecycle event handler.
- Components sometimes need to accept additional markup and display it inside the component called *content projection*. You saw how to use NgContent to insert external content into your component.

Advanced components

5

This chapter covers

- How to handle and optimize change detection

- Communication between different components

- Ways to style and different ways styles are
  encapsulated

- Rendering components dynamically on the fly

Chapter 4 covered many of the basics of components, but there is so much more! Here we'll dive into additional capabilities that will come in handy as you build more interesting applications.

We'll look at how change detection works in more detail, and look at how to use the OnPush capability to reduce the amount of work Angular has to do to improve rendering efficiency.

Although components can use inputs and outputs, there are additional ways to have components talk to one another. We'll look at why you might choose to use a different approach and how to implement it.

There are three primary ways to render styles for a component, and choosing different modes potentially has a significant impact on the way your components are displayed. You may want to internalize the CSS styling as much as possible, or you may not want any styling to be internalized, but to use the global CSS styles instead.

Finally, we'll look at how to render a component dynamically, and why you might want to do that. It's not very common, but there are moments where it's useful.

As discussed in chapter 4, I highly recommend that you keep your components focused. As we learn more about component capabilities, you'll see that it's important to avoid overloading your components.

This chapter will continue with the example from chapter 4, so refer to it for how to set up the example. Everything will build upon what you learned, so the examples will be expanded to demonstrate more advanced capabilities of components.

I can say with almost 100% certainty that no component will use every single capability, because it would most likely not function. However, mastery of these additional concepts will help you write more complex and dynamic applications. Let's start by taking a look at change detection and how to optimize performance.

5.1 *Change detection and optimizations*

Angular ships with a change detection framework that determines when components need to be rendered if inputs have changed. Components need to react to changes made somewhere in the component tree, and the way they change is through inputs.

Changes are always triggered by some asynchronous activity, such as when a user interacts with the page. When these changes occur, there is a chance (though no guarantee) that the application state or data has changed. Here are some examples:

- A user clicks a button to trigger a form submission (user activity).
- An interval fires every *x* seconds to refresh data (intervals or timers).
- Callbacks, observables, or promises are resolved (XHR requests, event streams).

These are all events or asynchronous handlers, but they may come from different sources. We'll dig deeper into the way that observables and XHR requests behave in other chapters, but here we're curious about how user actions and an interval trigger changes in Angular.

Angular has to know that an asynchronous activity occurred, but the `setInterval` and `setTimeout` APIs in JavaScript occur outside Angular's awareness. Angular has monkey-patched the default implementation of `setInterval` and `setTimeout` to have them properly trigger Angular's change detection when an interval or timeout is resolved. Likewise, when an event binding is handled in Angular, it knows to trigger change detection. There are some special things to do if you write code outside of Angular that needs to trigger change detection, but I won't cover that here.

One the change detection mechanism is triggered, it will start from the top of the component tree and check each node to see whether the component model has changed and requires rendering. That's why input properties have to be made known to Angular, or it would fail to know how to detect changes.

Angular has two change detection modes: Default and OnPush. The Default mode will always check the component for changes on each change detection cycle. Angular has highly optimized this process so that it's efficient to run these checks—within a couple milliseconds for most cases. That's important when data is easily mutated between components, and it can be difficult to ensure that values haven't changed around the application.

You can also use the OnPush mode, which explicitly tells Angular that this component only needs to check for changes if one of the component inputs has changed. That means if a parent component hasn't changed, it's known that the child component's inputs won't change, so it can skip change detection on that component (and any grandchild components). Just because an input has changed doesn't mean the component itself has to change; perhaps the input is an object with a changed property that the component doesn't use. Keeping tracking of your data structures in your application can help to optimize when values are passed around and how change detection fires.

Figure 5.1 illustrates the two types of change detection. Imagine there's a component tree with two properties, and the property 'b' is changed by some user input. The default mode will update the value in the component and then check all components underneath it for changes. The OnPush mode only checks child components that have an input binding specifically for the changed property and skips checking the other components.

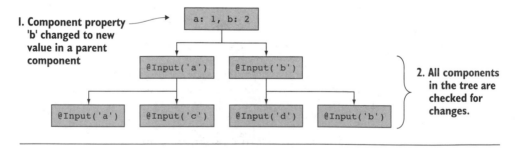

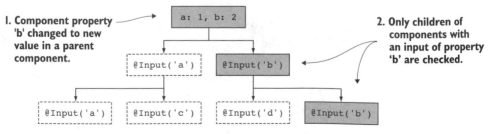

Figure 5.1   Change detection starts at the top and goes down the tree by default, or with OnPush only goes down the tree with changed inputs.

I recommend spending time reading about change detection in more detail from one of the people who helped create it, Victor Savkin: https://vsavkin.com/ change-detection-in-angular-2-4f216b855d4c.

Our Nodes Row component is a candidate for using OnPush because everything comes into the component via an input and the component's state is always linked to the values passed in (such as if the utilization is above 70% and the danger classes need to be applied). Open src/app/nodes-row/nodes-row.component.ts and we'll make a minor adjustment (see the following listing) to enable OnPush for it.

Listing 5.1 Nodes Row component using OnPush

```
import { Component, Input, ChangeDetectionStrategy } from '@angular/core';      ◄─┐

                                                        Imports ChangeDetectionStrategy │

@Component({
  selector: '[app-nodes-row]',
  templateUrl: './nodes-row.component.html',
  styleUrls: ['./nodes-row.component.css'],          Adds property to declare
                                                     it to use OnPush
  changeDetection: ChangeDetectionStrategy.OnPush   ◄─┘
})
```

That's it! Import and declare the component changeDetection property to OnPush, and your component is now only going through change detection when the inputs have changed. The strategy is a property of the component metadata, which is set to the Default mode by default (believe it or not!).

Now we can apply the same changes to our Metric component because it also only reflects the input values provided to it when rendered. Try to make the same change to that file yourself.

There's another way to intercept and detect changes using the OnChanges lifecycle hook, and because we're already intercepting the inputs with getter/setter methods in the Metric component, let's modify it again to use OnChanges and OnPush mode.

Open src/app/metric/metric.component.ts and update it to the code you see in listing 5.2. It replaces the getter and setter methods with an OnChanges lifecycle hook and also uses OnPush mode.

Listing 5.2 Metric component using OnPush mode and OnChanges lifecycle hook

```
import { Component, Input, ChangeDetectionStrategy, OnChanges } from    ◄─┐
    '@angular/core';
                                    Imports ChangeDetectionStrategy and OnChanges │

@Component({
  selector: 'app-metric',
  templateUrl: './metric.component.html',
  styleUrls: ['./metric.component.css'],              Turns on OnPush mode
  changeDetection: ChangeDetectionStrategy.OnPush   ◄─┘
})                                                     Declares the class should
                                                       implement OnChanges
export class MetricComponent implements OnChanges {   ◄─┘
  @Input('used') value: number = 0;          Still declares
  @Input('available') max: number = 100;     properties as inputs
```

```
ngOnChanges(changes) {
  if (changes.value && isNaN(changes.value.currentValue)) this.value = 0;
  if (changes.max && isNaN(changes.max.currentValue)) this.max = 0;
}

isDanger() {
  return this.value / this.max > 0.7;
}
}
```

Uses OnChanges lifecycle hook to detect invalid values

If you implemented the OnPush mode yourself, it should start by importing the strategy helper and then adding the `changeDetection` property. Here you also import the `OnChanges` interface and declare the class to implement it.

We still need to declare our input properties, so we go back to the previous way to declare them without the getter and setter methods. The `ngOnChanges` method implements the lifecycle hook for OnChanges, and it provides a single parameter as an object populated with any changed inputs, which then have their current and previous values available. For example, if only the `value` input was changed in the parent, then only the `change.value` property will be set on the lifecycle hook.

Inside the `OnChange` lifecycle hook, we run the same basic checks for whether the values are numeric or not, and if validation fails we reset the value. It should be noted that any changes to the inputs would propagate to any child components (should there be any). The value of using this approach is that we aren't creating private properties while still intercepting and validating the inputs, and the logic doesn't run when the component requests a property. It will only run the lifecycle hook for a component when the inputs have changed for that specific component.

If you ever need to run code every time that change detection is run on a component (regardless of whether you use OnPush or not), you can use the DoCheck lifecycle hook. This allows you to run some logic that can check for changes that exist in your component that Angular can't detect automatically. If you need to trigger your own type of change detection, this is the lifecycle hook that will help you do that. It's less commonly used, but do be aware of its existence for situations where OnChanges doesn't get you what you need.

In this section we've optimized the Nodes Row and Metric components' change detection by only checking them when an input has changed. The Metric component also now uses the OnChanges lifecycle hook to validate inputs, which can be more efficient and hooks into the change detection lifecycle.

5.2   *Communicating between components*

There are a number of ways to communicate between components, and we've already gone into depth about inputs as a way to communicate data from a parent component to its child. That doesn't give us a way to communicate back up to a parent, though, or to another component in the tree that isn't a direct descendent.

As you think about building your components, particularly ones that are highly modular, they will likely need to emit events when things happen so other components can easily take advantage of knowing when things are happening elsewhere. For example, you could create a tabs component and emit an event that describes what tab is currently visible. Another component might be interested in knowing when the tab selection changes so that you can update the state of that component, such as a nearby panel that has contextual help information based on the current tab.

You've seen inputs are the way to push data down the component tree to children, and events are the way to pass data and notifications up through the component tree to parents. When used this way, Angular considers these events outputs. We're going to use outputs to inform parent components of when changes happen so we can react to those events.

Additionally, we'll look at a couple ways to use other components in this section: using a View Child (which gives you access to a child component controller in a component controller) and using a local variable (which gives you access to a child component controller in a component's template). Each has a different design and might work in more than one use case, but we'll see each of them in action with our app.

Let's take a look at our application component tree again, but this time we'll annotate the inputs and communication flows (figure 5.2). We want to make it possible to click a button in the Navbar component and have it generate the data in the dashboard (like a refresh button). The Navbar component and the Dashboard component are child components of the App component, so how can we get them to talk? It's fairly simple using events and local template variables.

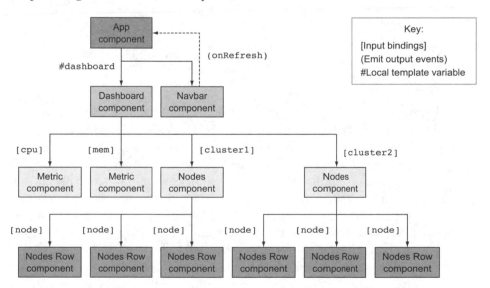

Figure 5.2 Components sharing data, emitting events, and accessing other components via local variables

In figure 5.2 you can see that the Dashboard component binds data into all child components, whereas the Nodes component also binds some data into its children. But all data flows from the Dashboard component down to children.

However, with the Navbar component we need a way to communicate with the Dashboard component to tell it to generate data again. We'll use an output event (onRefresh), which will alert the App component when the user clicks the refresh button. Then once the App component detects that the button was clicked, it can handle that event by telling the Dashboard to regenerate data, and it does that by referencing the Dashboard controller in the template using a local variable.

5.2.1   *Output events and template variables*

To illustrate how this works, we need to make a few changes to our Navbar and App components. Let's start by opening the src/app/navbar/navbar.component.ts file. We'll need to declare an output event, like we declare an input, so that Angular understands how to register and handle that event, as shown in the following listing.

> **Listing 5.3   Navbar component using an output**

```
import { Component, Output, EventEmitter } from '@angular/core';

@Component({
  selector: 'app-navbar',
  templateUrl: './navbar.component.html',
  styleUrls: ['./navbar.component.css']
})
export class NavbarComponent  {
  @Output() onRefresh: EventEmitter<null> = new EventEmitter<null>();

  refresh() {
    this.onRefresh.emit();
  }
}
```

Imports the Output decorator and EventEmitter factory

Creates a property with Output of an EventEmitter type

Implements a method to call on click that emits the event

We begin by importing the Output decorator and EventEmitter factory object. We need both of these to set up an output event. The EventEmitter is a special object that helps us emit custom events that work with Angular's change detection.

Next, we declare a new property called onRefresh and add the @Output() decorator to it. This will alert Angular that there is now an event output based on the name of the property, which will allow us to then use event binding to listen for this event in our template, like (onRefresh)="..expression..". As with the @Input() decorator, you could optionally pass an alias to change the event name that's used for event binding.

The output is typed to an EventEmitter<null> type, which means this variable will hold an EventEmitter that doesn't emit any data. Optionally, it could declare to emit data, such as a date object that contains the moment the event was fired.

At this point we've wired up the output properly, but we still need to devise a way to emit refresh events. We've added the refresh() method to the Navbar component to call the `onRefresh.emit()` method that's provided by the `EventEmitter` object. This is the line that will fire the event and alert the parent component that is listening.

Now we need to add the click event binding to the Navbar button so it will trigger the custom output event. Open the src/app/navbar/navbar.component.html file and update the button line to have the click handler, as you see in the following code. It should call the `refresh()` method:

```
<button class="btn btn-success" type="button" (click)="refresh()">Reload
    </button>
```

Clicking the Reload button in the navbar will now trigger the `refresh()` method, which will then emit the custom output event `onRefresh`. You can see what happens in figure 5.3.

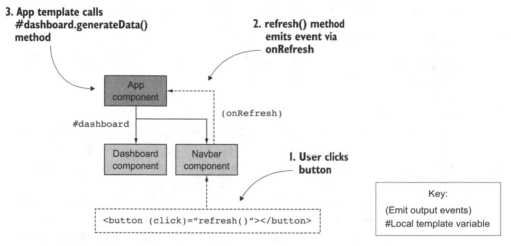

Figure 5.3 Overview of component tree, how user clicks button and it triggers refresh of data via an output event

Our App component (the parent of both Navbar and Dashboard) is now being alerted when the user clicks the button, but we haven't implemented an event binding to capture and respond to it. To do that, open the src/app/app.component.html file and modify it to the following:

```
<app-navbar (onRefresh)="dashboard.generateData()"></app-navbar>
<app-dashboard #dashboard></app-dashboard>
```

On the first line, we've added the event binding to react to the `onRefresh` output event when it fires, but it needs to call the method from the Dashboard component. Because the Dashboard component has the method to generate data, we need a way to call it from the App component. The second line adds `#dashboard` to the template on the Dashboard component. This denotes a local template variable, accessible as the variable `dashboard`, that references the Dashboard component controller so we can call methods from the Dashboard component—it allows us to call a method from the

Dashboard component anywhere in the App component template, even though we aren't inside the Dashboard component. But only public methods are available—private methods like randomInteger(), for example, aren't available.

If no components are listening to the event, then it *will not propagate* up the component tree. Output events only go to the parent component, unlike regular DOM events (such as click or keypress) that do propagate up the DOM tree.

This event emitting trick lets us use one component in another part of the template, and in this case we use it to handle the onRefresh event by calling the dashboard.generateData() method from the Dashboard component. This is handy for accessing components that exist in the same template. The major negative is that it only allows you to access the component controller from the template and not from the controller, meaning the App component controller can't call the Dashboard component methods directly. Luckily, there's another way to reference another component using a View Child.

5.2.2   *View Child to reference components*

In order to access a child component's controller inside a parent controller, we can leverage ViewChild to inject that controller into our component. This gives us a direct reference to the child controller so we can implement a call to the Dashboard component from the App component controller.

ViewChild is a decorator for a controller property, like Inject or Output, which tells Angular to fill in that property with a reference to a specific child component controller. It's limited to injecting only children, so if you try to inject a component that isn't a direct descendent, it will provide you with an undefined value.

Let's see this in action by updating our App component to get a reference to the Dashboard component and have it directly handle the onRefresh event from the Navbar. Open the src/app/app.component.ts file and replace it with what you see in listing 5.4.

Listing 5.4   App component controller

Imports ViewChild →
```
import { Component, ViewChild } from '@angular/core';
import { DashboardComponent } from './dashboard/dashboard.component';   ← Imports the Dashboard component

@Component({
  selector: 'app-root',
  templateUrl: './app.component.html',
  styleUrls: ['./app.component.css']
})
export class AppComponent {
  @ViewChild(DashboardComponent) dashboard: DashboardComponent;   ← Declares the dashboard property, decorated with ViewChild

  refresh() {
    this.dashboard.generateData();   ← Implements refresh method that calls Dashboard component method
  }
}
```

After we import the `ViewChild` decorator, we also need to import the `Dashboard-Component` itself. We need to make sure it's available during compiling and that we can directly reference it.

The App component then gets a single property, `dashboard`. The `@ViewChild()` decorator sits in front, and we pass a reference to the `DashboardComponent` so Angular knows exactly what component to use. We also give the property a type of `Dashboard-Component` because it's an instance of that controller.

Finally, we add a `refresh()` method, which calls the Dashboard component controller to generate the data. Compared to the template variable approach, this gives us an opportunity for additional work that might be difficult or not possible in the template.

We need to update the App component template to call the new controller method instead of using a template variable. Back in src/app/app.component.html, you should change the contents to the following:

```
<app-navbar (onRefresh)="refresh()"></app-navbar>
<app-dashboard></app-dashboard>
```

Now the template doesn't have a reference to the Dashboard component, but instead calls the App component's `refresh` method when the output event is fired. The result is the same—the Dashboard will generate a new set of data—but the approach is different.

You may be wondering which approach you should use, and it largely boils down to where you want to store the logic. If you ever need to do anything more than access properties or methods of a child controller, you probably need to use the `ViewChild` approach. This does cause a coupling between the two components, which should be avoided when possible. But if you can reference a child controller and call a method directly in the template, it can save code and reduce coupling.

5.3 Styling components and encapsulation modes

Angular can use different ways of rendering that change the way the component can be styled. Components are usually designed to manage their own state, and that includes the visual styling required for the component to display. There is almost always some kind of global CSS styling that you will apply to provide a functional base for your application default styling, but components can hold their own styles that are rendered in isolation from the rest of the application.

If you add CSS styles for a component, those styles aren't globally exposed, and you will avoid having to deal with CSS rules from one component overriding another component. There's a way to render component styles to the global styling that's only recommended in a few situations.

There are multiple ways to add styles to a component. It's best to add your styles in the same way across all of your components because mixing and matching can have some interesting (and sometimes unexpected) side effects. It can also be potentially challenging if you use an external library that does something differently, so keep an eye on how your dependencies work to ensure they don't conflict.

5.3.1   *Adding styles to a component*

Styles can be added several ways. You can always add CSS using a global approach, where you include a linked CSS file into your application index.html file or reference the file in the .angular-cli.json file `styles` property (which we already did for Ng-bootstrap). These styles are generic and will be applied to any matching elements in the page. That's good for common and shared styling that needs to go everywhere, but not good when you want to have isolated components that define their own styling.

To better isolate our styling, we can use one of the following approaches—these are ways to add styles that are specific to a single component:

- *Inline CSS*—Component templates can have inline CSS or style attributes to set the styles of the elements. These are the default ways to add style rules to HTML elements regardless of whether you're using Angular.
- *Component-linked CSS*—Using the component's `styleUrls` property with links to external CSS files. Angular will load the CSS file and inject the rules inside a `style` element for your app.
- *Component inline CSS*—Using the component's `styles` property with an array of CSS rules, Angular will inject the rules inside a `style` element for your app.

Let's take a look at how these different approaches can be used in an example. Here we have a simple component that has styling applied from five different approaches:

- Global CSS rules
- Inline CSS `style` element
- Inline `style` declaration
- Component `styles` property
- Component `styleUrls` property linked to a CSS file

We'll modify the Reload button in the navbar to have a different background color so we can see how these different approaches get applied. We'll start by adding some CSS to our CSS file that the CLI generates with each component, which is linked using the `styleUrls` property. Open the src/app/navbar/navbar.component.css file and add the following CSS rule to it:

```
.btn { background-color: #e32738; }
```

That overrides the global color set by the bootstrap CSS library and gives our button a red color (instead of the default green). Notice that the other buttons on the page (in the Nodes Row components) aren't changed, even though they also have the `.btn` class applied. We'll cover how that happens shortly, but that's the visual result of Angular's encapsulation features.

Next, we'll add some styles by updating the component metadata in the src/app/navbar/navbar.component.ts file with the following `styles` property:

```
@Component({
  selector: 'app-navbar',
  templateUrl: './navbar.component.html',
```

```
    styleUrls: ['./navbar.component.css'],
    styles: [`.btn { background-color: #999999; }`]
})
```

The `styles` property lets us provide an array of strings (here we're using the backtick character to make a string literal) that should contain valid CSS rules. Now when you look at the application, it should appear to be a gray button. That means that styles inside the `styles` property will override anything from the CSS files loaded through the `styleUrls` property. The trick here is that whichever is declared last will win, so when you have both `styles` and `styleUrls`, the one declared last will override the first regardless of which one is used, due to the way the compiling works. (At time of writing, the CLI complains if you declare both `styles` and `styleUrls` in the CLI, but it still seems to work.)

Now open up the navbar template at src/app/navbar/navbar.component.html and add the following style element into the template:

```
<style>.btn { background-color: #3274b8; }</style>
```

Once you save this, the application will reload, and all of a sudden your button will now be blue, which means that inline style declarations will override any values provide via the `styles` or `styleUrls` properties.

The last way to add styles is directly on the element itself using the `style` attribute. While still in the component template, modify the button to include this inline CSS declaration to make the button purple:

```
<button class="btn btn-success" type="button" style="background-color:
    #8616f6" (click)="refresh()">Reload</button>
```

This exercise showed us that if a CSS rule is set with a different value in all of these places, you might be surprised which rule is applied. It should be noted that using the `!important` value will raise that particular rule above any others, should you dare to use it. Here's the priority order in which the rules are applied if the same rule is declared in multiple places, with each item overriding any rules below it:

1 Inline style attribute rules
2 Inline style block rules in the template
3 Component `styles` rules or `styleUrls` rules (if both, then last declared has priority)
4 Global CSS rules

Declaring a rule using inline styles is always going to be the highest priority rule. This is probably expected because, except for when the `!important` value is declared, inline styles are given highest priority by the browser. The style block from the template is the next highest priority. Then the next highest are rules declared in the component `styles` array or `styleUrls` external files, and lastly any global styles.

All CSS rules are added to the end of the document head inside a new `style` element. As the application is rendered, components will get loaded, and those styles will get added to the document head. But depending on the encapsulation mode, the way those styles are rendered can change the way those styles are processed.

One important note: all these guidelines are based on using the CLI for building. It's possible to change the build process and obtain different priorities or results, just so you're aware. Now let's look at how different encapsulation modes work and why we might want to change the default settings.

5.3.2   *Encapsulation modes*

Angular wants to ensure that you can build modular components that can be easily shared. One key capability is the ability to ensure that CSS styling for a component doesn't bleed over into the rest of the app, which is called *styling encapsulation*. Have you ever used a third-party library that included some CSS which conflicted with something else in your application and caused something to display improperly? Most likely you've run into this situation, and Angular offers some options to avoid it.

Until recently, there was no certain way to encapsulate CSS styling or HTML elements of a particular DOM element. The most common approach is to use specific class naming conventions, as are found in most popular CSS libraries. These conventions provide a specific nomenclature for CSS classes that limits the chances of the same class being used elsewhere. Although these might typically be effective, there's no guarantee that class names or styles won't collide, and it provides no encapsulation for inner HTML elements.

Enter the Shadow DOM, the official native browser standard for encapsulating styles. Shadow DOM provides us with a good set of features to ensure that our styles don't conflict and bleed in or out of a component, except that it might not be available on older browsers. If you need to brush up on Shadow DOM, refer to chapter 1.

Angular comes with three encapsulation modes for a view. In the earlier styling example, you were using the default Emulated mode.

- *None*—No encapsulation is used during rendering of the view, and the component DOM is subject to the normal rules of CSS. Templates aren't modified when injected into the app except for the removal of any CSS style elements from the template to the document head.
- *Emulated*—Emulated encapsulation is used to simulate styling encapsulation by adding unique CSS selectors to your CSS rules at runtime. CSS can cascade into the component easily from the global CSS rules.
- *Native*—Uses the native Shadow DOM for styling and markup encapsulation and provides the best encapsulation. All styles are injected inside the shadow root and are therefore localized to the component. None of the templates or styles declared for the component are visible outside the component.

Each encapsulation mode applies styles in a different manner, so it's important to understand how encapsulation modes and styling render the view. The order in which styles are applied remains constant regardless of which encapsulation mode is used, but the way in which the underlying styles are injected and modify the app does change.

Now let's take a closer look at the different modes, how they behave, and why you might decide to select a different mode than the default mode. As we look at each mode, try setting the mode in the Metric component and inspecting the output as it's rendered in the page to see how it adds styles into the document head.

NO ENCAPSULATION MODE

If you use no encapsulation by setting in the component, you'll bypass any native or emulated Shadow DOM features. It will render the component into the HTML document as is, as if you had written the HTML markup directly into the body yourself. This is the default mode for components without any styles.

To set this mode, you would use the `encapsulation` property of the component metadata to set it like so—of course, you'll need to import the `ViewEncapsulation` enum from `@angular/core`:

```
encapsulation: ViewEncapsulation.None
```

Once the mode is set, any styles you declare for the component will be hoisted up from the component template into the document head, and this is the only real modification made to the markup. The `style` element is moved into the document head as is, which is a way of injecting global CSS rules. It's possible another component rendered later would inject a competing CSS rule, so render order matters as well.

Here's a summary of reasons why you might use, or avoid using, components with no encapsulation mode:

- *Styles bleed out*—Sometimes applications are designed with CSS libraries where encapsulating the internal styling of each component is unnecessary or undesired. If you don't put styles into your components, then encapsulation may not be necessary.
- *Global styles bleed in*—The global background style for a header element is applied because of the lack of encapsulation, which may or may not be desired behavior.
- *Templates are unmodified*—Because this mode injects the template as is (after relocating the styles), your DOM elements won't have any special transformations applied.

When using no encapsulation mode, you can't use any of the special Shadow DOM selectors like `:host` or `::shadow`. These have no context because no Shadow DOM (native or emulated) features are enabled.

Now let's look at the emulated mode and see how it behaves in comparison.

EMULATED SHADOW DOM ENCAPSULATION MODE

Emulated mode applies some transformations to any styles by adding unique attributes to HTML markup and CSS rules to increase the specificity of the CSS rules by making them unique. Because this isn't a true encapsulation, it's referred to as *emulated*, but it has many of the same benefits. This is the default mode for Angular components that have any styles declared (regardless of how they're declared in the component).

Emulated mode is primarily about preventing styles in the component from bleeding out to the global rules (which happens when no encapsulation is used). In order to accomplish this, the view will render the template and styles with unique attributes to increase the specificity of the CSS rules inside the component. Emulated mode is the default mode, but if you want to explicitly declare it, you would set the property on the component metadata:

```
encapsulation: ViewEncapsulation.Emulated.
```

During the render, the styles are first extracted from the component template or component properties. Then a unique attribute is generated, something similar to _ngcontent-ofq-3. It uses the _ngcontent prefix with a unique ending so each component can have a unique CSS selector. Multiple instances of the same component have the same unique attribute. Lastly, the view renders by adding the unique attribute to the component DOM nodes and adding it into the CSS selector rules.

Here's a quick overview of the behaviors of emulated encapsulation mode and why you would (or wouldn't) want to use it:

- *Styles are isolated*—The rendering of the styles and markup adds the unique attributes to ensure that CSS rules don't collide with global styles.
- *Styles bleed in*—The global styling can still bleed into the component, which can be useful to allow a common styling to be shared. It also could conflict with the component if a rule is added somewhere globally that you didn't intend to bleed into the component.
- *Unique selectors*—The rendered DOM gets a unique attribute, which means if you have global styles that you want to apply into the component, you'll need to write CSS selectors accordingly.

Now let's finish the encapsulation modes by looking at the native mode and how it uses Shadow DOM.

NATIVE SHADOW DOM ENCAPSULATION MODE

The Shadow DOM is a powerful tool for encapsulating markup and styles from the rest of the application. Angular can use Shadow DOM to inject all the content instead of putting it into the primary document. This means that the template and the styles are truly isolated from the rest of the application.

Native browser support for Shadow DOM is limited and can be checked at http://caniuse.com/#feat=shadowdom. The benefits of Shadow DOM may not extend to all the browsers you need to support, but there is also a good polyfill to backfill the support at http://webcomponents.org/polyfills/shadow-dom/. Even with a polyfill, older browsers may not be supported, so you should consider all of your needs.

While the component renders, it creates a shadow root in the component. The template is injected into the shadow root, along with the styles from the sibling and any parent component. As far as the rest of the document goes, this shadow root protects the contents from being visible to anything outside of the component.

Angular intends that nested components should be able to share styling, but with the shadow root, Angular makes those styles available to the component by injecting them into the shadow root as well.

Here's a summary of the way that the native mode works and why you might or might not want to use it:

- *Uses Shadow DOM*—For true encapsulation, the native option is the best bet. It will protect your components from the styles of the document and encapsulate the markup as well.
- *Parent and sibling styles bleed in*—Due to the way Angular renders the component, it also injects the parent and sibling components' styles, which can cause issues like styles bleeding in (which you might not want).
- *Limited support*—Browser support for Shadow DOM is limited and may require the use of a polyfill to allow its use in applications.

So far, we've looked at how to bind data into the view from the component. This is important to allow us to inject data and modify properties of the view dynamically. We also looked at how to use event bindings to call from the view back to the component, which can be used to update values or call methods. And we've looked at the various ways to style a component and how to encapsulate styles.

We've covered a lot of ground, but now we're going to look at Angular directives and pipes. They provide additional options to modify the display of data or elements in our view and add additional logic to templates.

5.4 Dynamically rendering components

Applications sometimes need to dynamically render a component based on the current application state. You may not always know what component needs to be on the screen, or perhaps the user interactions call for a new component to display in the page.

There are a few fairly common situations that you've seen where a dynamic component is often a good solution. For example

- Modals that display over the page with dynamic content
- Alerts that conditionally display
- Carousel or tabs that might dynamically expand the amount of content
- Collapsible content that needs to be removed afterward

These situations all have something in common: They don't always need to be on the screen or are dependent on conditions outside of their own power. Angular gives us the ability to use lower-level APIs to call, that let us render a component that doesn't already exist in a template, on demand.

I'll show two examples of using ng-bootstrap to generate a modal and then talk about how to do it all ourselves using Angular's APIs to create an alert component. With ng-bootstrap, most of the magic is hidden behind a helpful service, but it will give us the ability to quickly get the capability working before we build it by hand.

5.4.1   *Using the ng-bootstrap modal for dynamic components*

Let's start by generating a new component. This component is going to show details about the node when you click the View button in the Nodes Row component. We're going to call this the Nodes Detail component:

```
ng generate component nodes-detail
```

Now replace the component's controller, found in src/app/nodes-detail/nodes-detail.component.ts, with the code in listing 5.5. This controller has similar logic to determine whether the node exceeds its utilization or not. This is the component that will open inside the modal and won't be loaded until called for.

Listing 5.5   Nodes Detail component controller

```
import {Component, Input} from '@angular/core';
import {NgbActiveModal} from '@ng-bootstrap/ng-bootstrap';    ◄── Imports the
                                                                   NgbActiveModal
                                                                   service
@Component({
  selector: 'app-nodes-detail',
  templateUrl: './nodes-detail.component.html',
  styleUrls: ['./nodes-detail.component.css']
})                                                   Declares an
                                                     input for the
export class NodesDetailComponent {                  component
  @Input() node;    ◄──────────────────────────────┘
                                                          Adds the NgbActiveModal
                                                          service to the controller
  constructor(public activeModal: NgbActiveModal) {}   ◄──┘

  isDanger(prop) {
    return this.node[prop].used / this.node[prop].available > 0.7;
  }

  getType(prop) {
    return (this.isDanger(prop)) ? 'danger' : 'success';
  }
}
```

The Ng-bootstrap library provides a useful service called NgbActiveModal, which is an instance of the modal controller that loads the Nodes Detail component. It will allow us to dismiss the modal when we like, either on demand or based on user action. This will be more apparent when we add the template for this component.

Unlike other components so far, this component won't be called from a parent's template. But we will need to pass it an input for the data, so we still need to declare the input property.

Now we need the template to make the component functional. Open src/app/nodes-detail/nodes-detail.component.html and replace the existing code with the following listing.

Listing 5.6 Nodes Detail component template

```html
<div class="modal-header">
  <button type="button" class="close" aria-label="Close"
    (click)="activeModal.dismiss()">
    <span aria-hidden="true">&times;</span>
  </button>
  <h4 class="modal-title">{{node.name}}</h4>
</div>
<div class="modal-body container">
  <div class="col-xs-6">
    <app-metric [used]="node.cpu.used" [available]="node.cpu.available">
      <metric-title>CPU</metric-title>
    </app-metric>
  </div>
  <div class="col-xs-6">
    <app-metric [used]="node.mem.used" [available]="node.mem.available">
      <metric-title>Memory</metric-title>
    </app-metric>
  </div>
</div>
```

Use the NgbActiveModal service to close the modal on click

Using the Metric component for CPU

Using the Metric component for Memory

There's a lot of markup here needed for the display of a modal with bootstrap's CSS styling, but it has a modal header with a title and close button and a body containing two Metric components. Notice that we can use any components that have been registered with our Application module inside of a dynamic component, which is handy.

Remember in our controller we had a property named `activeModal`, and it was an instance of the NgbActiveModal service. We use that in the template to call the `dismiss` method, which will close the modal itself. This is why we included that property in our controller. You can also see how the `node` property, which is our only input binding, is used to display data or pass data into the other components.

The contents of this component are fairly similar to the rest of the application, so we don't need to spend time on it. What we're now interested in is how to trigger the modal to open from the Nodes Row component. Open the src/app/nodes-row/nodes-row.component.html file and add the following event binding to the button:

```html
<td><button class="btn btn-secondary" (click)="open(node)">View</button></td>
```

Now we need to open src/app/nodes-row/nodes-row.component.ts and implement this new method. The code in the following listing contains the updated controller, and changes are annotated for you.

Listing 5.7 Nodes Row component template additions for modal

Imports the NgbModal service

```typescript
import { Component, Input, ChangeDetectionStrategy } from '@angular/core';
import { NgbModal } from '@ng-bootstrap/ng-bootstrap';
import { NodesDetailComponent } from '../nodes-detail/nodes-detail.
    component';
```

Imports the Nodes Detail component

```
@Component({
  selector: '[app-nodes-row]',
  templateUrl: './nodes-row.component.html',
  styleUrls: ['./nodes-row.component.css'],
  changeDetection: ChangeDetectionStrategy.OnPush
})
export class NodesRowComponent {
  @Input() node: any;

  constructor(private modalService: NgbModal) {}        ◄─── Adds property to inject
                                                             NgbModal service

  isDanger(prop) {
    return this.node[prop].used / this.node[prop].available > 0.7;
  }

  open(node) {
    const modal = this.modalService.open(NodesDetailComponent);
    modal.componentInstance.node = node;                    Implements method
  }                                                         to open modal
}
```

Here we import the NgbModal service that will allow us to create a new modal. We saw the NgbActiveModal service in the Nodes Detail component, which, once the modal and its component has been created, will allow the Nodes Detail component to reference the active modal instance. We need to import the Nodes Detail component as well. The constructor also sets the `modalService` property with an instance of the NgbModal service.

In the `open()` method, we pass in a reference to the node data to use. Then we create a new modal instance using the `modalService`, which takes as a parameter the component to be rendered in the modal. It stores a reference to this newly created component in the `componentInstance` property, which allows us to set the `node` input binding that was passed in during the click.

That wires up all we need to trigger the modal from the Nodes Row component. But if you try it, the modal doesn't work quite yet because there are a few minor details we need to implement that will allow us to open this modal.

First, open the src/app/dashboard/dashboard.component.html file and add the following code line to the bottom of the template—we need to give the Modal service a place to render the component:

```
<template ngbModalContainer></template>
```

This is a placeholder template element that has the NgbModalContainer directive on it, which tells Ng-bootstrap where in the template to render this component. Components have to be rendered somewhere in the template, and this is Ng-bootstrap's way of defining the location to render.

Secondly, we need to add a new entry to our App module. When the CLI processes Angular, it needs to know what components might be rendered dynamically because it will process them differently. Open the src/app/app.module.ts file and add a new line to the NgModule decorator:

```
entryComponents: [NodesDetailComponent],
```

Entry components are any components that need to be rendered dynamically in the browser, which will also include components that are linked to routes (more on this in chapter 7). The CLI will try to optimize components by default and not include the component factory class. But to dynamically render, the component factory class is needed to render, so this tells the CLI compiler how to properly process it during build time.

This example is a bit specific for Ng-bootstrap's implementation of the modal, so it will only get us so far in understanding how to build our own dynamic components.

5.4.2 *Dynamically creating a component and rendering it*

The Ng-bootstrap modal example is a nice way to create a modal, but it abstracts some of the capability away from us. We want to see how it works directly and will build upon the knowledge of our components that we have so far to create our own dynamically rendered component.

When we dynamically render a component, Angular needs a few things. It needs to know what component to render, where to render it, and where it can get a copy of it. This all happens during the compilation process for any template, but in this case we have no template and have to invoke the APIs ourselves. These are the Angular capabilities we'll use to handle this process:

- `ViewContainerRef`—This is a reference to an element in the application that Angular understands and that gives us a reference point to where we can render our component.
- `ViewChild`—This will give us the ability to reference an element in our controller as a `ViewContainerRef` type, giving us access to APIs needed to render components.
- `ComponentFactoryResolver`—An Angular service that gets us the component factory (which is needed to render) for any component that has been added to the entry components list.

As we build our example, you'll see these three capabilities working together. We're going to build an alert box that appears when the data is refreshed and then removes itself after a certain amount of time. This will give us insight into how to dynamically render a component and remove it from the page, which accomplishes much the same thing as what you get from the Ng-bootstrap modal service.

Start by generating a new component. From the CLI, run the following command to set up this new component:

```
ng generate component alert
```

The template for this component is going to be simple; it has some bootstrap-flavored markup that makes an alert box and binds the date of the last refresh. Open src/app/alert/alert.component.html and replace its contents with the following:

```
<div class="container mt-2">
  <div class="alert alert-warning" role="alert">
    The data was refreshed at {{date | date:'medium'}}
  </div>
</div>
```

Likewise, the component controller is going to be empty except for a single input property. Open src/app/alert/alert.component.ts and replace its contents with the code from the following listing.

Listing 5.8   Alert component controller

```
import { Component, Input } from '@angular/core';

@Component({
  selector: 'app-alert',
  templateUrl: './alert.component.html',
  styleUrls: ['./alert.component.css']
})
export class AlertComponent {
  @Input() date: Date;
}
```

So far, so good. There's nothing special about this component that we haven't already seen in this chapter, so I'm going to move to the next step. Because this component will be dynamically rendered, we need to add it to the list of entryComponents, so open up src/app/app.modules.ts again and add it to the list. At this point, our component itself is ready to be dynamically rendered:

```
entryComponents: [
  NodesDetailComponent,
  AlertComponent
],
```

Now we can start to work on the mechanics that will trigger the rendering of the component out to the screen. As with the modal example, we'll need to create a template element in our application that can be used to render out, so open the src/app/dashboard/dashboard.component.html file and update it to have the following template:

```
<app-navbar (onRefresh)="refresh()"></app-navbar>
<ng-template #alertBox></ng-template>
<app-dashboard></app-dashboard>
```

The #alertBox attribute is another template local variable that we can use to identify this element later on. This will be the element that we render the component alongside. Open up the src/app/app.component.ts file and replace it with the code from the following listing.

Listing 5.9   App component controller

Imports a number of new entities

```
import { Component, ViewChild, ComponentFactoryResolver, ComponentRef,
    ViewContainerRef } from '@angular/core';      ◄──────
import { DashboardComponent } from './dashboard/dashboard.component';
import { AlertComponent } from './alert/alert.component';   ◄──────

                                                  Imports the Alert
                                                      component
@Component({
  selector: 'app-root',
```

```
        templateUrl: './app.component.html',
        styleUrls: ['./app.component.css']
    })
    export class AppComponent {
        alertRef: ComponentRef<AlertComponent>;
        @ViewChild(DashboardComponent) dashboard: DashboardComponent;
        @ViewChild('alertBox', {read: ViewContainerRef}) alertBox:
            ViewContainerRef;

        constructor(private ComponentFactoryResolver: ComponentFactoryResolver) {}

        alert(date) {
            if (!this.alertRef) {
                const alertComponent = this.ComponentFactoryResolver.
                resolveComponentFactory(AlertComponent);
                this.alertRef = this.alertBox.createComponent(alertComponent);
            }

            this.alertRef.instance.date = date;
            this.alertRef.changeDetectorRef.detectChanges();

            setTimeout(() => this.destroyAlert(), 5000);
        }

        destroyAlert() {
            if (this.alertRef) {
                this.alertRef.destroy();
                delete this.alertRef;
            }
        }

        refresh() {
            this.dashboard.generateData();
        }
    }
```

Injects the component resolver into the controller

Creates two new properties for a reference to the component and a ViewChild

Implements the alert method to create the component

Implements the destroyAlert method to remove the component

This might look complicated at first, so let's break it down. It's fairly plain how it's working and constructed.

First we must import a few additional objects, and we'll look at their roles as we go along. We also import the Alert component itself so we can properly reference it during rendering.

We then add two properties, with alertRef being a component reference to the Alert component (which is the declared typing). We will want to have this reference so we can keep track of the alert and later remove it if we want. The second property is another View Child, called alertBox. The ViewChild syntax is different because it allows us to pass in a string to reference a local template variable by that name and then "read" it as a particular type of entity—in this case, a ViewContainerRef. It will get the element based on the template variable and then parse it as a ViewContainerRef type. This will give us access to a critical API shortly. These are only properties, though. So far, nothing has been instantiated.

The constructor sets the `ComponentFactoryResolver` property to the Factory Resolver service, which is what we'll need in order to look up a copy of the component factory class before rendering it.

The primary magic of this occurs inside the `alert()` method. We'll walk through this line by line. First, it looks to see if there is already something stored on the `alertRef` (meaning the Alert component has already been created), and if so it skips past the creation of another alert and moves on to update the binding. But if no Alert component exists yet, it uses the `ComponentFactoryResolver.resolveComponentFactory()` method to get an instance of the component factory (it seems a bit redundant, but it's the API name). At this point, the component will be available in its raw form (not yet rendered).

The next line uses the `alertBox` to create the component from the factory instance we received previously. Remember, `alertBox` is the instance of the element where we will inject the component, wrapped in a `ViewContainerRef` instance. At this point, the component will be rendered into the template where the template element was declared.

The next two lines (outside of the conditional) set the binding data for the component and then trigger change detection to run. Because we changed binding data manually, we need to alert Angular to check something (this was asynchronous from Angular's typical rendering process!).

Lastly, a timeout is set to call the `deleteAlert` method after five seconds so the alert doesn't remain on the screen forever. If we look at this method more closely, you can see it will check if there is an existing instance of an Alert component. If so, it will use the `destroy()` method that all components have to remove it from the page.

If you're trying to run this example, you'll find it doesn't work yet. We've missed an important step! Nowhere do we call the App component's `alert()` method, so it won't appear. To do that, we'll emit an event from the Dashboard component that will fire when data is generated, along with the timestamp when it was updated.

Open up src/app/dashboard/dashboard.component.ts. We're going to add a new output event. Be sure to import the `Output` and `EventEmitter` objects at the top of the file. Then add a new property like you see here:

```
@Output() onRefresh: EventEmitter<Date> = new EventEmitter<Date>();
```

Now inside the `generateData()` method add this line to the end of the method:

```
this.onRefresh.emit(new Date());
```

This sets up a new output event from the Dashboard component, and this time we're passing some data during the emit phase. We can capture this information in the App component and use it to pass into our Alert component. This is simple now—all we have to do is update the src/app/app.component.html file one more time by adding an event binding to the Dashboard component:

```
<app-dashboard (onRefresh)="alert($event)"></app-dashboard>
```

Voila! Our Alert component should now appear after every data generation event, regardless of whether you click the button in the top right or wait 15 seconds for it to automatically regenerate. It will also automatically close the alert after five seconds.

That was a whirlwind tour of dynamic components. There are several different ways to generate a component besides this one, but this is a solid approach that you can use in your own applications.

Summary

We've been busy in this chapter. We covered a lot of content about components, how they work, their various capabilities, and much more. Here's what we talked about in this chapter:

- We looked at change detection in more detail, along with how to leverage the OnPush mode to better optimize when a component is rendered.
- We looked at several lifecycle event handlers. There are a number of other ones that have their own use cases as well:
- The OnInit lifecycle hook fires only once after the constructor and when the input properties are available.
- The OnChanges lifecycle hook fires whenever an input property changes.
- The OnDestroy lifecycle hook fires whenever a component is about to be removed from the page.
- We talked about how to communicate between components using output properties and the built-in `EventEmitter`, and how to reference child components as a View Child.
- We talked about the styling of components using CSS in various ways and how different encapsulation modes can affect the way that content is rendered on the page.
- We finished by looking at how to render out components dynamically, with two examples. The first was a prebuilt service using the Ng-bootstrap modal service to render our component on demand, whereas the second was managed entirely by us.

Services

This chapter covers

- Services and their role

- Creating many different types of services

- Using services to help retrieve and manage data

- Replacing logic from controllers with services

- Understanding how dependency injection works with services

In chapters 4-5, we had the Dashboard component, which generated some data for the rest of the application to consume. But that was only because we didn't want to introduce more complexity into the example. This isn't ideal in most scenarios, because that logic is hard to reuse and makes the component unnecessarily complex.

Your application will need to manage many tasks, and many of them will fall outside of the responsibility of components, such as managing data access, managing configuration across the app, and utility functions. The Angular HttpService is a great example of a service that makes it easy to reuse logic for making HTTP requests without having to implement it repeatedly. Although Angular and many libraries provide services for you to consume, you can and should make your own too.

Services are fundamentally JavaScript objects that provide commonly used logic in a way that other parts of the application can easily consume. For example, applications that require a user to log in will need to have a service to help manage the user's state. Or you might have a service that helps manage how you make requests to your API and encapsulates the logic necessary away from the components using it.

Shared code across your application is almost always best placed inside of a service. In Angular, most of the time a service also is something that you can inject into your controllers using dependency injection, though there is no exact definition of what makes an object a service.

To help you out, I've come up with several loose classifications that are useful in providing insight into the various ways a service can be created. A service could fit into more than one of these categories, but I usually try to keep my services focused on one of these roles:

- *Injectable* services are the typical Angular services that provide a feature for the application and work with Angular's DI system to be injected into components. An example would be a service that handles how to load data from an API.
- *Non-injectable* services are JavaScript objects that aren't tied into Angular's DI system and are just imported into the file. This can be useful to make a service available outside of Angular's DI, such as in the application's main file.
- *Helper* services are services that make it easier to use a component or feature. An example would be a service to help manage the currently active alert on the page.
- *Data* services are for sharing data across the application. An example is an object holding data for the logged-in user.

In chapter 4, it would have been more appropriate to extract data logic into a service to separate it from the component. In chapter 5, we talked about designing components to focus on a particular role, and that should include keeping the controller focused on the minimal tasks needed to manage data by delegating those responsibilities to services. *Components* are for displaying the UI, and *services* are meant to help manage data or other reusable snippets of logic.

The goal of a service is to be responsible for a specific set of tasks, which in turn helps keep other aspects of your application focused. The size of a service isn't as important as keeping it on task.

We're going to look at different ways to use services, and I've even named a few service patterns that I find to be most common.

6.1 Setting up the chapter example

We're going to build a fantasy stock-trading application that uses generated data which changes several times a minute to simulate real market changes (see figure 6.1). You'll be able to buy and sell stock, but unlike the real stock market, you can always reset your account if you lose it all.

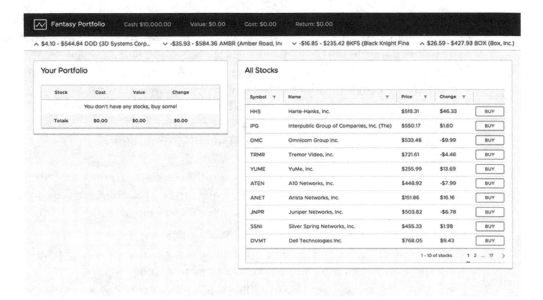

Figure 6.1 **Fantasy Portfolio stock trading application, powered by services**

The stock prices change steadily over time (for better or worse), just like a real stock market. The stock API automatically handles the changes, so every time data is requested it will be refreshed with new values. If you hold onto a stock for a few minutes, you can easily gain or lose money. If you want to see how your portfolio holds, check it the next day and see whether you made good or bad investments, because the value might have drifted up or down by 25%. Your portfolio is also stored, so if you return later it will remember your status, but you'll also be able to start over if you lose too much money.

We'll use several services to help us manage this application. First we'll create a service to help manage the user's account data, such as what stocks they've purchased and how much money they have left in their account. Another service will help us provide configuration data to the application to tell us where the API service is located. We'll use the Http library from Angular inside of a service to help us load data from the API. Finally we'll create a service that helps us manage the storing of data in local storage, so the experience persists between reloads. Each of these fits into one of the categories discussed in the chapter introduction.

Unlike previous chapters, this time we'll start with an application that already has some components set up, which will let us focus on building services and not worry about implementing other aspects already covered in previous chapters. Some code snippets are commented out because they'll throw errors if enabled, and we'll uncomment them as we build the services that will support them properly.

In this chapter, we'll use the Clarity UI library from a team at VMware. It builds on top of Bootstrap 4 for the CSS grid and layout, but provides a design specification that fits their company guidelines. We'll use a few of the components, and you can quickly get a feel for how this particular UI library behaves in comparison to ones we've used in other chapters.

6.1.1 Getting the chapter files

You have two choices for setting up this chapter project. You can download the project as a zip file from GitHub or clone the repository using Git. If you're using Git, run the following command:

```
git clone -b start https://github.com/angular-in-action/portfolio.git
```

Alternatively, you can download and unzip the project files from https://github.com/angular-in-action/portfolio/archive/start.zip. Either way, you should now have a copy of the code on your computer, and you'll need to also install the node modules for the project. Navigate to the directory and run the following to install the modules, and then preview the project:

```
npm install
ng serve
```

Initially, the application looks a little empty, because it can't properly render until we set up the services to help manage data. As you see in figure 6.2, the application has a basic layout, with a header and two cards.

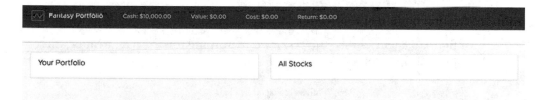

Figure 6.2   Starting point of chapter example; basic header and cards as placeholders

Most of the display is currently commented out (because it would throw many errors at this point), so we just see the scaffolding. As we generate services, data will start to appear, as you saw in figure 6.1. However, the layout and structure are fairly straightforward, and you can review it if you're interested in using the Clarity UI library.

6.1.2 Sample data

This application requires stock data, and I'll quickly cover how it's being generated and provided to the application. The list of stocks that are loaded by the application are a subset of the technology stocks from the New York Stock Exchange, which is about 160 stocks. You'll likely recognize some of the stocks but not others; they're real companies and symbols. But the prices associated with each one are randomly assigned. There is a back-end process running that changes the price values every 5 seconds. The calculations are weighted so that most of the changes are 1–2 cent changes, but stocks can also quickly swing up to 40 cents every 5 seconds, though that's far less likely.

We'll create a service that will help us load this data into our application from the remote service. Using it, we'll refresh the data in our application regularly to show the latest stock data to the user.

You can also see the code powering the API changes by looking at the API project at https://github.com/angular-in-action/api. You could also run the services locally yourself, but that's not covered here. If you need help, it would be best to post an issue on the API repository. It's unlikely that you'll need to run it yourself, but you might in case you want to tweak its behavior or the service is down.

All right, let's get to building some services. We're going to start with a service that will help us load those stock prices so we can start to see data in our application.

6.2   *Creating Angular services*

We'll build our first service, which will help us maintain account information for our fantasy portfolio. It will help provide data to the rest of the application about how much money is available in the account, how much has been invested, the current list of stocks owned, and so on. The focus of this service is to manage the account, just as you would manage a bank or investing account.

The application already has a file generated for you, but if you were to create a new service yourself, you can use the CLI like you see here. The last parameter is the name of the service, which is used in the filename as well as the class name, so this would generate a service named `AccountService`:

```
ng generate service account
```

In figure 6.3 you can see the result we're working toward. The header will soon display some basic account information for the user.

Figure 6.3   The result of creating the Account service is a display of account information in the top bar.

Open up src/app/services/account.service.ts. We're going to add some of the basic properties that are needed by replacing its contents with what you see in the following listing. We'll expand this service several times throughout the application, but this will get us started with showing some of the basic data.

Listing 6.1   Account Service Basics

```
import { Injectable } from '@angular/core';          Imports dependencies
import { Stock } from './stocks.model';

                                                      Defines a variable
const defaultBalance: number = 10000;                 outside of the class

                                 Annotates class with
@Injectable()                    @Injectable()
export class AccountService {
  private _balance: number = defaultBalance;          Declares private
  private _cost: number = 0;                          properties
  private _value: number = 0;
  private _stocks: Stock[] = [];

  get balance(): number { return this._balance; }     Defines getter
  get cost(): number { return this._cost; }           methods for
  get value(): number { return this._value; }         properties
  get stocks(): Stock[] { return this._stocks; }

  purchase(stock: Stock): void {
    stock = Object.assign({}, stock);
    if (stock.price < this.balance) {
      this._balance = this.debit(stock.price, this.balance);
      stock.cost = stock.price;
      this._cost = this.credit(stock.price, this.cost);
      stock.change = 0;
      this._stocks.push(stock);
      this.calculateValue();
    }
  }
                                                      Methods to handle
  sell(index: number): void {                         purchasing and
    let stock = this.stocks[index];                   selling a stock
    if (stock) {
      this._balance = this.credit(stock.price, this.balance);
      this._stocks.splice(index, 1);
      this._cost = this.debit(stock.cost, this.cost);
      this.calculateValue();
    }
  }

  init() {

  }

  reset() {
    this._stocks = [];
    this._balance = defaultBalance;                   Methods to handle
    this._value = this._cost = 0;                     various calculations
  }

  calculateValue() {
    this._value = this._stocks
      .map(stock => stock.price)
      .reduce((a, b) => {return a + b}, 0);
  }
```

```
  private debit(amount: number, balance: number): number {
    return (balance * 100 - amount * 100) / 100;
  }

  private credit(amount: number, balance: number): number {
    return (balance * 100 + amount * 100) / 100;
  }
}
```

> Methods to handle various calculations

This service contains several properties and methods to manage an account. At the top we import our dependencies, which include the `Injectable` decorator and the `Stock` interface (which describes the typing information for a stock). The `defaultBalance` constant is declared, because eventually we'll use it in several places and want to have one place to reference it.

The `Injectable` decorator is used to wire the class to work with the Angular dependency injection system. It doesn't take any parameters, like the `Component` decorator does. Any class that you want to register with DI, you'll need to decorate with `Injectable`. This doesn't immediately make the service available to use elsewhere in the application—we'll get to that shortly.

The rest of the class implements logic of the Account service, which includes having a number of private properties that can't be manipulated directly and getter methods for those properties to read the values.

The service exposes two methods: one to purchase and one to sell a stock. An important aspect of this application is that you can only buy a single instance of a stock, which simplifies a few other aspects of our application. The Account service will retain a list of the stocks that have been purchased at what price, and when they're sold it can calculate the return on that investment.

The last few methods are for calculating various values, such as the current value of all the stocks or debits and credits, and resetting the values. In JavaScript, adding or subtracting float numbers can sometimes cause odd results, such as 0.1+0.2=0.30000000000000004—many pixels have been spent on the topic if you search for it. To avoid such behaviors, currency values are first converted to cents, then the math is done, and then they're converted back to currency.

We wanted to use this service to show data in the header, which is defined in the App component. We need to make it available so that the App component template can read the property values from the Account service. Open up the src/app/app.component.ts file and modify the top part of it to match what you see in the following listing. The rest of the file will remain the same for now.

Listing 6.2   App Component Consuming the Account Service

```
import { Component, OnInit, OnDestroy } from '@angular/core';
import { AccountService } from './services/account.service';

@Component({
  selector: 'app-root',
  templateUrl: './app.component.html',
```

```
    styleUrls: ['./app.component.css']
})
export class AppComponent implements OnInit, OnDestroy {

    constructor(private accountService: AccountService) {}
```

Injects service as a private property ◄

```
// skipping some content

    reset(): void {
        this.accountService.reset();
    }
```

Enables resetting the application state

```
// file continues
```

In the constructor method, Angular can use the type annotation of a property to determine what should be assigned to that property. In this example, that means the DI system will provide a copy of `AccountService` and store it on the `accountService` property. We'll dig a bit further into how this works shortly, but first let's finish up our first service.

We use the Account service inside of the `reset` method, which will allow the user to click a button to start the simulation over again. In this listing, I've also skipped over a lot of code to focus on the changes.

For the Account service to be injectable, we need to make sure it's registered in the providers array. Open up src/app/app.module.ts and import the Account service:

```
import { AccountService } from './services/account.service';
```

Then in the NgModule, add the `AccountService` to the `providers` array:

```
providers: [
  LocalStorageService,
  CurrencyPipe,
  AccountService,
]
```

This is the second part of wiring up a service to be consumed, as it makes the component (or more specifically, the injector) aware of how to inject the service. If you don't add a service to the `providers` array, the DI system will never be aware of it and will fail to compile the service.

We need to take a quick look at our Investments and Stocks components, so we can implement the purchase and sale of a stock. These both need to use the Account service in nearly the same way.

The Stocks component gets the list of all stocks through an input binding (passed from the App component), and has a button to buy a stock. It uses a paginated data grid to allow the user to look at the whole list of stocks without having to display them all at once. We'll need to call the Account service's `purchase` method when the Buy button is clicked. To do this, we need to open up the src/app/stocks/stocks.component.ts file and implement the buy method:

```
buy(stock): void {
  this.accountService.purchase(stock);
}
```

The Investments component displays a list of the stocks the user currently owns, and it looks at the Account service for this information. Instead of using a binding, it looks at the service to determine whether the list of stocks owned has changed, and also calls the Account service's `sell` method when the Sell button is clicked. We need to make the changes to the Investments component to support these two scenarios.

Open up src/app/investments/investments.component.ts and replace its contents with the code you see in the following listing.

Listing 6.3   Investments Component Controller

```
import { Component, DoCheck } from '@angular/core';
import { AccountService } from '../services/account.service';

@Component({
  selector: 'app-investments',
  templateUrl: './investments.component.html',
  styleUrls: ['./investments.component.css']
})
export class InvestmentsComponent implements DoCheck {
  cost: number = 0;
  value: number = 0;
  change: number = 0;
  stocks: any = [];

  constructor(private accountService: AccountService) {}

  ngDoCheck() {
    if (this.accountService.stocks.length !== this.stocks.length) {
      this.stocks = this.accountService.stocks;
    }
    if (this.cost !== this.accountService.cost || this.value !== this.
     accountService.value) {
      this.cost = this.accountService.cost;
      this.value = this.accountService.value;
      this.change = this.accountService.value - this.accountService.cost;
    }
  }

  sell(index): void {
    this.accountService.sell(index);
  }
}
```

Annotations:
- **Declare we'll implement the DoCheck lifecycle hook.** (points to `export class InvestmentsComponent implements DoCheck {`)
- **Injects the Account service** (points to `constructor(private accountService: AccountService) {}`)
- **Implements the DoCheck lifecycle hook to update the state when a stock is bought or sold** (points to the ngDoCheck method)
- **Provides a method that sells a stock** (points to the sell method)

The Investments controller doesn't accept an input binding for the list of stocks the user has bought, so instead it implements the `DoCheck` lifecycle hook. If you recall from chapter 4, this hook runs anytime the change detection runs.

In the `ngDoCheck` method, we first check whether the list of owned stocks has changed, and if so we update the internal `stocks` value. Then we check whether the local `cost` or `value` properties have changed on the service, and if so we update our internal properties. It's a way to grab the values from the service and store them in the component. This allows us to maintain an internal state that only changes when the values change in the service, much like an input binding.

We also implement the `sell` method so the button to sell a stock calls the Account service to sell the item. Once the item is sold, the Account service will update its own values, and then change detection will trigger the `ngDoCheck` method to run and update with the current values.

Look at the templates for these components and see how the templates directly bind to values stored on the service. This is entirely valid, and change detection will still fire when those values change.

Finally, update the src/app/app.component.html file by uncommenting the `div` with the class `header-nav`. This will show the top bar, which will now be populated with the values from the Account service.

Now that we've seen a service in action, we can spend a little more time looking at how the services are injected.

6.3 *Dependency injection and injector trees*

Services usually rely on Angular's dependency injection system, which is how we're able to include dependencies in our components. To get a sense of how services are injected into your application, we should dig a little further into how DI works. The basic rules aren't complex, but they do allow you to create some interesting and potentially complex scenarios (on purpose or by accident).

You've seen it working in all the chapters with examples, and in the last section we injected the Account service into the Investments component, like you see here:

```
constructor(private accountService: AccountService) {}
```

Chapter 3 discussed the basics of dependency injection. *Dependency injection* works by having an injector (the entity that can inject a dependency when requested) and a provider (an entity that knows how to construct and instantiate objects). A module has the top-level injector for all the entities inside that module.

In chapter 4, we saw how components are constructed into a component tree, with the App component being the root that the rest of the components stem from. What we haven't discussed yet is the fact that every component has an injector.

Anytime you declare a `providers` array in the component metadata, that component will get its own injector. For a component that doesn't have any providers declared, it will share the injector of its parent (or its parent's parent if it doesn't have one, or parent's parent's parent, and so on). This is similar to how events bubble up—the injector will look up the injector tree until it finds what was requested (or throws an error when it cannot find it).

This is the foundation of the hierarchical injection system, which is a fancy name for what the previous paragraph described. Injectors are created in a hierarchy (the injector tree that mirrors the component tree), but they also allow us to isolate what parts of the application can inject a particular object or even override how a higher-order injector works.

In larger applications, isolation becomes more important for managing complexity and preventing conflicts. Imagine a large application, like an accounting program or an e-commerce platform. In that situation, it's realistic for multiple teams to work on the same application, and it's likely that some services will be named the exact same thing. If these services were all registered at the topmost level, they would conflict. But if they're properly managed and registered at a lower level, closer to where they're used, then conflicts could be avoided. This is the principle of isolation at work.

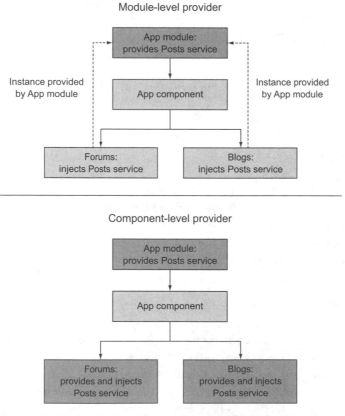

Figure 6.4   Module level providers are injected from the module, and component level providers create individual instances at their level in the component tree. Highlighted blocks are where services are provided.

In figure 6.4, the left side shows that if you declare the provider for the Posts service at the module level, it's available to anything inside of that module. When the Blogs or Forum components request the service to be injected, it goes up through the component injector hierarchy to the App component and then App module to find the provider. Both components get a reference to the same instance of the service, because the service was provided by the same provider.

On the right side, the Forums and Blogs components both provide and inject the Posts service themselves, so they don't have to go up the hierarchy to find the service, which means they're getting separate instances created. Even though the App module has the provider, it's never reached, because the components both provided a service by the same name.

This means there's not a single global registry of all of the dependencies to inject (unlike how NodeJS modules are a flat list of packages), but (potentially) numerous injectors that each maintain their own list. This grants us a level of flexibility not found in flat dependency lists.

We're also able to remap a provider at one node in the tree. Like our Posts service example earlier, imagine that the Forums component wanted to inject a different version of the service (perhaps due to refactoring or needing to pass in a value that isn't a service). Using this syntax, we can provide a different class that will be injected as the same name:

```
providers: [
  { provide: PostsService, useClass: PostsServiceV2 }
],
```

There are several different ways to override a provider, depending on exactly how you need to modify the provider. Table 6.1 has a list of the providers and basic examples with the different capabilities they enable.

Table 6.1 Ways to override a provider with a secondary value or implementation

Provider type	Purpose
Alias	You can have the injector remap one service to another. This might be useful if you can't modify a component directly but need to change the service. It doesn't create a new instance of the service. `providers: [{provide: PostsService, useExisting: PostsServiceV2}]`
Class	The injector can inject a new instance of a different service in place of an existing service. This is useful if you want to replace an existing service with a new instance. `providers: [{provide: PostsService, useClass: PostsServiceV2}]`
Factory	In some cases, you'll need to use a Factory pattern to construct the instance of a service yourself, typically because a configuration type value is needed during construction that isn't known ahead of time. You would need to create a factory function that returns a new instance of the service and that's used by the injector. You'll have to declare any dependencies of that service that need to be injected. `providers: [{provide: PostsService, useFactory: PostsServiceFactory, deps: [HttpClient]}]`
Value	A value can be injected in place of a service, meaning you don't need to create a full class. For example, a static value is already injected, such as a configuration object, and you want to override it at runtime. You can also replace a service with a simple object definition, which is particularly useful for mocking during testing. `providers: [{provide: PostsService, useValue: PostsServiceV2}]`

There's one more nuance to be aware of: When you register a provider, the name of the object is captured as a token and used to look up the value later. While you're passing a reference to the service itself in the `providers` array, internally DI takes the name of the service as the token to look up that service.

When we inject a service and give it a type value, internally DI looks for a service based on the name of that type and returns the corresponding value. In cases where we override the default provider value, DI understands to return the overridden value.

Why do we want to use DI instead of regular module loading in JavaScript? There are a few key reasons you'll usually want to make your services injectable:

- It allows you to focus on consuming services and not worry about how to create them.
- It resolves external dependencies for you, simplifying consumption.
- It's easier to test your Angular entities because you can always inject a mock service instead of the real thing.
- It can allow you to control the injection of a service without having to worry about where another piece of the application might also inject the service.
- It gives you a clean instance of the service for each injector tree.

DI is powerful and is vital for our applications to be easy to manage, but keeping up with the nuances can be a little challenging if you try to combine these capabilities all of the time. Here are a few tips to keep in mind when it comes to DI and services:

- *Inject at the lowest level*—Instead of adding everything to the App module `providers` array, try to add it to the lowest component `providers` array. This will minimize the "surface area" of your service to only be available to the components that might use it.
- *Name your services wisely*—Give your services semantic and meaningful names. PostsService might be clear enough, or perhaps BlogPostsService, depending on the context. I find it's easier to type a few more characters than it is to guess what a service named BPService might be, especially when multiple people are working on your application.
- *Keep services focused*—Rather than creating one mega service that you inject everywhere with lots of abilities, make a sensible number of services that do specific tasks. The longer your service is, the harder it is to maintain and test, and it will likely become tangled in your application.
- *Keep services meaningful*—On the flip side of keeping services focused, you'll need to balance the utility of adding another service. Do you need a service for something that's used only once? It may add more complexity for little benefit, so strike the right balance between number of services and their roles.
- *Use consistent patterns*—Follow the same design for your services for consistency. For example, if you have several services that handle making REST API calls, you'd likely want to give them the same kinds of methods, like `get` to load an object, or `save` to store a record.

That wraps up most of what you'll want to know about DI in Angular. The many ways it can be used make it flexible and powerful. But you can also bypass DI for some scenarios where it's not required or available, as we'll discover next.

6.4 *Services without dependency injection*

Now that you've seen how to use services and dependency injection together, let's look at services that bypass DI. There are some situations where you may not need to use dependency injection, or you may need to have a service that can be used before Angular is fully ready. For example, you may want to create a service that can be used to set configuration before Angular starts or you may want to create a helper service for generic actions.

This approach is using JavaScript modules for exporting and importing values across files. This is no different than how you'd use JavaScript modules in any project. In short, most of the time you'll make your services injectable. There is very little reason not to, except when your service is used outside of Angular's application lifecycle. Think of it like this: If Angular hasn't started to render the application yet, there's no way for Angular to inject a service for you to consume.

We're going to build a class with static methods for getting and setting configuration values to be used throughout the application. We won't make this an injectable service, because we want to use it before the application is bootstrapped—we want to set the configuration values before Angular starts rendering, so there's no chance of a configuration value not being set when Angular needs it.

Start by opening up the src/app/services/config.service.ts file and use the code from the following listing to replace its contents. This is a basic static class to maintain configuration, though we only have one property in this example.

Listing 6.4 Config service without using DI

```
export class ConfigService {
  private _api: string;

  static set(property, value) {
    this['_' + property] = value;
  }

  static get(property) {
    return this['_' + property];
  }
}
```

In this service, there's a single property for storing the URL to the API and two static methods for getting and setting that property. We could add more properties as needed, but for this application it's the only configuration we'll use. There are many ways you could have written this service, but the key here is that it's a plain JavaScript class and doesn't use DI.

Now let's use this to set the value in the src/main.ts file before the application is bootstrapped. Open up the file and add the two lines in bold in the following listing after the current imports.

Listing 6.5   Main file

```
import { enableProdMode } from '@angular/core';
import { platformBrowserDynamic } from '@angular/platform-browser-dynamic';

import { AppModule } from './app/app.module';
import { environment } from './environments/environment';
import { ConfigService } from './app/services/config.service';

ConfigService.set('api', 'https://angular-in-action-portfolio.firebaseio.com/
    stocks.json');

if (environment.production) {
  enableProdMode();
}

platformBrowserDynamic().bootstrapModule(AppModule);
```

If you recall, the main.ts file is our entry point for the application. This is the first code to be executed when the application starts, so this will set the API URL immediately. That allows us to use the Config service anytime in the application to get this value.

You could certainly use DI and make a service that handles configuration that way, but this is an alternative you may consider if you need configuration set as early as possible.

Now we'll use this Config service in another service that will manage loading the stock data, and we'll dig into the HttpClient service that Angular provides.

6.5   *Using the HttpClient service*

Angular comes with its own HttpClient service that helps with requesting data from an API. We saw the Http service in action in the chapter 2 example application, but we need to give it a little more attention. In addition, we'll use the Config and Account services we created to enable most of the rest of the application to start working.

HttpClient is part of its own module, so you have to make sure it's included in your project. It's part of the @angular/common package, which you've probably installed, but if not, use npm to install it. If you're using your own tooling and module loader, like SystemJS, you'll have to ensure it's aware of this module.

It's considered best practice to never use HttpClient in the component controller directly (yet many articles and even the documentation may demonstrate this case), because this helps create a separation of concerns. That's why we'll create a new service that will use the HttpClient service and abstract some of the logic from the controller.

The HttpClient service uses observables for handling aspects of the response. Because it returns an observable, you could also use RxJS to convert it to a promise (not covered here, but found in RxJS documentation), though I generally discourage that unless there's a strong reason.

By the end of this section, the application will look like figure 6.5, where data gets loaded, and the data will finally fill in the cards. It will display the list of stocks in the data grid and in the price ticker.

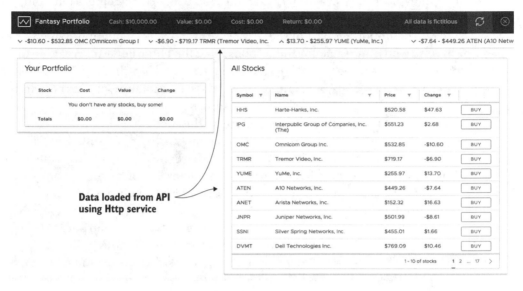

Figure 6.5   Data loaded into the application using the Stocks service with the HttpClient

To get started, open up src/app/services/stocks.service.ts and replace the contents with what you see in the following listing.

Listing 6.6   Stocks service wrapping the use of the HttpClient service

```
import { Injectable } from '@angular/core';        Imports
import { HttpClient } from '@angular/common/http'; dependencies
import { ConfigService } from './config.service';
import { Stock } from './stocks.model';

@Injectable()                                   Creates injectable class
export class StocksService {
                                                Constructor is used to inject
  constructor(private http: HttpClient) { }     services into the class

  getStocks() {
    return this.http.get<Array<Stock>>(ConfigService.get('api'));
  }                                                   Method that uses the HttpClient
}                                                     to request data
```

The Stocks service serves one primary function: to facilitate the loading of data. We keep the focus on this by having one method that uses the HttpClient service to request data and return a subscription for the result. It starts by importing dependencies, as you should expect by now, and that includes the Config service we created earlier and the HttpClient service from the @angular/common/http package. Then the StockService class is decorated with Injectable.

The constructor injects the HttpClient service into the class, but notice we don't do the same for Config because it isn't an injectable service, remember—it's only an object with static methods, so we can call it directly.

Now the important part of the service is the getStocks method. When it's called, it will return an observable for the response that the HttpClient will create so we can elsewhere use subscribe to get the response data. The HttpClient has methods for other HTTP verbs, like post, put, and delete. You can read more about these in the documentation at https://angular.io/guide/http. There's no error handling here because that will need to be handled at the call site of this method.

In some ways, this simple service abstracts away the use of HttpClient from our components, because we shouldn't have to care where the data is coming from. Controllers should ask for data and receive it from a service instead of having to construct the URL and make HTTP requests directly. This is considered a best practice in most programming paradigms.

When put all together, we'll use the getStocks method to set up our HTTP request and then subscribe to it to trigger the request and handle the response. Note that calling get-Stocks won't fire the HTTP request—only when we subscribe to it will it fire. Open up the src/app/app.component.ts file and replace it with the code from the following listing.

Listing 6.7   App component controller to use Stocks service

```
import { Component, OnInit, OnDestroy } from '@angular/core';
import { AccountService } from './services/account.service';
import { Stock } from './services/stocks.model';
import { StocksService } from './services/stocks.service';

@Component({
  selector: 'app-root',
  templateUrl: './app.component.html',
  styleUrls: ['./app.component.css'],
  providers: [
    StocksService
  ]
})
export class AppComponent implements OnInit, OnDestroy {
  refresh: boolean = true;
  stocks: Stock[] = [];
  interval: any;

  constructor(
    private accountService: AccountService,
    private stocksService: StocksService) {}

  ngOnInit() {
    this.load();

    this.interval = setInterval(() => {
      if (this.refresh) {
```

Imports and marks Stocks service as provider

Injects Stocks service

Calls the load method on an interval to automatically refresh data if enabled

```
      this.load();
    }
  }, 15000);                      Calls the load method on an interval to
}                                 automatically refresh data if enabled

toggleRefresh(): void {
  this.refresh = !this.refresh;   Method to toggle the
}                                 automatic refresh

ngOnDestroy() {
  clearInterval(this.interval);   Lifecycle hook to
}                                 clear the interval

reset(): void {                                 Method to call Stocks
  this.accountService.reset();               service to request data and
}                                             store data on property

private load() {
  this.stocksService.getStocks().subscribe(stocks => {
    this.stocks = stocks;
  }, error => {
    console.error(`There was an error loading stocks: ${error}`);
  });
}
}
```

Before we can use the service, it has to be imported and added to the providers array. Then it gets injected into the component as an argument for the constructor. This is the same thing we did for the Account service, except here we're doing it in the component itself. This means only the App component and any child components will have access to this service, instead of the entire module.

When the App component initializes, it will call the ngOnInit method to load the data once and then set an interval to reload every 15 seconds. Note that it will also check whether the refresh property is true before reloading, because we'll have a toggle to optionally disable refreshing data. When the component is destroyed, we use ngOnDestroy to clear the interval to prevent memory leaks.

The load method is a private method that uses the Stocks service in order to load the data. We call getStocks().subscribe() to construct the HTTP request and fire it. When the response is received, we store the result on the stocks property. We also have an error handler to log in to the console if there was an error.

The last step we'll take is to uncomment everything else inside of the src/app/app. component.html file, except for the first line that has the alert component. Doing this will make all the components now appear in our application, filled in with data! You'll notice that the App component binds the data into the different components, as in the following sample code. Anytime the data is reloaded, the binding will update, and the components will refresh their copy of data and display:

```
<app-ticker [stocks]="stocks"></app-ticker>
```

Because we created a service to handle the complexities of building the HTTP request to load data, we kept our controller much more focused. The component doesn't have to know how data was returned—it could be hard coded or loaded dynamically—it only knows how to ask the service for data. You'll want to follow this pattern anytime you have data access. The component does need to understand how to handle the response from the service, and in this case the component only needs to understand that it's given back an observable.

You'll likely create several services like this in your applications, and over time you'll probably come up with specific patterns that you prefer to reuse. I've found it useful to create a base HttpClient service and extend that to create specific services for various API endpoints. The design you choose for your services can depend greatly on the API design.

Although HttpClient is the most common service to use to load data, your application can still use other protocols like Websockets, push notifications, or other APIs such as audio recording. Services can be designed to abstract the complexities of each data source and allow your components to remain focused.

Now let's look at how we can intercept requests and responses to handle scenarios where we want to do additional work, such as adding common headers or even targeting a specific type of response. We can easily transform both requests and responses from a common point, and that's powerful.

6.5.1   *HttpInterceptor*

Often you'll want to intercept HTTP requests or responses before they're handled elsewhere in the application. For example, you may want to add an authorization header to all outgoing requests to a particular domain or you may want to capture any error responses and log them. The HttpClient provides a nice way to intercept requests and responses for these types of purposes by making a service that implements the `HttpInterceptor` interface.

In our case, we'd like to add a bit of logic when the Stocks API data is returned so that we can update our account balance. When we buy some stocks, the current value of the stocks and our portfolio are tracked in the Account service. When we get the latest data from the API, we want to also update the Account service state to reflect the most recent pricing (and hopefully we've made money and not lost it).

An `HttpInterceptor` is crafted like most Angular services, but it must have a method by the name of `intercept`. You'll always intercept the request and then optionally follow it through to also intercept the response. To see this in action, let's make an interceptor that will intercept any requests for the stock data and update the Account service with the latest prices. Generate a new service using the following:

```
ng generate service services/interceptor
```

Open up the new file at src/services/interceptor.service.ts and replace its contents with the values from the following listing.

Listing 6.8 HTTPInterceptor

Creates service class, implements
HttpInterceptor, and injects Account service

```
import { Injectable } from '@angular/core';
import { Observable } from 'rxjs/Observable';
import 'rxjs/add/operator/do';
import { HttpEvent, HttpInterceptor, HttpResponse, HttpHandler, HttpRequest }
    from '@angular/common/http';
import { AccountService } from './account.service';
import { Stock } from './stocks.model';
import { ConfigService } from './config.service';


@Injectable()
export class StocksInterceptor implements HttpInterceptor {
  constructor(private accountService: AccountService) {}

  intercept(req: HttpRequest<any>, next: HttpHandler):
      Observable<HttpEvent<any>>
    const request = req.clone();
    request.headers.append('Accept', 'application/json');
    return next.handle(request).do(event => {

      if (event instanceof HttpResponse && event.url === ConfigService.
  get('api')) {

        const stocks = event.body as Array<Stock>;
        let symbols = this.accountService.stocks.map(stock => stock.symbol);
        stocks.forEach(stock => {
          this.accountService.stocks.map(item => {
            if (stock.symbol === item.symbol) {
              item.price = stock.price;
              item.change = ((stock.price * 100) - (item.cost * 100)) / 100;
            }
          });
        });
        this.accountService.calculateValue();

        return stocks;
      }
    });
  }
}
```

Defines the intercept method → (points to `intercept` method)

Gets clone of request object → (points to `const request = req.clone();`)

Modifies our new request object → (points to `request.headers.append` line)

Returns the handler, passing our version of the request and chaining an event handler → (points to `return next.handle(request).do(event => {`)

Checks the event type and URL ← (points to `get('api')) {`)

Accesses the response body → (points to `const stocks = event.body as Array<Stock>;`)

Logic to update Account service values

There's a bit of setup required, and we can take this slowly. After we import dependencies, we declare a service with `Injectable` and have it implement the `HttpInterceptor` interface. This interface checks whether we have the `intercept` method on our class and throws a compile error if not. We also need access to the Account service, so we inject it in the constructor.

The `intercept` method is what will be called for any HTTP request, and you're given two parameters. The first is the `HttpRequest` object, which has data about what URL is being called, the payload, any headers, and so forth. The second parameter is the

HttpHandler object, which is how we'll tell Angular that we're done modifying the request. If we don't, the request will fail.

If we want to make changes to the request before it's fired, we would modify those values at the top of the intercept method. The HttpRequest object is immutable, so if you want to modify a request you have to first clone the object, as we do here. Then we add a new header to the request to say we want to accept JSON data. You can review all the properties for the request at https://angular.io/api/common/http/HttpRequest.

Once we've made our changes to the request, we then need to tell Angular to handle them. The HttpHandler object has a method called handle (aptly named) that will take our modified request and pass it along to the HttpClient to use for making the HTTP request.

We could end it here if we only wanted to modify the request, but because we also want to use the response, we're using the RxJS operator do to run our custom logic on the response after it arrives. The do operator allows us to do actions that receive the data on the stream, but don't modify the response itself. This is appropriate in this case because we only want to use the response to modify the Account service, and it would also make sense in a case where you'd do something like logging or caching of the response. If you wanted to modify the response object directly, you'd most likely use the RxJS map operator to modify the stream.

Once we're inside of our do method, we grab a copy of the data and then implement some logic to look through the stocks we've purchased in the Account service and update their current price and value based on the latest prices. When the Account service gets the updated values, the portfolio values will update.

Now that we have our interceptor, we need to correctly set it up so the application is aware of it. Because there may be multiple interceptors, we have to declare our service provider in a different manner. It will be declared in the App module providers array, but in this case we're going to use a *multiprovider*. That means you can provide a new service that gets bundled into a list of other providers. This makes sense if you want to have more than one interceptor (which is possible), but want to be able to refer to all interceptors as a single entity.

Open up src/app/app.module.ts and import the HTTP_INTERCEPTORS token:

```
import { HttpClientModule, HTTP_INTERCEPTORS } from '@angular/common/http';
```

Modify the providers array like this:

```
providers: [
  LocalStorageService,
  CurrencyPipe,
  AccountService,
  {
    provide: HTTP_INTERCEPTORS,
    useClass: StocksInterceptor,
    multi: true
  }
],
```

Here we use an object that will attach our StocksInterceptor to the list of HTTP_INTERCEPTORS. This allows us to define multiple interceptors, all to be added to the same list, which is a realistic scenario.

There are so many potential uses for HttpInterceptors, and in my experience they're often the best solution. Although this example is useful, the best uses are when you want to apply changes to all HTTP requests or responses. In this case, we're only applying the response logic if the URL matches our stock endpoint, so it could be better to handle this logic elsewhere. But I like this interceptor because the logic it powers is about the Account service and not directly about the Stocks service, so it makes sense to separate it like this. That said, I'd recommend that you use interceptors when you need to apply logic to more than one type of request or response, or when the additional action is beyond the scope of the normal service.

Next we'll take a look at helper services that have a more limited role in the application and are primarily there to keep complexity down or reduce code duplication.

6.6   *Helper services*

As you build your application, you may see some code start to reappear in various places. That's what all services help to reduce, but sometimes you'll find that some code feels out of place and needs to be extracted into a service. When you do that, you're creating a service that exposes helper functions to simplify your components. We haven't seen much of this in our examples yet because our applications have been fairly compact.

Imagine you have some custom sorting logic that you want to use when the user selects various filters for a list of items, but that the logic might be used in multiple components. That would be an example of reusing the same logic in multiple places, but also extracting the complexities from the component level to a service to keep your components focused.

I have a few ways to identify code that would be good to be extracted into a helper service. First, if I have to unit test similar logic in multiple places, I know there's a chance to simplify my application and my tests. I also look for code that's particularly difficult to read, often because it's nested several blocks deep. That kind of code becomes challenging to unit test (though you might also want to think about how to reduce the depth as well). Finally, I try to keep track of code that does tasks that are secondary to the primary goal of a function, such as a block that has to do some JSON parsing and validation before being stored on the model.

In our application we'd like to make it easy to access local storage so we can cache the current application state. I think of it as a data access helper service. Getting and storing data in local storage isn't terribly difficult, except we're putting in JSON data that has to be parsed or stringified before local storage can handle it.

We'll create a local storage service to help us manage accessing and storing JSON data and then update our application to check for any cached data on initialization. This will allow us to remember the purchase history for the user (in the current browser only).

Open up app/src/services/local-storage.service.ts and add the code from the following listing. This is a fairly simple service, but it helps us abstract these steps from the controllers.

Listing 6.9   Local storage service

```
import { Injectable } from '@angular/core';

@Injectable()
export class LocalStorageService {
  get(key: string, fallback: any) {
    let value = localStorage.getItem(key);
    return (value) ? JSON.parse(value) : fallback;
  }

  set(key: string, value: any) {
    localStorage.setItem(key, JSON.stringify(value));
  }
}
```

> Method to get a value from local storage

> Method to store a value into local storage

This class is much more basic than the Stocks service, but it still performs an important function. The `get` method lets us request an entry from local storage based on a key and parse it into an object for us. It also accepts a fallback value, which is returned if there is no cached data. The `set` method stores some data into local storage but will stringify the data before it's stored, because local storage only stores strings.

This service is built assuming that you want to store objects or arrays into storage, but you can also store some primitive values like numbers or strings. If you wanted to better handle some of those data formats, it would require more complexity, and later on you could easily expand the service to handle those situations without having to change any of your current uses. That's another great benefit to abstracting this type of logic: You can improve upon it and give it more capabilities as long as you support the current functionality.

In order to use this service, we'll want to cache the application state anytime users buy or sell stocks. That's handled by our Account service, so we'll want to open up src/app/services/account.service.ts and add the bold sections in the following listing. The entire file is included for your convenience.

Listing 6.10   Account service using Local storage service

```
import { Injectable } from '@angular/core';
import { Stock } from './stocks.model';
import { LocalStorageService } from './local-storage.service';

const defaultBalance: number = 10000;

@Injectable()
export class AccountService {
  private _balance: number = defaultBalance;
  private _cost: number = 0;
  private _value: number = 0;
  private _stocks: Stock[] = [];

  constructor(private localStorageService: LocalStorageService) {}

  get balance(): number { return this._balance; }
```

> Imports the Local storage service

> Injects Local storage service into class

```
get cost(): number { return this._cost; }
get value(): number { return this._value; }
get stocks(): Stock[] { return this._stocks; }

purchase(stock: Stock): void {
  stock = Object.assign({}, stock);
  if (stock.price < this.balance) {
    this._balance = this.debit(stock.price, this.balance);
    stock.cost = stock.price;
    this._cost = this.credit(stock.price, this.cost);
    stock.change = 0;
    this._stocks.push(stock);
    this.calculateValue();
    this.cacheValues();          ◄
  }
}

sell(index: number): void {
  let stock = this.stocks[index];
  if (stock) {
    this._balance = this.credit(stock.price, this.balance);
    this._stocks.splice(index, 1);
    this._cost = this.debit(stock.cost, this.cost);
    this.calculateValue();
    this.cacheValues();          ◄
  }
}

calculateValue() {
  this._value = this._stocks
    .map(stock => stock.price)
    .reduce((a, b) => {return a + b}, 0);
}

init() {
  this._stocks = this.localStorageService.get('stocks', []);
  this._balance = this.localStorageService.get('balance', defaultBalance);
  this._cost = this.localStorageService.get('cost', 0);
}

reset() {
  this._stocks = [];
  this._balance = defaultBalance;
  this._value = this._cost = 0;
  this.cacheValues();
}

private cacheValues() {
  this.localStorageService.set('stocks', this.stocks);
  this.localStorageService.set('balance', this.balance);
  this.localStorageService.set('cost', this.cost);
}
```

On purchase or sell, calls cacheValues to store state

Method to store data into local storage

Method to initialize the application state on startup

```
  private debit(amount: number, balance: number): number {
    return (balance * 100 - amount * 100) / 100;
  }

  private credit(amount: number, balance: number): number {
    return (balance * 100 + amount * 100) / 100;
  }
}
```

As you should expect by now, we start by importing the service into our file and then inject it into the class. I hope you're wondering how this works, since there is no `providers` array like in the components. Services must be injected somewhere into a provider, and before you started, the Local storage service was already added to the app module's `providers` array. See src/app/app.module.ts to confirm that the Local storage service is imported and added into the `providers` array. That means this provider is available anywhere in this module, so the Account service can inject it.

We added the new method `cacheValues` to our list of private methods, which will call the Local storage service to save the requested properties. Then both the `purchase` and `sell` methods call `cacheValues` to save the application state.

The last method is an `init` method, and this is used to initialize the data from local storage if it was stored previously. Otherwise, it uses the default values and starts the application with a fresh session. This doesn't get called automatically, because this isn't a lifecycle hook like NgOnInit. I'll address this in a moment.

Since we moved the local storage work into a helper service, it's much easier to use and allows us to keep the Account service more focused as well. You could imagine extracting the Account service's debit and credit methods into a helper service if you needed to do a lot of financial calculations. I find opportunities for helper services easy to spot after I've written some code, though not always obvious when I first write the code.

The last little change we'll make is to call the `init` method, which we'll do from the App component. Open up the src/app/app.component.ts file and add a call to the `init` method as the first line of `ngOnInit`, like this:

```
ngOnInit() {
    this.accountService.init();
    this.load();

    this.interval = setInterval(() => {
      if (this.refresh) {
        this.load();
      }
    }, 15000);
}
```

This will initialize the data from local storage when you start up the application, allowing you to continue an existing session. The Account service is already injected, so we need to use it.

These kinds of helper services can take many different forms, so don't worry too much about making them until you see similar or repeated logic in multiple places or a code snippet is clearly best separated. As you create more Angular applications, you'll get better at creating services earlier on, but I suggest focusing on components first and refactoring to services after you get more familiar.

6.7 Services for sharing

There are many ways to deal with application data and sharing state, as we've already seen in our components in previous chapters' examples. Remember, the primary way to pass data between components is through using input or event bindings, but another option is to store data in a service and use dependency injection to make it available anywhere it's needed.

What you do is externalize some data into a service, and anywhere you need to use it, you inject that service. If you use it in a component's template with data bindings, then change detection will automatically catch any changes on the service and render. Alternatively, you can implement your own change detection in cases where that might be needed using the DoCheck lifecycle hook (similar to what we did earlier).

The service can share data and also methods. You may want to protect access to data, similar to the Config service, or you may make it more public. Over time, as you build larger and more complex applications, you'll likely want to ensure that you lock down the way your services expose data so it doesn't get messed up.

We're going to create a small service to help us display alerts when certain events occur, as you see in figure 6.6.

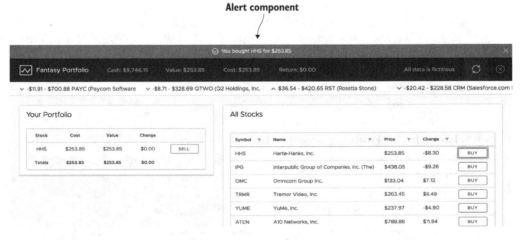

Figure 6.6   Alert component and service appears on purchase

For example, when the user purchases or sells a stock, we can show an alert with the details of the exchange. Open up the src/app/services/alert.service.ts file and update it to match the code in the following listing.

Listing 6.11 Alert service

```
import { Injectable } from '@angular/core';

@Injectable()
export class AlertService {
  show: boolean = false;
  type: string = 'info';          Sets properties to describe the alert state
  message: string;
  timer: any;

  alert(message: string, type: string = 'info', autohide: number = 5000) {

  alert(message: string, type: string = 'info',
autohide: number = 5000) {
    this.show = true;
    this.type = type;
    this.message = message;
    if (this.timer) {
      clearTimeout(this.timer);          Method to display an alert
    }                                     based on configuration
    if (autohide) {
      this.timer = setTimeout(() => {
        this.close();
      }, autohide);
    }
  }

  close() {
    this.show = false;          Method to close the alert
  }
}
```

The Alert service contains three properties that describe whether the alert is visible,
what type it is, and the message to display. These values are initialized with default
values, and the `alert` method accepts arguments that will change the state. The `close`
method changes the state to disable the alert. This service exposes three properties
and two methods that mutate those properties.

This service doesn't do anything on its own—it has to be linked to the Alert component to bind these properties into the component's behaviors. I've already set up
the component template to correctly bind these values where needed if the service is
injected into the component, which is what we need to do next. Open up src/app/
alert/alert.component.ts—we need to import and inject the service. At the top of the
file, make sure to import like you see here:

```
import { AlertService } from '../services/alert.service';
```

Then the class needs to inject the service in the constructor method, like this:

```
export class AlertComponent {
  constructor(private service: AlertService) { }
}
```

While we're looking at the Alert component, note that the template found in src/app/alert/alert.component.html is already trying to reference the service to bind to these properties, such as `*ngIf="service.show"`. The template directly references the values in the service, so if the service property changes, so will the binding.

Now that the Alert component and service are wired up, we can start to use the alerts, right? Not quite. We haven't yet registered the provider, so we need to add it to the App module. Open up src/app/app.module.ts and import the Alert service:

```
import { AlertService } from './services/alert.service';
```

Then add it to the `providers` array to make it available to the application for injection:

```
providers: [
 AlertService,
 LocalStorageService,
 CurrencyPipe,
// ... rest of the providers
```

The App component template should still have the Alert component commented out, so we need to fix that. Open up src/app/app.component.html and uncomment the top line so it will render:

```
<app-alert></app-alert>
```

Now we need to call the Alert service and have it trigger an alert! We'll do this in two different places. In the Account service, we'll show an alert when you buy or sell a stock, and in the App component, we'll show an alert when you toggle the refresh or reset the app state.

While we're still in the App component, let's add the first set of alerts. Update the `toggleRefresh` method to call the service, like you see here:

```
toggleRefresh(): void {
  this.refresh = !this.refresh;
  let onOff = (this.refresh) ? 'on' : 'off';
  this.alertService.alert(`You have turned automatic refresh ${onOff}`,
    'info', 0);
}
```

This calls the Alert service, passing in a message and type and disabling the auto close feature. Likewise, modify the `reset` method like this:

```
reset(): void {
  this.accountService.reset();
  this.alertService.alert(`You have reset your portfolio!`);
}
```

This calls the service but only sets a message and leaves the other defaults in place. Now we can implement the alerts in the Account service. Open up src/app/services/account.service.ts and import the Alert service:

```
import { AlertService } from './alert.service';
```

Then make sure to inject the service onto the controller constructor:

```
constructor(private localStorageService: LocalStorageService,
  private alertService: AlertService) {}
```

Now update the purchase and sell methods, as you see in the following listing.

Listing 6.12 Account service with alerts

```
purchase(stock: Stock): void {
  // ... The rest of the method should remain
    this.cacheValues();
    this.alertService.alert(`You bought ${stock.symbol} for $${stock.
  price}`, 'success');      ◄─────────────────────────────────────┐
  } else {                                                         │
    this.alertService.alert(`You have insufficient funds to buy ${stock.
  symbol}`, 'danger');    ◄──────────── Displays an alert on success or failure of purchase
  }
}

sell(index: number): void {
    // ... The rest of the method should remain
    this.cacheValues();
    this.alertService.alert(`You sold ${stock.symbol} for $${stock.price}`,
    'success');    ◄──────────────────────────┐
  } else {                                      Displays an alert on
    this.alertService.alert(`You do not own    success or failure of sale
  the ${stock.symbol} stock.`, 'danger');
    #B
  }
}
```

Now when the user purchases or sells a stock, the Alert service will get called and trigger the alert to display. In each use, it passes a different message and type based on the circumstances. If you run the application at this point, you'll now see the alert slide in when you buy and sell.

That completes the Alert component and service, and it allows us to easily display an alert from anywhere in the application. We already have a service that shares data, the Account service, but I want to cover one more service and look at it from this perspective. I suggest that you go back and look at the Account service more closely, see how it shares data and makes it available, and consider the pros and cons that it may bring.

Using a service like you see here couples the service and component and means that you can only have one instance of the Alert component. If you had more than one, they'd share the same state, and you'd get multiple copies of the same alert. You could design the service to manage multiple components with some logic if you wanted to, but I suggest thinking about other options.

Although I demonstrate services for sharing data and state here and in chapter 2, I want to emphasize that this can be a tricky approach to scale as you build your application. It can also be problematic if you don't provide the service at the module level, or if you provide it again (by accident of course) elsewhere and get a different copy.

Let's wrap up services by looking at a few less-common services provided by Angular and how you can learn to use them.

6.8   Additional services

Angular has a few other services you can use, like the Http service. To find all the services Angular has to offer, the API documentation lists hundreds of objects that Angular exposes. Sadly, none of them is listed as a service. But here's a little secret: Some of those objects can be used like services!

When you view the API documentation (https://angular.io/api), you'll notice the API is coded with different categories, including Pipe, Class, Function, and Decorator. What this list includes is everything that Angular itself exports, which means you can import any of these items and use them, and some of them can even be injected.

One example is the Location service, which is a class by definition, but acts as a service by providing functionality to read and write values to the browser's URL. Another example is the Date pipe, which can be used to format dates outside of a template. As you explore the API, you'll find other entities that can be used as a service. Although you could import and use any of the API entities, many are only useful in specific situations or for Angular's implementation details.

I'll use the Currency pipe in our example. You'll recall that we show an alert when you buy or sell a stock that shows the sales price. We want to format that number, as we do when we use the Currency pipe in a template. But that isn't possible because the message is set inside a service.

If you remember from our previous chapter examples, the Currency pipe is used like in the following code snippet. It has a binding value and then the pipe symbol with various arguments to configure how it will process the values. In this case, the configuration formats the value in USD, with a dollar symbol, and formats the value to two decimal points:

```
{{stock.price | currency:'USD':true:'.2'}}
```

I want to point out that the Currency pipe is already added as a provider in the App module, which means we can use it with dependency injection in our services. Open up src/app/services/account.service.ts. We're going to start by importing the Currency pipe. Add the following to the imports at the top of the file:

```
import { CurrencyPipe } from '@angular/common';
```

We need to inject the Currency pipe directly into the service through the `constructor`:

```
constructor(private localStorageService: LocalStorageService,
    private alertService: AlertService,
    private currencyPipe: CurrencyPipe) {}
```

Now we can use this pipe in our service when a stock is bought or sold. Look for the line in the `purchase` method that calls the Alert service and modify it to the following:

```
this.alertService.alert(`You bought ${stock.symbol} for ` + this.
    currencyPipe.transform(stock.price, 'USD', true, '.2'), 'success');
```

Likewise, find the corresponding line in the `sell` method and modify it like this:

```
this.alertService.alert(`You sold ${stock.symbol} for ` + this.currencyPipe.
    transform(stock.price, 'USD', true, '.2'), 'success');
```

That's all we need to do to use the Currency pipe. Pipes always have a `transform` method, which is how the pipe is internally processed when the template encounters a pipe, and because we're calling the pipe directly, we follow the same process. It takes the input value (which in the template would be the binding value) as the first argument, and then additional arguments are passed in the same as if it were used in the template.

There are many more services and capabilities in the API that you'll find uses for over time that I don't have room to cover. But before you build a service, you can look through the API to see if Angular exposes something that handles it already.

Summary

We've gone through a lot of capabilities for services and how they work. Services are fundamental for Angular applications, and you'll be building or using many of them. Here is a quick recap of what you've learned in this chapter:

- Services are best for taking on specific tasks, such as data access and managing configuration.
- Services can be injected anywhere in the application as long as they've been registered with a provider.
- Angular provides an HttpClient service that helps manage making XHR requests, and you can wrap your own services around it to simplify data access.
- Services can hold values that get propagated, but you need to be aware of the injection tree to avoid getting different copies of the service.
- A class could be used like a service, without having to use dependency injection, but it should be limited to only situations that make sense.
- Angular exposes many entities in the API that you can use in your application, such as a Location service for managing URLs.

Next up, we'll talk about routing and how to create different types of navigation for your Angular application.

Routing

7

This chapter covers

- What routes are and demonstrates how to create them

- Different patterns for navigation and their merits

- How to protect pages from access without authorization

- Organizing code into modules

- Using secondary routes for multiple routes

Most applications require the ability to navigate between different pages during the lifecycle of the application. Typically, an application has at least a few basic pages, such as a login page, home page, user's account page, and so forth. *Routing* is the term used to describe the capability for the application to change the content on the page as the user navigates around. Our previous chapter examples haven't used routing; they've been limited to displaying all the content at once.

The web has a well-established pattern of using URLs to maintain the current location of a user. This has traditionally happened (and often still does today) by the browser requesting a page from a server and the server responding with the necessary

HTML, CSS, and JavaScript assets. When single page applications (SPAs) became viable, the role of routing had to move fully into the browser, by allowing JavaScript to manipulate the current URL in the browser to maintain the current location within the application, even if the application runs entirely in the browser.

Angular provides a comprehensive routing library that makes it straightforward to create simple and complex navigation patterns. Angular's router library gives us the ability to easily define routes and replaces the need for the server to handle resolving what to display based on the current URL. Instead of using the term *page* to describe different places the user can access, I'll use the term *view* to describe these different contexts, such as login view or dashboard view.

You'll see an example of how to structure your application into different feature modules. Thus far, we've only created one module for our application. When we introduce routing into our application, the complexity and size of our applications are likely to increase. We'll see how to create different modules to keep parts of the application separate from one another. Although we could have done this in other chapters, this chapter example has the most distinct separation between different capabilities.

The first thing we'll do is get the chapter example set up.

7.1   *Setting up the chapter example*

In this chapter, we're going to set up a basic community website where the user can browse forums, blogs, and chat with other users (figure 7.1). I've already created the components and services you'll need for displaying these features, but I've left out the capabilities that will make it functional with routes.

In the example, there's a Forums section where you can view all topics in a forum and then view all of the posts of a particular topic. There's also a Blogs section, where you can see a list of blog posts you can view individually. Lastly, there's a chat feature that pops up over the rest of the content so you can chat with an automated robot while browsing the rest of the site. The application also has login ability and an error page if you navigate to an unknown URL.

Each of these features has at least one route, often more. Let's look at a short list of routes that we'll build in this chapter. These routes represent an important place inside of the application that a user can land in:

- List of forums, which also acts as the default view
- Individual forum, which shows a list of topics
- Individual topic, which shows the posts in the topic
- List of blog posts
- Individual blog post
- Chat box for selecting another user to chat with
- Chat box for talking with another user
- Login view
- Not found error view

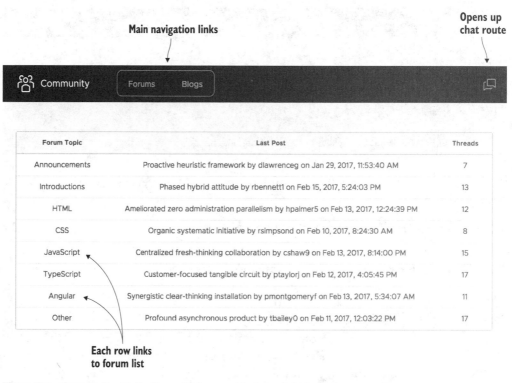

Figure 7.1 Community application with forums, blogs, and chat chapter example

Because I've already created much of the application, we'll start by downloading the existing code either with Git or by downloading the archive from GitHub. This helps us focus on adding only the necessary pieces for routing. If you're using Git, then you can run the following command:

```
git clone -b start https://github.com/angular-in-action/community.git
```

Otherwise, you should download and unzip the project from GitHub: https://github.com/angular-in-action/community/archive/start.zip. You should now have a copy of the code on your computer. You'll need to also install the node modules for the project. Navigate to the directory and run the following to install the modules and then preview the project:

```
npm install
ng serve
```

Initially, the application looks empty, but when we start to set up routes, pages will begin to function. It should appear as you see in figure 7.2. The data for this application is stored in a couple of static TypeScript files (named data.ts), just to avoid having to build an API for this demo and keep it fast. I've also kept the application simpler by avoiding the complexities of allowing users to create new forum posts or blog posts. The routing knowledge you gain from this chapter will help you to easily add those abilities after we cover the forms in the next chapter.

Figure 7.2   What the application should look like based on the starting point

Now that you've got the files and everything set up, let's get to creating our first set of routes!

7.2   *Route definitions and router setup*

There are a few basic concepts that the Angular router leans on, but it's very flexible, and you can create many combinations of various types of navigation experiences. A router is responsible for coordinating the navigation options for a user as they click and interact with your application.

At its most basic, the router handles rendering a component based on the current URL, such as having a Home component render on the main view. It also allows you to create child routes, where only inside portions of a component change based on the route, such as when you have commonly shared portions of the page that always exist, but the inner content swaps based on the URL. It also can support auxiliary routes that sit "above" the current route and have a separate routing history entirely, like live support chat boxes.

Our first step is to get the router included in the project, and then we'll get to create our first couple of routes, as follows:

- /login—Displays the login page
- /—Redirects to the default /forums page in case they load the root page
- **—Fallback for matching any route that isn't defined, like a 404 page

Our goal in this section is to get the router set up, to set up a default route, and to define a fallback route. You'll likely follow these steps for each of your projects in which you use a router.

The Angular router is included as a separate package (@angular/router), which the CLI includes as part of the npm packages, but doesn't actually load into the Application module. If you have a project that doesn't have the module package, you can install it via npm like so:

```
npm install --save @angular/router
```

When we include the router, we'll also need to define a set of routes that are valid for our application. To start off, we'll have two routes. The first is a login screen, and you should notice the corresponding Login component in the app. The second is a 404 not found page, which also has a corresponding NotFound component in the app.

All routes have to be defined, and a definition is only a basic object with at least one property. There are more than a dozen properties you can use to define a route, but a typical route contains a path (or the URL) and a component (the component to display based on the path). We'll see some other properties in action in this chapter as well, but we'll focus first on these two.

Let's define the login route first as we set up the router in the app. Open the src/app/app.module.ts file and add the following imports to the file—this includes the Router module and an interface that describes how routes should be defined:

```
import { RouterModule, Routes } from '@angular/router';
```

We can now define our first routes. Create a new variable with the following values, and then we'll look at both to understand the type of route they define. You can place this right after the last import statement:

```
const appRoutes: Routes = [
  { path: 'login', component: LoginComponent },
  { path: '', redirectTo: '/forums', pathMatch: 'full' },
  { path: '**', component: NotFoundComponent },
];
```

The appRoutes variable, which is typed to Routes, is an array of simple objects. These objects can have different properties, and we'll use many of them in this chapter. You can see all the properties here: https://angular.io/api/router/Routes. Table 7.1 lists the properties we'll use in this chapter, which is most of them.

Table 7.1 Route properties used in this chapter and their purposes

Property	Accepted values	Purpose
path	A string, or wildcard matcher **	Defines the URL path to use for a route; it's appended to any parent paths if routes are nested
component	Reference to a component	Identifies which component is tied to a particular route
redirectTo	A string of another valid route	Redirects a user from one route (the path) to the route defined in redirectTo
pathMatch	'full', 'prefix'	Determines the matching strategy, whether to match a partial or full URL for a route
children	An array of routes	List of routes that are loaded as children of this route
outlet	String of a named outlet	Tells the route to load in a specific router outlet
loadChildren	A string with a path to a module	Allows you to lazy load a new module when a particular route is requested
canActivate	Array of references to guards	Allows you to prevent a route from being used under certain conditions, such as not being logged in

The first route is the most basic and probably most common type of route. It defines that when a certain path is found in the URL, Angular should render the specified component. The path can't start with the backslash. This route means that if the browser is at the URL http://localhost:4200/login, it will render the Login component.

The second route is a redirect route. Angular allows you to redirect paths to other URLs, just as you might with your back end server. The `redirectTo` property defines the new URL to navigate to, and the `pathMatch` property declares that the path must match exactly before the redirect will trigger. If you want to redirect a path and all its children, you could set the `pathMatch` to the value `'prefix'`. In this case, the root path http://localhost:4200/ will redirect to http://localhost:4200/forums. We haven't implemented the forums link yet, so it will render the third route.

The third route is similar to the first in that it defines a path and a component, but the path with two asterisks makes this a wildcard, catch-all type route. If you go to any route that isn't known by Angular, such as http://localhost:4200/not-a-route, it will render the NotFound component.

You'll want to have a wildcard route in your application to prevent navigational errors. I recommend setting up a component like the NotFound component in all your applications from the start.

We've defined our routes. Now we need to set up the router to use them. Inside of the `imports` section of the module, you need to add the Router module, as you see here. I've bolded the new line to add:

```
imports: [
  BrowserModule,
  FormsModule,
  ClarityModule.forRoot(),
  ForumsModule,
  RouterModule.forRoot(appRoutes)
],
```

What we've done is include the router in our application, and we've used the `for-Root()` method to declare that we're using the router in the main App module. It also takes a parameter, which should be an array of routes declared by this module. If you don't pass anything here, the router won't know about any of your routes, so it's the way to pass configuration into the router.

The last step is to make sure there's a Router Outlet component somewhere in your application. You may have been wondering where exactly it will render these components. If you recall from chapter 2, the router needs to know where to render the content for a given route, and the router outlet is the location marker. You'll need at least one router outlet in your application.

Open the src/app/app.component.html file and note that it contains markup for a header and navigation, as well as a content area, which right now contains a single header element. Because the navigation will remain consistent between all routes, it exists outside of the router outlet. This means we don't have to redefine the navigation in every route, and I like to think of this as a "global template" that's always active. Often global navigation or footers are good candidates, but anything that you would have to copy and paste into every component is likely best in the global template.

Replace the header element with the following element to define the router outlet. I've bolded the change for you:

```
<div class="content-container">
  <div class="content-area">
    <router-outlet></router-outlet>
  </div>
</div>
```

When you run the application, go to http://localhost:4200 and you should see the Not-Found component rendered in the screen. Type into the address bar *http://localhost:4200/login* and navigate to the page, and you should see the Login component render.

So far, we've seen a basic route definition, the wildcard matcher, and how to set up the router library with an outlet. You'll go through these basic steps anytime you use the router. In some applications, you might not even need it to get more complex than this!

But most of the time you'll need to navigate to different URLs and pass in information such as IDs for navigating to specific items. Let's look at this now and see how we can build routes that have parameters as we look at how to use a feature module with our application.

7.3 Feature modules and routing

The intention of Angular feature modules is to create isolated code that's easier to maintain and that keeps things together that are logically connected. This is considered a best practice to implement when you have distinct parts of your application that can be split. I think the most important benefit is the isolation of code, but it also can help with creating tests, optimizing the build process, and implementing lazy loading of routes (which we're more interested in right now).

A feature module can include the route definitions for the feature set (see figure 7.3). For example, our Forums section of the application should be its own feature module, and all routes that are related to the forum can be defined inside of it. This is best for decoupling, so we don't have to define routes for a feature module outside of the feature module.

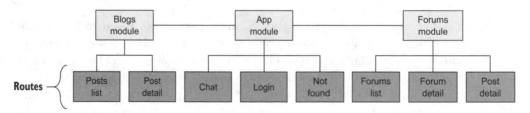

Figure 7.3 Routes are defined by different modules.

This chapter example has two additional modules: the Forums module and the Blogs module. The Forums module has components and services for the Forums section of the site, and the Blogs Module has its own components and services to render the Blogs section. They're already created in the repo, and if you've not spent time with feature modules before, you can take a look at them in the src/app/forums and src/app/blogs directories.

We can declare some routes in our feature modules, but we'll have to include the router and define routes similarly to the previous step. There's one key difference we'll cover, but to get started, open the src/app/forums/forums.module.ts file and import the Router module:

```
import { RouterModule, Routes } from '@angular/router';
```

Now we'll create another array with route definitions. After the last `import` statement, create the following route definition variable:

```
const forumsRoutes: Routes = [
  { path: 'forums', component: ForumsComponent }
];
```

This will define a route to display a list of the available forums on the site by rendering out the Forums component. Now we need to register this list of routes with the router, but we need to use a slightly different syntax to make it work for feature modules. In the `imports` section of the Forums module, add the Router module like you see in bold here:

```
imports: [
  BrowserModule,
  FormsModule,
  ClarityModule.forChild(),
  RouterModule.forChild(forumsRoutes),
],
```

Here we use `forChild()` instead of `forRoot()`, because we're declaring routes that belong to an imported module instead of the main App module. Otherwise, the process is the same, and the route definitions follow the same rules.

The feature module is already included in the App module as one of the imports. You must import a feature module into the main App module for it to be activated. Once you save these changes, you can view the forums page by going to http://localhost:4200/forums.

When you're planning your application, I've found it best to look for opportunities to organize features into separate modules. It's always possible to move things into feature modules later, but if you know that you'll have several key features that can be organized, you can set up modules early in development.

When trying to determine what kinds of things belong together, I often look at the URL structures I expect my application to have. In this chapter example, I expect to put functionality under /forums and /blogs as two separate root paths, so these are good candidates for their own modules.

7.4 Route parameters

URLs are designed to hold information, and sometimes that information tells you important details such as the ID of a resource to load or other stateful data. Depending on how you want to structure your URLs, values might be part of the path or the query.

We'll look at how to use query variables later; right now let's focus on how to use a URL parameter to indicate a record ID. In our example, we have a list of forums displayed and we will want to click on a forum to see the threads inside it. The URL for these routes will be something like this:

```
/forums/1-announcement
```

The difference here is that the second part of this URL will change depending on the forum we want to view, because it contains the alias (which is the ID and title together). Angular supports this with route parameters, which are straightforward to implement. First let's add a new route to our Forums module that will denote the path with a parameter. Open the src/app/forums/forums.module.ts file and add a new route to the forumsRoutes array, as you see here in bold:

```
const forumsRoutes: Routes = [
  { path: 'forums', component: ForumsComponent },
  { path: 'forums/:forum_alias', component: ForumComponent }
];
```

Here we've defined a path with a parameter, which is any name we want to declare preceded by the colon (:) symbol. This will try to match any route that starts with *forums* and has a second part of the path, which could be any value, but if there's a third segment to the path, the router wouldn't match to this route.

7.4.1 Creating links in templates with routerLink

In order to allow users to navigate in the application, we need to create links that work with the Angular router. The way to do that is by using the special routerLink directive from Angular on an element that you want to be a clickable link.

Let's add one routerLink to the top header bar to link to the forums page and see how to create a link using the basic implementation. Open src/app/app.component. html and update the line that contains the currently dead link to the forums with a routerLink, as you see in bold here:

```
<a class="nav-link" routerLink="/forums"><span class="nav-text">Forums</
    span></a>
```

In this use of routerLink, it accepts the string with the appropriate path to use. If the path starts with a forward slash, it will treat the URL as an absolute path from the domain. It could also be a relative path without the slash. This is probably the most common way to use routerLink.

We saw routerLink in chapter 2, but let's take a moment and talk about why it exists and what it does. In order to facilitate navigating around, links must know which URL to go to, and typically href is the attribute for an anchor tag that gives the browser that information. When you use `href` with links, the browser will request a new URL from the server, which isn't what we want. With Angular, `routerLink` is the attribute directive that denotes the expected route to navigate to and allows the Angular router to handle the actual navigation. In short, if you use `href` to link to a page, it will trigger a page load from the server, even if it's a valid Angular route, and that's much slower than using the router. This is a primary tenet of client-side routing.

That's all it takes to create a link, but you can also bind an expression with `router-Link` for more dynamic links. To demonstrate this, we'll add a link from the forums list to load the individual forum page. Open src/forums/forums/forums.component.html (yes, I know the file path is a bit redundant) and update the table row with the `NgFor` to include a `routerLink` to link to the forum:

```
<tr *ngFor="let forum of forums" [routerLink]="[forum.alias]">
```

You'll notice in this case we're binding a value to it (by wrapping it with the [] notation). When you bind a value, it expects an array of path segments that it will use to construct the complete URL. In this case, we're setting the forum alias value in this array. By default, it will treat routes as relative to the current URL, which means it will append to the current route. On this page, the URL is /forums, and each link will be routed to the forum by alias, like /forums/1-announcements.

I like to use `routerLink` in this manner for any paths that don't have any parameters, and I like to bind an array of values to `routerLink` when there are params. I find it easier to read this way, but you can settle on your own approach.

Notice that we also put a `routerLink` on a table row element, which is traditionally not a link. Angular is smart enough to add the correct click event listeners on any element with a `routerLink` to handle navigation, so you're free to use it anywhere. Just be aware that it won't add an `href` attribute to any element that isn't an anchor tag.

7.4.2   *Accessing the route parameters in a component*

Now we need to get the route parameter information into our Forum component so it knows which forum to display. Often, you'll use this route parameter information to call one of your services to load data, and we'll do that here.

Angular provides a service that contains the currently active route metadata. It gives you access to a wealth of information, described at https://angular.io/api/router/ActivatedRoute. It contains details such as the current URL, query or router parameters (and their current values), information about any children or parent routes, and more.

Using this service, we'll access the current parameter information. Open src/app/forums/forum/forum.component.ts and update the class as you see in the following listing. It will inject new services and handle getting access to the route parameters.

> **Listing 7.1   Forum component getting access to route parameters**

```
export class ForumComponent implements OnInit {
  forum: Forum;
```

```
                    constructor(
Calls service          private route: ActivatedRoute,
    to get             private router: Router,              │ Injects the router and current active route
  requested            private forumsService: ForumsService) { }
forum by alias                                                        Subscribes to the
specified by        ngOnInit() {                                      parameters observable
  the route            this.route.params.subscribe((params: Params) => { ◄──
  parameter └──►         this.forum = this.forumsService.forum(params['forum_alias']);
                         if (!this.forum) this.router.navigate(['/not-found']); ◄──
                       });                                          If forum wasn't found,
                    }                                               navigate to error page
                    }
```

This component is activated when the user navigates to a page like /forums/ 1-announcements. We start off by injecting the active route into the route property, and the router service into the router property. You'd normally need to import them into the file at the top, but that should already be done for you.

Inside of OnInit, we then create a subscription to listen for when the parameters change. Many of the values returned by ActivatedRoute are exposed as observables, so you'll have to subscribe to get the values. The primary reason why is that when you have nested routes where a parent and child route are active at the same time, a parent component can subscribe to get updates as any child routes are loaded.

The params observable you subscribe to will return a Params object type, which allows you to access the properties like params['forum_alias']. We then use our service to get the requested forum by passing in the forum alias from the params, and set that to the forum property.

Just because a parameter is provided to a component doesn't guarantee that the alias provided is a valid one, which is a case we should handle. Therefore, if the forum doesn't exist, we'll redirect the user to a not found page.

Throughout the rest of the chapter we'll write this same basic active route observable anytime we need access to the parameters. There are other ways to access the current parameters on the page, but they have some weaknesses and aren't typically used or recommended. One example is being able to get the values one time using a promise instead of an observable, but the drawback there is that you'd only get the parameters one time, and the component wouldn't know about new parameters if the route changed without the component being recreated.

If you're familiar with observables, you may have noticed we didn't unsubscribe from the params observable, because an observable typically persists after a component is destroyed, as an event listener can do. Typically, you should manually unsubscribe or you'll end up with memory leaks, but in this case it's allowed because Angular will destroy this observable as soon as the active route is no longer active. You could unsubscribe in the component's OnDestroy hook if you prefer.

At this point, if you go to http://localhost:4200/forums, you should be able to click a forum and see the title of that forum appear in a new page with the URL changing. Try a few forums to make sure the values change depending on the forum you view.

Now we need to see the threads in a single forum, and we'll use child routes to help us define these routes that are organizationally linked to the specific forum.

7.5   *Child routes*

Having just one component per route can be somewhat limiting and could cause additional complexity in having to re-declare commonly used pieces across multiple components. We talked about how the top navbar remains active and visible across all routes, because it exists outside of the router outlet. We can apply this same principle to our routes so a portion of the route remains active even while you navigate between child routes.

For example, in our application there is a Forum component that contains a header with the forum title (figure 7.4). This will remain active regardless of whether you're looking at the list of threads or at a specific thread. You could imagine that this header bar could also contain common features, such as buttons for creating a new thread in this forum or a button to report spam.

Forums component inside
App component's router outlet

Forum component inside
Forums component's router outlet

Figure 7.4   A child route renders inside of the parent component, as you see here with the Forums component hosting the Forum component.

We just defined a route with the path /forums/:forum_alias. We will continue to use this path base when we start to view a specific thread inside of our forum, and we want it to be like this: /forums/:forum_alias/:thread_alias. When you look at the URL structure here, it shows that you expect both a forum and thread alias to correctly navigate, and that's an indication of a good place to use child routes.

Based on this, you can see that child routes always share their parent route's path and extend it for a new child route. Here is a basic list showing the relationship of these various routes:

- */forums*—Forums component, top-level route
- */forums/:forum_alias*—Child route to show a specific forum
- */forums/:forum_alias/:thread_alias*—Also a child route of a specific forum, showing a particular thread

Child routes work by creating another router outlet that's localized to the parent component, and then all child routes will render inside of this new router outlet. Figure 7.4 shows how nested router outlets will work in our example, by having two routes and components active. There's no limit to how many nested router outlets you could have, though in my experience I recommend no more than three, because it gets more challenging to define the correct routes with more children.

Let's start by adding this new router outlet, which should help you see where the child routes will go, and then we'll define these routes. Open src/app/forums/forum/forum.component.html, and add a new router outlet to the bottom of the file:

```
<header class="header">
  <div class="branding">
    <span class="title">{{forum?.title}}</span>
  </div>
</header>
<router-outlet></router-outlet>
```

This defines where any children will be rendered, so the header will always remain rendered even when the child component routes are active. Now you can think of our routing as two levels: the router outlet in the App component and this localized router outlet.

Next we'll define our routes, and then we can step back and see how it all comes together. Open src/app/forums/forums.module.ts and update the forumsRoutes to match the following listing.

Listing 7.2   Forums module routes with children

```
const forumsRoutes: Routes = [
  { path: 'forums', component: ForumsComponent },          Adds new children
  {                                                        property to forum route
    path: 'forums/:forum_alias',
    component: ForumComponent,
    children: [                                            Defines default path to render
      { path: '', component: ThreadsComponent },           Threads component
      { path: ':thread_alias', component: ThreadComponent }
    ]
  }
];                                                         Defines path with thread alias to
                                                           render Thread component
```

Here we've added a new `children` property to the forums/:forum_alias route. This is how we denote which routes we want to load into the new router outlet of the Forum component.

We've added two routes. The first has an empty path, and will render when we are on the parent route. That will display the list of threads that belong to the forum. The second is to display a single thread by accepting a thread alias parameter. These two routes are now child routes for the forum route.

Child routes also help demonstrate how important it is to use observables when getting route parameters. Parent components remain active and onscreen even as the child components may be destroyed.

Now we can round off the Thread and Threads component capabilities to load the correct data and link to threads. We'll start by helping the Threads component load the correct list of threads to display. Open src/app/forums/threads/threads.component.ts and update it as you see in the following listing.

Listing 7.3   Threads component getting list of threads

```
export class ThreadsComponent implements OnInit {
  threads: Thread[];

  constructor(private route: ActivatedRoute, private forumsService:
    ForumsService) { }

  ngOnInit() {
    this.route.params.subscribe((params: Params) => {
      this.threads = this.forumsService.forum(params['forum_alias']).threads;
    });
  }
}
```

Gets list of threads from service

This is nearly identical to the way we got parameters and loaded the forum data from the Forum component. The only real difference is that we're grabbing the threads instead of the forum data from the service. This pattern will repeat, and I won't belabor the details.

Next open the src/app/forums/threads/threads.component.html file and we'll add a `routerLink` to individual thread routes. Replace the existing table row with this:

```
<tr *ngFor="let thread of threads" [routerLink]="[thread.alias]">
```

Notice again this is a relative link, so it will append the thread alias to the current URL, which would be like /forums/:forum_alias/:thread_alias. That will activate the correct route.

Now that we can navigate to a specific thread, we just need to update the Thread component to grab the active route to have access to the parameters. This will be slightly different due to the way routes are activated, so let's take a look. Open src/app/forums/thread/thread.component.ts and update as you see in the following listing.

Listing 7.4 Thread component loading a thread and accessing parent route

```
export class ThreadComponent implements OnInit {
  forum: Forum;
  thread: Thread;

  constructor(private route: ActivatedRoute, private forumsService:
    ForumsService) { }

  ngOnInit() {
    this.route.params.subscribe((params: Params) => {
      let forum = this.route.snapshot.parent.params['forum_alias'];
      this.thread = this.forumsService.thread(forum, params['thread_alias']);
    });
  }
}
```

Uses the snapshot to access the parent parameters ──→

Subscribes to the params observable

Loads the specific thread from the service

As usual, we inject the active route and subscribe to params. But in this route we have access to the parent route information, because the currently active route information doesn't contain all the parameters we need. The active route information contains that information, so we look at the snapshot property to dig into the parent route. Once we get it, we then use the service to load data for the thread.

You may wonder why we didn't have to do this with the other child route. Since this child route has no path (remember we defined the path as "), it will share the params and the path with the parent route. You will need to keep that in mind as you design URLs.

Make sure you've saved the changes and preview the application again. At this point, you should be able to click the Forum link in the top navbar to see forums, select a forum to view, and then select a specific thread. We've created two child routes by adding a new router outlet and defining them as children of that same route.

Sometimes you need something that's like a child route but that's disconnected from a specific parent route. Let's dive into secondary routes, talk about what they are, and see how you can use them.

7.6 *Secondary routes*

In desktop applications, email applications (such as Outlook or Apple Mail) often will open a new window for composing a new email, and the user can flip between the windows to continue their work. Gmail has a feature that allows you to create a new email in a little window inside the application while you continue to navigate around the rest of the application—which is the same concept as a secondary route. *Secondary routes* are designed to allow the user to draft an email while continuing to use the email application.

These are examples of secondary routes, sometimes also called *auxiliary* routes, where some part of the application appears but maintains a different state from the main application. Chat, help, or documentation windows are also examples of secondary routes.

Angular supports these types of routes, and they behave like having a new root-level router outlet for a set of routes. You can create multiple secondary router outlets, though typically one is enough to satisfy most use cases. The rules for secondary routes are mostly the same as other routes, except sometimes we'll have to specify additional details to ensure the correct router outlet is used, as shown in figure 7.5.

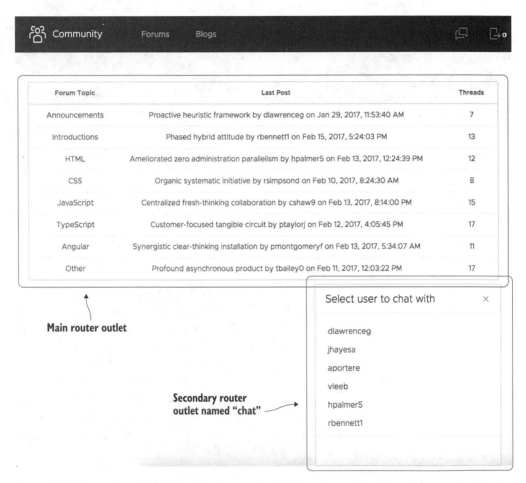

Figure 7.5   The main outlet and the secondary router outlet can be active at the same, and can change their routing states independently of each other.

In this example, we want to have a chat feature that would allow any user to open a chat box with another user, as you see in figure 7.5. This will sit atop the current page so the user can continue to browse the site and read forum or blog posts.

7.6.1   Defining a secondary route

Open src/app/app.component.html and at the bottom of the file add a new line with another router outlet. This outlet has a name attribute to allow us to target loading routes into this outlet instead of the primary outlet:

```
<router-outlet name="chat"></router-outlet>
```

Next we need to define some routes that will be attached to this route. They are as follows:

- */users*—This will show a list of the users you can chat with.
- */users/:username*—This will be the chat experience with another user.

Open src/app/app.module.ts and update the appRoutes to contain these two new routes, as you see here in bold:

```
const appRoutes: Routes = [
    { path: 'login', component: LoginComponent },
    { path: 'users', component: ChatListComponent, outlet: 'chat', },
    { path: 'users/:username', component: ChatComponent, outlet: 'chat', },
    { path: '', redirectTo: '/forums', pathMatch: 'full' },
    { path: '**', component: NotFoundComponent },
];
```

Notice they have a path and component like other routes, but we also declare the outlet property. This is how we'll tell the router to render this component inside of the new router outlet with the name chat. Notice we can use route params in secondary routes as well, so we'll be able to access those params in the same way we have elsewhere. I also placed these routes before the redirect and wildcard routes, because those are meant to act like fallback routes.

The top right of the application has two buttons: a speech bubble button for the chat and a logout button (which we'll implement soon). We want to add a routerLink to the speech bubble button to open this chat box. Go back to the app.component.html file and update the link surrounding the icon like you see here in bold:

```
<a class="nav-link nav-icon" [routerLink]="[{outlets: { chat: ['users']}}]">
    <clr-icon shape="talk-bubbles"></clr-icon>
    </a>
```

Here we use the binding version of the attribute on the routerLink and we pass in an array with an object. The syntax here is more verbose, because we have to pass in additional data for the router to understand that this is meant to be a secondary route. The object contains the outlets property, which then has an object that maps the name of the outlet to the specific route requested. In this case, we're passing {chat: ['users']}, which tells it to use the chat outlet, and then go to the path users. This pattern will repeat for using the secondary routes, so you'll get to see a couple more examples of the structure.

At this point, we've got a secondary route and a way to trigger it. View the application and click the speech bubble icon in the top right to open a new window with a list of users. It allows you to select a user to talk to but doesn't navigate to the chat window with that user. Let's add the ability to navigate within a secondary route now.

7.6.2 *Navigating between secondary routes*

Once you're rendering a component inside of a secondary route, you still link different routes together using the same rules. You don't have to specify the outlet as long as you use relative links. The context of the route will be understood by the router, so this will help simplify your links.

You can change the primary route from a secondary route as long as you provide an absolute path (such as /forums). Using an absolute path from a secondary route will change the primary outlet, but the secondary route will remain at the same route.

To get this working, let's open src/app/chat-list/chat-list.component.html and update the link to start a chat. When you click a username, it sets a property called `talkTo` with the username. We then want to navigate to a relative path with this username, because we defined the secondary route to be /users/:username. Add the bolded `routerLink` to the link:

```
<a class="btn btn-sm btn-link btn-primary" *ngIf="talkTo"
    [routerLink]="[talkTo]">Start Chat with {{talkTo}}</a>
```

The binding will now navigate the user to the Chat component to engage in a fun discussion with that user. But the Chat component doesn't yet get access to the route params to know which user to talk to, so we need to add that to our Chat component.

Open src/app/chat/chat.component.ts and update the constructor and `ngOnInit`, as you see in the following listing. The rest of the controller is focused on handling the chat experience.

> **Listing 7.5   Chat component accessing route params**
>
> ```
> constructor(
>   private route: ActivatedRoute,
>   private router: Router,              Injects the active route and router
>   private chatBotService: ChatBotService,
>   private userService: UserService) { }
>
> ngOnInit() {
>   this.route.params.subscribe((params: Params) => {
>     this.messages = [];                    Subscribes to the
>     this.user = this.userService.getUser();   params and sets
>     this.guest = params['username'];          up chat experience
>   });
> }
> ```

There is nothing new about this, except it sets up the component model to have a new chat experience. You can review the remainder of the component controller to see how it behaves, but at this point the chat box will start to work correctly. You can type a message and hit Enter, and after three seconds the other "user" will reply with some anecdote. This is obviously not a real chat experience, but I wanted to make it realistic.

7.6.3   *Closing a secondary route and programmatic routing*

All good things come to an end, and at some point you'll need to exit this secondary route. For example, you'll likely want to end the chat session at some point. We can close a secondary route, and if we ever need it back we just open it up again. To close a secondary route, you set the current route to null and that will remove it.

I'd also like to show you how to use programmatic (or imperative) routing. Sometimes you'll need to have your controller or services change the route for you instead of always waiting for a user to click an element with a `routerLink`.

If you look at the Chat and ChatList component templates, you'll notice there is a close button near the top of the file. Right now it has a click handler to call the close() method, which is currently empty. Although you could use a routerLink, I wanted to demonstrate programmatic navigation here.

Open the src/app/chat/chat.component.ts and src/app/chat-list/chat-list.component.ts files and update the close method to be the following. You will need to ensure that the router is properly injected in the constructor as well (hint: the Chat component already has it, but ChatList does not):

```
close() {
  this.router.navigate([{outlets: {chat: null}}]);
}
```

The router service provides a navigate method that takes the exact same syntax as routerLink. In this case, we're declaring that the chat outlet should navigate to null, which tells Angular to remove the secondary route. We'll see another use case for programmatic routing next, but I usually find it best to use routerLink whenever possible over programmatic routing.

Now that the secondary route is cleared, there's no other cleanup. It will be removed from the application, and to open it again you just have to reactivate it with a new valid route.

I suggest that you limit using secondary routes to when they provide the most value. They're very useful in the right situations, but it's best to keep it simple. Similar to avoiding too many nested child routes, adding a lot of secondary routes will add complexity that can probably be avoided.

We have a bit of a problem now. We're allowing any user to open a chat window with other users regardless of whether they're logged in. Using routes, we can guard our routes from being activated unless certain conditions are met, to secure them from unauthorized access.

7.7 Route guards to limit access

Angular allows you to control the conditions that allow a route to render, which usually is done to prevent the application from going into a bad state. For example, you shouldn't allow an unauthenticated user to view portions of the application that require them to be logged in or they will likely get a lot of errors.

A *guard* is like a lifecycle hook for route changes that allows an application to verify certain conditions or load data before a change occurs, as you see in figure 7.6. When a route change is triggered (either by the user clicking a link or the app programmatically changing routes), Angular will check to see whether any guards are registered. For example, if an unauthenticated user tries to load the page that displays a logged in user's account details, the application should implement a guard that checks the user's logged in state before activating the route. The term *activate* is used to describe if a route is allowed to be loaded.

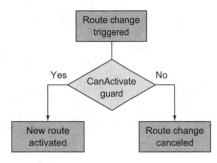

Figure 7.6　Guards run before a route is activated and can prevent access.

There are several types of guards that give you different options when managing how routes are activated. They're defined as a service and then linked to a particular route to take effect. This allows you to use the same guard multiple times. Here are the five types of guards and their basic roles:

- *CanActivate*—Used to determine whether the route can be activated (such as user validation)
- *CanActivateChild*—Same as CanActivate, but specifically for child routes
- *CanDeactivate*—Used to determine whether the current route can be deactivated (such as preventing leaving an unsaved form without confirmation)
- *CanLoad*—Used to determine whether the user can navigate to a lazy loaded module prior to loading it
- *Resolve*—Used to access route data and pass data to the component's list of providers

We're going to implement a guard for the chat routes so that the user is forced to log in first. From that list, the CanActivate guard is the best option for us to accomplish this.

We'll generate a new service to solve this problem, so run the following command to set up the AuthGuard service:

```
ng generate service services/auth-guard
```

Now open the src/app/services/auth-guard.service.ts file and replace its contents with the code from the following listing.

Listing 7.6　AuthGuard service for limiting access to routes

```
import { Injectable } from '@angular/core';
import { CanActivate, Router, ActivatedRouteSnapshot, RouterStateSnapshot }
    from '@angular/router';
import { UserService } from './user.service';

@Injectable()
export class AuthGuardService implements CanActivate {

  constructor(
    private userService: UserService,
    private router: Router) {}
```

Imports dependencies

Implements the CanActivate interface

Injects services into class

```
canActivate(route: ActivatedRouteSnapshot, state: RouterStateSnapshot) {

    if (!this.userService.isGuest()) {
      return true;
    } else {
      this.router.navigate(['/login'], {
        queryParams: {
          return: state.url
        }
      });
      return false;
    }
  }
}
```

Checks if user is logged in

Implements CanActivate method, which gets two params

If user isn't, redirect to login page

It starts like a normal service by importing dependencies, and we want to implement the CanActivate interface to make sure we correctly set up our service. The constructor injects the UserService and Router into the object, which allows us access to the router inside of the service.

The canActivate method must be implemented with this name, because Angular is expecting it that way. That's why the interface is useful to implement; it will warn you if you didn't set it up correctly. It receives two parameters: first the snapshot of the current route activated, and second the new route the application is trying to activate. I only use the new route metadata in this example, but they allow you to inspect the current route and requested route details.

Once inside the method, we check our UserService to see if the user is logged in or not. If they are, we return true to tell the guard that it's acceptable to allow the route to be activated. Otherwise, we tell the route to navigate to the login route, and we also pass an object that contains some metadata. We'll look at this more closely in a moment.

At this point, we've implemented the guard to return true or false, depending on whether the user is valid. If they're not, it redirects to the login screen. After the login process, we want to redirect them back to the page they attempted to view, which is where the metadata object comes into play. Let's look at it again:

```
this.router.navigate(['/login'], {
  queryParams: {
    return: state.url
  }
});
```

The router takes an optional object as a second parameter, and here we're using it to set a query parameter. These are variables that are found in the URL after a question mark, like you see here in bold:

/login?**return=/forums**(chat:user).

We're using this to remember the URL that the user attempted to navigate to by looking at the state.url property (which is the route that the router attempted to activate but couldn't). This is a common pattern in login flows, and you can certainly use query parameters for many other reasons as well in the same way.

That's our guard; now we need to apply it to some routes. To do this, we'll update our appRoutes from the src/app/app.module.ts file; add the following in bold. We need to first import the new `AuthGuardService` and then add a new `canActivate` property to the routes to secure:

```
import { AuthGuardService } from './services/auth-guard.service';

const appRoutes: Routes = [
  { path: 'login', component: LoginComponent },
  { path: 'users', component: ChatListComponent, outlet: 'chat', canActivate:
    [AuthGuardService] },
  { path: 'users/:username', component: ChatComponent, outlet: 'chat',
    canActivate: [AuthGuardService] },
  { path: '', redirectTo: '/forums', pathMatch: 'full' },
  { path: '**', component: NotFoundComponent },
];
```

We also need to add the `AuthGuardService` to our list of providers for the application to know it exists. Add it in the module providers array like this:

```
providers: [
  AuthGuardService,
  UserService
],
```

We've now attached the service as a guard to our chat routes. If you preview the application and attempt to open the chat, it will redirect you to the login screen. The guard fires prior to the chat route being completely activated, and therefore the component will never render, so you don't have to worry about that component having an unauthenticated user.

We want to update the Login component to help with the redirect back to the requested URL once the user logs in. For this login form you can use any values. It's happy as long as you input any random username and password. It also persists the login into localStorage, so it will remember you. Update the src/app/login/login.component.ts file with the contents from the following listing.

Listing 7.7   Login component with redirect after login

```
import { Component } from '@angular/core';              ┐
import { UserService } from '../services/user.service';  ├ Imports dependencies
import { Router, ActivatedRoute } from '@angular/router'; ┘

@Component({
  selector: 'app-login',
  templateUrl: './login.component.html',
  styleUrls: ['./login.component.css']
})
export class LoginComponent {
  username: string = '';
  password: string = '';
  return: string = '';
```

```
constructor(
  private userService: UserService,        Injects services into controller
  private router: Router,
  private route: ActivatedRoute) {}

ngOnInit() {
  this.route.queryParams
    .subscribe(params: Query => {
      this.return = params['return'] || '/forums';
      if (!this.userService.isGuest()) {      Subscribes to queryParams
        this.go();                             observable to get redirect URL
      }
    });
}

login() {
  if (this.username && this.password) {
    this.userService.login(this.username);    Method to validate login
    this.go();
  }
}

private go() {
  this.router.navigateByUrl(this.return);    Method to call router to navigate
}                                             back to return URL
}
```

After you import the dependencies and inject the services into the component, you will implement another observable to get the queryParams just like you would for getting the route params. Because this is a different type of value, you have to subscribe on a different property of the activated route.

Inside of the callback, the return URL is grabbed from the URL (or if it doesn't exist, it sets it to /forums). Then it checks whether the user is already logged in and redirects immediately to the page. This is to help the situation where someone is already logged in but somehow lands on the login page erroneously.

The login() method is called by the component when the user clicks the Login button, and handles logging in the user by calling the user service and redirecting. Then the go() method calls the router.navigateByUrl() method, which is different from the typical router.navigate() method in that it takes a string. Because we're getting a return path from the URL, it will rely on the route to parse the URL and determine the correct URL.

We now need to update the logout feature, which will remove the current user state from the UserService. The service is already there to handle this, but we need to enable the button to call the service.

First open src/app/app.component.ts and update the link to the Logout button like you see bolded here:

```
<a class="nav-link nav-icon" (click)="logout()" *ngIf="!userService.
    isGuest()">
  <clr-icon shape="logout"></clr-icon>
</a>
```

This will disable the Logout button if the user is a guest, and also call the `logout` method to handle the logout. The issue that we might run into is that if you have the chat outlet activated and then you click Logout, it doesn't close the secondary chat outlet. That's because it's only checked on route activation, so we need to manually check whether it's open and close it.

In order to solve this, we need to make a few small changes to the `UserService`. Open src/app/services/user.service.ts. First make sure to import the Router and Activated-Route services:

```
import { Router } from '@angular/router';
```

Then we want to inject those dependencies into the constructor like you see here:

```
constructor(private router: Router) {}
```

Finally we need to update the `logout` method with the bold parts, which will always ensure the router outlet is closed on logout:

```
logout() {
  username = '';
  guest = true;
  localStorage.setItem('username', '');
  this.router.navigate([{outlets: {chat: null}}]);
}
```

This is the same code we used earlier to close the chat outlet, and here we run it to ensure that the outlet is closed. If it's not currently active, nothing will happen.

You'll likely need guards anytime you have to deal with application state, such as logged in users or forms. They're very helpful, but like most things they're best used sparingly. You can have multiple guards on the same route, but the more you have, the more difficult it is to keep track of application logic.

On the other hand, you should be sure to use guards instead of relying on adding logic into a component controller directly to check whether the user can activate a route. Components shouldn't be concerned about router configurations as much as possible (with the obvious exception of getting parameter information from URLs).

Our last major feature is to lazy load Angular modules into the application only when they're needed, which can be a boost to initial load time for large applications.

7.8   *Lazy loading*

If you're building your application and using feature modules to organize code, then you can use *lazy loading* (or *asynchronous loading*) with the router (figure 7.7). Doing so will allow an entire module to load only when required, which can save on file size of the core bundles, perhaps even limiting access to bundles for only those who are authorized to use it (like administrative modules).

If you haven't organized your application into different modules, then lazy loading them into the application isn't possible, because there's no logical isolation. The basic idea is that the Angular build process can analyze the code paths and optimize the code based on how it's used to generate different files, but it depends on Angular modules as the primary way to determine how code is related.

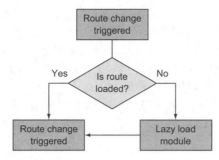

Figure 7.7 Lazy loading a module happens only when the route is requested and must be loaded before the route can activate.

In our chapter example, we have three modules (excluding Angular or third-party modules):

- AppModule
- ForumsModule
- BlogsModule

The AppModule is our primary application, and the ForumsModule is directly imported into the AppModule. But we haven't imported the BlogsModule yet, and when we want to lazy load, we don't want to import the module into our application directly.

Let's see this in action by setting it up ourselves with the BlogsModule. Open src/app/app.module.ts and update the routes as you see here in bold:

```
const appRoutes: Routes = [
  { path: 'login', component: LoginComponent },
  { path: 'users', component: ChatListComponent, outlet: 'chat', canActivate:
    [ AuthGuardService ] },
  { path: 'users/:username', component: ChatComponent, outlet: 'chat',
    canActivate: [ AuthGuardService ] },
  { path: 'blogs', loadChildren: 'app/blogs/blogs.module#BlogsModule' },
  { path: '', redirectTo: '/forums', pathMatch: 'full' },
  { path: '**', component: NotFoundComponent },
];
```

The new route contains a path and blogs, and the `loadChildren` property is used to define a path to the module that should be lazy loaded when the browser tries to access any URLs starting with /blogs. The `loadChildren` property takes a file path pointing to the actual module file, starting from the src directory and excluding the .ts extension. It then has a hash (#) symbol, followed by the module name. This special syntax lets Angular know both the location of this module and the name so it can properly create it.

This is all the configuration you need to do to enable lazy loading of a module, but we still have a little bit of work to do to the BlogsModule for it to function as expected. So far, it doesn't have any routes declared, which means this won't work just yet.

In the AppModule and ForumsModule, we created a variable in the file and stored the routes in the same file. But you can also create what's called a *router module* to store this configuration. This may be favorable if your configuration is complex and you want to keep your module files cleaner.

I personally have found that routing modules are just extra files if my application is small, but they're more meaningful as my application gets larger. I think it's more important to be consistent in how you declare your routes rather than which you choose. But if you need a generic guideline, then I suggest that if you have more than three modules, you use a routing module. The choice is yours.

When you create modules with the Angular CLI, you can have it generate a routing module for you by adding the `--routing` flag:

```
ng generate module mymodule --routing
```

Because the BlogsModule already exists, we'll need to manually create the routing module for the Blogs module. Create a new file at src/app/blogs/blogs-routing.module.ts and add the contents from the following listing.

Listing 7.8   Routing module for blogs

```
import { NgModule } from '@angular/core';
import { Routes, RouterModule } from '@angular/router';          Imports dependencies

import { BlogsComponent } from './blogs/blogs.component';
import { BlogComponent } from './blog/blog.component';

const routes: Routes = [
  { path: '', component: BlogsComponent },
  { path: ':post_id', component: BlogComponent }          Defines routes for this module
];

@NgModule({
  imports: [RouterModule.forChild(routes)],          Uses the RouterModule.forChild() method to
  exports: [RouterModule],                           register routes, and exports RouterModule
  providers: []
})
export class BlogsRoutingModule { }
```

This module is a bit different from normal modules, as it's focused only on setting up the necessary pieces for routing. After you import all the dependencies, you still declare a variable with the routes as we have in the other examples. Notice that these paths don't contain a prefix of blogs, because we already defined that prefix in our lazy load route definition. These routes are simple in that they map to a component to render.

Finally we declare the `RouterModule.forChild()` method in the module `imports`, just as we did with the ForumsModule. Then we also add the RouterModule in the `exports`, which makes the router directives available to this module's templates.

We didn't declare any redirect or fallback routes here. That's because the one we defined in the AppModule will still catch any unknown URLs. Routes can be declared anywhere in the application, and Angular will try to match to the best URL, which demonstrates the importance of good URL planning.

To consume the router module, we need to import it into our BlogsModule. Open src/app/blogs/blogs.module.ts and add the new import line here:

```
import { BlogsRoutingModule } from './blogs-routing.module';
```

Then we need to add it to the imports for the module like this:

```
imports: [
  CommonModule,
  BlogsRoutingModule,
],
```

That completes the routing module setup, and if you had generated it with the CLI, the files would already exist for you to add your routes. Now we want to make use of the BlogsModule by adding a link to the Blogs section in the navbar. There's already a link for it, so we'll just need to add `routerLink`. Open src/app/app.component.html and update the link to the blogs:

```
<a class="nav-link" routerLink="/blogs"><span class="nav-text">Blogs</span>
    </a>
```

Now when you run the application and click Blogs in the navbar, it will take you to the Blogs section. If you open the developer tools, you can also watch the HTTP requests to see that the Blogs module is loaded asynchronously on demand. It happens so fast when you work locally that there shouldn't be any lag, but there would be a slight lag for that file to download from a remote server.

The rest of the blog components already have `routerLinks` set up for you, but you can stop and review them if you like. There's nothing new in there that we haven't already done a few times already.

That wraps up the primary Angular routing capabilities you'll likely need to use in most of your applications. Although there are some features that I wasn't able to cover, I haven't had many occasions to use capabilities that aren't outlined in this chapter.

Before closing out this chapter, I'd like to review a few best practices from my experience for crafting good routes and using the Angular router.

7.9 Routing best practices

There have been a lot of debates around how to design your application URL structures, and I have some particularly strong opinions about what constitutes good design. There are also debates about whether URL design is really all that important, because most of the time users don't type URLs into the address bar, anyway.

I can't force you to follow any specific rules, but I do want to share my beliefs and experiences with you. I believe that URL design is essential to quality applications. Good URL structure makes applications easier to maintain, can help users navigate your website, and should help maintain navigational state. Just as you might spend time planning a page's layout, you should take time to plan your application's URL structure.

I would like to suggest the following as best practices, which I put into practice with my applications and believe are the most likely to provide you with a solid foundation:

- *Keep URLs short*—When possible, URLs should be only as long as they need to be. This can be tricky as your application grows, so being vigilant from the start is the best way to keep on track. There may be some SEO considerations for your URLs, for which I suggest you just keep it simple.

- *Favor path parameters over query variables*—The use of query variables should be limited to transient stateful data, such as search filter variables. When you use IDs or resource aliases in the URL, they should almost always be path parameters.
- *Prefer to spell out words*—I have a strong preference for not abbreviating variables or paths, because it's harder to read and some abbreviations are not always clear. Although you should keep URLs short, you shouldn't shortcut the words you use.
- *Use hyphens when using multiple words*—The readability of a URL is important, and if you have multiple words together (like /forums/2-introductions/89-cloned-didactic-knowledge-user), using hyphens between words is the easiest way to read. It's also easy to parse.
- *Limit the use of secondary routes*—As fun as secondary routes can be, they add complexity. If a secondary route is contextual to only some of the application routes, then you'd have to keep track of when to enable or disable that secondary route. For example, if you have an application for a bank and there is a secondary route for opening a new account, you would need to pay attention to what the user does and determine when it might be appropriate to close it.
- *Carefully consider the correct guard to use for your use case*—There are five types of guards, and sometimes they can be bent to do different tasks. Be aware of the purpose of your guard and use the correct one.
- *Use feature modules so you can use lazy loading*—Feature modules are helpful for code isolation, but being able to lazy load modules is extremely useful. It's much easier to start with feature modules and not use lazy loading than it is to later have to refactor to feature modules to use lazy loading.
- *Keep it simple*—This is true of all things, but I think it's the most important underlying principle in routing. Things can quickly get out of hand if you have 100 routes when you only needed 10 that had better parameters. Look for ways to simplify all the time!

The rules for the Angular router are fairly straightforward, and most of the complexity comes from combining these features. That's the inherent power of the Angular router and its design. It's simultaneously simple and capable of complex scenarios. I caution against making a simple scenario into a complex one unnecessarily, but given some mastery of the router you'll be able to craft routes to handle any use case.

Summary

The Angular router is quite powerful, and yet the basic principles are easy enough to pick up quickly and put into practice. We've gone through a lot of capabilities for services and how they work. Services are fundamental for Angular applications, and you'll be building or using many of them. Here's a quick recap of what you learned:

- The RouterModule needs to be included in any module that uses routing. When you set it up in the AppModule, you call the `forRoot()` method to set it up for the application.

- Routes are defined as arrays of objects that contain properties applicable for those routes, such as a path, a component to render, and/or child routes.

- Routes can accept parameters, both in the path or as query variables, to allow you to reuse a route with different parameters. These parameters are made available to the component controller through the activate route details.

- Using `routerLink` you can link any element to a particular route. It can be given a basic string with a valid path, or you could also use the binding syntax to pass in additional data as an array.

- Child routes render inside of a parent component and allow you to reuse code, such as sharing common navigation or resolving data.

- Secondary routes are useful to create routes that are standalone and detached from the primary routes. This can be useful for experiences that are active regardless of which page you are on, such as documentation windows.

- Use guards to limit access to routes, resolve data prior to activating a route, or prevent a route from being deactivated. You'll have to create a service to include in the route definition to enable the guard.

- Feature modules can be lazy loaded into the application, giving you the ability to reduce the file size of the code that's initially downloaded to users. It only loads the module when the user navigates to a route that's part of the feature module.

In the next chapter, we're going to look at forms in depth and make it easy to capture user input.

Building custom directives and pipes

This chapter covers

- How to create your own directives
- The difference between structural and attribute directives
- How to use a directive to modify another component
- How to craft custom pipes
- What pipe purity is and how to design stateful or stateless pipes

Angular ships with a number of directives and pipes for the broadest use cases. Chapter 3 covered the defaults, so you can review what they are and how they're used. This includes directives such as NgFor and NgIf for iterating over a list or conditionally displaying items, and pipes such as Currency and Number for formatting values for currency or number display.

This chapter focuses on creating custom directives and pipes and talks about why you might create them. The built-in pipes and directives may fill many of the use cases, but sometimes your application requirements will benefit from a custom implementation to make things easier to use.

There are two types of custom directives, which have their own use cases and capabilities. We'll create one that modifies some attributes of an element, one that modifies the default behaviors of a component, and one that changes the way the elements are added to the page.

Likewise, we'll also be building some custom pipes to demonstrate what value they can provide you. Just like directives, there are two types of pipes that you can build depending on your needs. We'll create three different pipes to demonstrate the scenarios in which they're useful and discuss best practices and design for performance.

The bundled directives and pipes cover a lot of the primary use cases, but often developers will need to craft their own. I find the early stages of building an application can often be accomplished without any, but once I start to notice places of duplication or unnecessary complexity, I start to create my own. Sometimes I don't always see the best way to design a custom pipe or directive until I've already built something else that needs to be improved.

That's why in this chapter I'm tackling the perspective of adding custom pipes and directives to the chapter 2 example application that you should already be familiar with. I believe it's easier to see the role and value of them in the context of an existing application rather than just building isolated examples.

To be completely honest, it's entirely possible to never create your own directives or pipes by just adding more logic into components—so why even bother? The main reasons apply to both directives and pipes:

- *Reuse and reduce*—Instead of each component having to implement similar logic, it can be abstracted out and easily reused. This also reduces code footprint and helps standardize logic.
- *Maintainability and focused components*—Components sometimes become a dumping ground for code and logic that are tangential to the component itself. Removing that from the component makes it easier to maintain your components.
- *Testability*—Moving everything into smaller blocks means you can create smaller test cases and limit permutations.

There are certainly a few scenarios where custom directives or pipes are required or the best solution. For example, custom directives are useful when we want to create some custom form validation, as we'll investigate in the next chapter.

The number of situations in which you'll need to create your own will vary from project to project, and I've found that the ones I've created once are often useful for other projects.

8.1 Setting up the chapter example

In this chapter, we'll take the stock application example from chapter 2 and add some custom pipes and directives to it. Doing it that way will help us minimize the number of new things to review during this chapter while giving us some useful examples.

If you skipped chapter 2 or don't recall the specifics of that example, the application is a basic stock tracking application. It displays a list of stocks and their current statuses and allows you to add or remove items from that list. It loads real data from a service as well. We won't make any drastic changes to the way the application behaves, but we will simplify a few things with the use of custom pipes and directives. You can see what it will look like in figure 8.1.

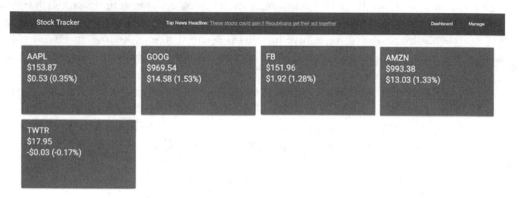

Figure 8.1   What we'll build in this chapter extends the example from chapter 2.

Regardless of whether you have the chapter 2 sample already or not, we'll be starting from a new repository. To download with Git, clone the repo and check out the starting point using the following:

```
git clone https://github.com/angular-in-action/stocks-enhanced
cd stocks-enhanced
git checkout start
```

Otherwise, you can download the archived files from https://github.com/angular-in-action/stocks-enhanced/archive/start.zip and unzip the files.

As usual, you'll need to run `npm install` to download all the dependencies. Then run `ng serve` to start the local development server.

8.2   *Crafting custom directives*

There are two types of directives: *structural* and *attribute*. The way they're declared and used is essentially identical, but they have one key difference that you've seen in use in previous chapters. When we want to change a property of an element (such as the background color or height), we'll need to use an attribute directive. But if we want to have control over how the element itself is rendered into the page, we'll rely on the structural directive.

We've had use cases where we wanted an element to appear on the page only when certain conditions were true, specifically a loading indicator. This is a great example of how we use a directive to change how the element is rendered. Likewise, we've needed to dynamically change the background color of an element, and we did that by modifying the classes on the element with a directive.

More specifically, recall that you must prefix ngIf with *—for example, *ngIf="loaded = true". This means that NgIf is a structural directive and is able to control whether the DOM element is rendered or not. On the other hand, the ngClass directive is an attribute directive and doesn't have the * when it's used, such as [ngClass]="{active: true}". NgClass simply modifies the properties of the element—in this case, the CSS class is applied—but doesn't render DOM.

The difference is in the structural directive's ability to add or remove DOM elements from the page. It's similar to the idea of construction: You can remodel an existing building (attribute directive) or handle the creation of the building itself (structural directive). A structural directive can render DOM, but an attribute directive can only modify properties. The structural NgIf directive can determine if the DOM element is rendered based on the conditional value provided. The NgClass attribute directive doesn't create elements, but rather changes the element's class list.

In figure 8.2, you can see how attribute directives modify a component and how a structural directive creates (or destroys) components. In this chapter's example, the NgFor structural directive creates multiple instances of the Summary component, whereas the NgClass attribute modifies the background color of those same instances.

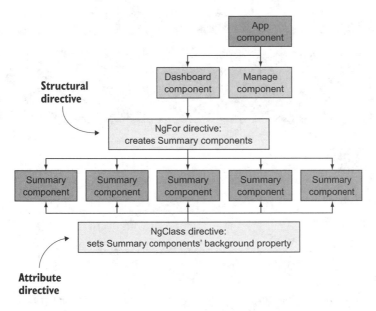

Figure 8.2 **How a structural or attribute directive modifies the DOM**

Therefore, the primary difference between structural and attribute directives is that a structural directive is designed to modify the DOM tree of an element, whereas an attribute directive is designed to only modify the properties or DOM of a single element. We'll build an example of both types in this chapter.

Remember, neither structural nor attribute directives have a template. Technically, *components* are a third type of directive, and the only type that has a template. If you ever need a template for your implementation, you should use a component.

Directives can inject services just like a component, which gives you access to some interesting capabilities. If you have custom services, your directives could leverage them for use cases such as knowing whether the user is logged in and conditionally showing or hiding content.

We'll start by building an attribute directive, a second attribute directive to modify a component, and then a structural directive. Let's get to it!

8.2.1   Creating an attribute directive

Our first directive is going to help us manage the color of the Summary component, which is the card that displays the current stock information. The result won't change the visual experience for the user but will abstract the capability so it can be reused. Right now, the Summary controller contains logic that's used by the NgClass directive to change the background color to green or red based on the day's change in value.

Although this isn't necessarily a problem, we can abstract this into its own attribute directive in case we ever want to use it again. That's a great use for attribute directives, because it's simply managing the list of classes applied to an element, as shown in figure 8.3.

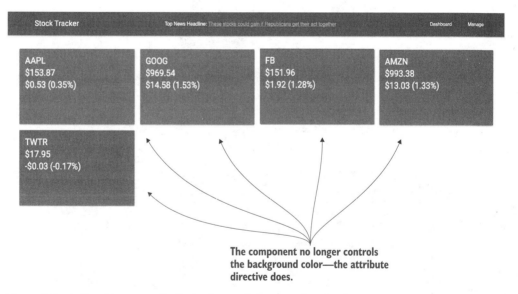

The component no longer controls the background color—the attribute directive does.

Figure 8.3   A directive can modify the background property of an element, so the component doesn't have to manage the logic.

The Angular CLI allows us to generate the directive scaffolding quickly, so we'll use the following command to generate the files we need—the files will be placed inside of the src/app/directives directory:

```
ng generate directive directives/card-type
```

As with a component, it will also add the directive to the App module for you, saving a little bit of effort. We'll implement this directive to also take an input that contains the stock data used by the component so we can detect the correct class to attach.

Let's go ahead and create our directive. Open src/app/directives/card-type.directive.ts and replace its contents with what's shown in the following listing.

Listing 8.1   Card type directive

```
import { Directive, ElementRef, Input, OnInit } from '@angular/core';
                                                        Imports dependencies

@Directive({
  selector: '[cardType]'            Declares directive using decorator,
})                                   and defines the selector
export class CardTypeDirective implements OnInit {
  @Input() cardType: number = 0;
  @Input() increaseClass = 'increase';     Creates an input by the same name as
  @Input() decreaseClass = 'decrease';      the selector, and two more with defaults

  constructor(private el: ElementRef) {}        Injects a reference to the element
                                                 the directive is applied onto

  ngOnInit() {
    if (this.cardType) {
      if (this.cardType >= 0) {
        this.el.nativeElement.classList.add(this.increaseClass);
        this.el.nativeElement.classList.remove(this.decreaseClass);
      } else if (this.cardType <= 0) {
        this.el.nativeElement.classList.add(this.decreaseClass);      Implements a
        this.el.nativeElement.classList.remove(this.increaseClass);  lifecycle hook to
      } else {                                                        change the classes
        this.el.nativeElement.classList.remove(this.increaseClass);  based on daily
        this.el.nativeElement.classList.remove(this.decreaseClass);  change
      }
    }
  }
}
```

The first thing you should notice is how similar this looks to a component, because a component is really a special type of directive that has a template. Directives use the template of the element they are applied to instead of having their own template.

The directive starts by importing a few things that we'll need, and then we have the Directive decorator. Here we only define the selector, [cardType], which is the CSS form of making it work as an element attribute. This decorator is applied to the exported class CardTypeDirective.

Directives can take inputs, and we define some properties to accept input bindings. By defining one by the same name as the directive selector, we can then bind to the directive, like <div [cardType]="stock"></div>. The cardType property will accept a number, and, depending on whether the number is positive or negative, will apply the appropriate class. The other two inputs are to allow someone to change the class names applied, and they have defaults set in case we choose not to define them. This enables this directive to be flexible and more reusable than having everything hard-coded.

The constructor is used to inject a property that contains a reference to the element that the directive is applied to. We then use that in the lifecycle hook to change the classes based on the cardType number being positive or negative. If the card is neither positive nor negative, it won't apply any class.

Now let's put this directive to use and see how it works out. Open src/app/components/ summary/summary.component.html and update the first line of the template to the following, which will remove the NgClass and add the fade-in animation that's on the card:

```
<div class="mdl-card stock-card mdl-shadow--2dp" [cardType]="stock.change" [@
    fadeIn]="'in'" style="width: 100%;">
```

You can also open the src/app/components/summary/summary.component.ts file and remove the isNegative and isPositive methods from the controller, as they're no longer used. We didn't end up using the increaseClass or decreaseClass input bindings, but you can try them out.

When you run the code at this point, you should in fact see no change, except the animation of the cards while they fade in on load. We were able to refactor the logic into a separate directive and make it more flexible for reuse without breaking the current implementation.

A primary role of directives is to facilitate reuse. The cardType attribute directive allows this by decoupling the specific implementation of using NgClass into a more abstract directive that accepts a number to add the same classes. You might not initially build your application with these types of smaller directives, but keep an eye out for opportunities for reuse like this.

Another key aspect of this example is how it simplified the Summary component by removing logic that wasn't essential to the component itself. Though there was nothing inherently bad about how it was before, it did require the Summary component to contain methods to manage how it adds classes. Again, look for opportunities to keep your components focused and simplify their roles by moving unnecessary capabilities outside.

8.2.2   *Modifying a component with a directive with events*

The cardType directive was used to modify a div element, but we can also apply custom directives to components to modify them. Many times you'll use an external library of components and wish it did something slightly differently. To some extent, you can modify those components without having to reimplement them yourself. This doesn't require a different type of directive—it's still an attribute directive—but it does show how you can modify components that you didn't write yourself.

Let's imagine that the Summary Card itself is a third-party component that we didn't write ourselves. We don't like the way it behaves out of the box, and we can craft a directive to let us change its default behavior or add new abilities. Fundamentally, this is no different from putting a directive on a normal HTML element, but people don't often consider this approach instead of hacking the third-party library. In our particular example, we want to add a hover effect and shadow to the cards on hover to give it a unique feel.

The examples in figure 8.4 are useful for showing how to modify a component without changing it directly. We'll add event listeners to handle mouse events and override the background color.

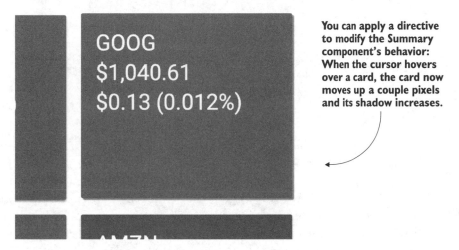

You can apply a directive to modify the Summary component's behavior: When the cursor hovers over a card, the card now moves up a couple pixels and its shadow increases.

Figure 8.4   Directive that handles hover events and modifies a component indirectly

To get started we need to generate another directive. Run the following in the terminal to create the CardHover directive:

```
ng generate directive directives/card-hover
```

Now open the src/app/directives/card-hover.directive.ts file and replace its contents with the code from the following listing.

Listing 8.2   CardHover directive

```
import { Directive, ElementRef, OnInit, HostListener } from '@angular/core';
```
Imports dependencies
```
@Directive({
  selector: '[cardHover]'
```
◄──── Notes the selector is the cardHover attribute
```
})
export class CardHoverDirective implements OnInit {
  card: any;

  constructor(private el: ElementRef) {}

  ngOnInit() {
    this.card = this.el.nativeElement.querySelector('.mdl-card');

    if (this.card.classList.contains('increase')) {
      this.card.style.backgroundColor = 'rgb(63,81,181)';
    } else if (this.card.classList.contains('decrease')) {
      this.card.style.backgroundColor = 'rgb(255,171,64)';
    } else {
      this.card.style.backgroundColor = '';
    }
  }
}
```
OnInit method to override the background colors of the cards

```
@HostListener('mouseover') onMouseOver() {
  this.card.style.boxShadow = '2px 2px 1px #999';
  this.card.style.top = '-2px';
}

@HostListener('mouseout') onMouseOut() {
  this.card.style.boxShadow = '';
  this.card.style.top = '';
}
}
```

HostListener events to handle mouse events for hover states

This directive is structured similarly to the previous one, with importing dependencies and defining a selector attribute. The focus for this directive is the three methods for ngOnInit, onMouseOver, and onMouseOut.

In the ngOnInit method, we start by getting a reference to the card by querying the element. Then we inspect the classes to determine whether the stock price is positive or negative, and change the background color property of the element to override the default provided by the component.

Then inside of the onMouseOver and onMouseOut methods, we change styles to give the cards a box shadow and move them slightly up to make them appear to hover slightly above the page. The event listener is triggered by using the @HostListener decorator, which takes a single argument for the event to listen to. This is an event binding, but done through the context of a directive. There are many cases where you will need a directive to listen for events to handle your logic.

To use this, we just need to update the use of the Summary component in the src/app/components/dashboard/dashboard.component.html file, like this:

```
<summary [stock]="stock" cardHover></summary>
```

Just by adding the attribute, the new behaviors will attach to the Summary component, and the new background colors should appear along with the hover affects. This directive is designed specifically to modify an existing element, which I find to be a good solution to the problem of components not doing everything exactly as we need.

This example shows one way to modify a component, but you could also implement an Input that would capture data to help you do additional processing if you need more data than just the element itself.

These two attribute directive examples describe a number of concepts that interplay as you think about how to craft your own directives for maximum impact. Sometimes they will need to be generic for maximum reuse, but it's often useful to create them for specific use cases as we've done here.

You may be wondering why we used JavaScript to change element styles. We certainly could have written some CSS to handle some of this logic, since appropriate class names were applied to use in selectors. But I wanted to demonstrate the use of element manipulation using JavaScript because you can do so much more with it than CSS. Keep your use cases and needs in mind, and if you can use CSS only, then that's perfectly fine, but directives give you access to the entire element and DOM APIs.

Let's shift gears and talk about the other type of directives that allow us to manipulate the existence of the element itself.

8.2.3 *Creating a structural directive*

Structural directives allow you to modify the DOM tree of the element, not just the element itself. This includes being able to remove the element and replace it with something else, creating additional elements, and so forth.

As discussed earlier in the chapter, the use cases for structural directives are more limited, and the built-in examples of NgIf, NgFor, and NgSwitch are likely to provide you with everything you need.

But you still want to learn about it, right? Let's create a directive that will delay the rendering of the element for a certain number of milliseconds. You can use this to fade elements into the page—in our case, we want each card to have a different delay so they appear to fade in sequentially, as shown in figure 8.5.

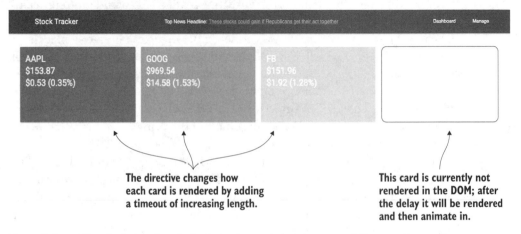

Figure 8.5 Adding the Delay directive to have the cards fade in sequentially, one after another

We'll build one and then come back to a key point about why they're always preceded with a * symbol when they're used. It'll be easier to see why after we walk through the example.

Start by generating a new directive by running the following command in the terminal:

```
ng generate directive directives/delay
```

Open src/app/directives/delay.directive.ts and replace its contents with the code you see in the following listing.

Listing 8.3 Delay directive

```
import { Directive, Input, TemplateRef, ViewContainerRef } from
    '@angular/core';                        ◀── Imports the necessary
                                                dependencies
@Directive({
  selector: '[delay]'
})
```

```
export class DelayDirective {
  @Input() set delay(ms: number) {
    setTimeout(() => {
      this.viewContainer.createEmbeddedView(this.templateRef);
    }, ms);
  }

  constructor(
    private templateRef: TemplateRef<any>,
    private viewContainer: ViewContainerRef
  ) { }
}
```

Defines an input as a setter method, which delays the rendering of the template

Injects the necessary dependencies

In this directive, we're importing dependencies, of which `Input`, `TemplateRef`, and `ViewContainerRef` are required. `TemplateRef` and `ViewContainerRef` are references to the template of the element our directive is attached to and a reference to the view that contains it, respectively.

When the structural directive is rendered by Angular, it creates a placeholder space, called an *embedded view*, where the directive can decide what to insert inside of this new view container. Using the `ViewContainerRef`, we can access this view and create any number of views. The documentation for `ViewContainerRef` can be found at https://angular.io/api/core/ViewContainerRef and is a good place to go to learn more in-depth about how views work in Angular. But the primary point is that we end up with an empty container that we can add one or more views into.

After it renders the view container, it takes the template and extracts it into a template so that it's removed from the page but still accessible and available via the `TemplateRef`. That means Angular won't render out the template unless our directive explicitly calls the necessary methods to render it out. This is how you can handle the lower-level rendering of an element.

Now our constructor injects both of these references into our directive so we can use them in the setter method. The `Input` is defined as a setter (which is a feature of Java-Script) and uses the same name as the selector, so we can bind data into the directive easily. The `delay` property accepts a number, which is the number of milliseconds to delay the rendering of the element. This is immediately passed into a `setTimeout` function that calls the following line after the specified delay:

```
this.viewContainer.createEmbeddedView(this.templateRef);
```

This line is where we create a new view inside of the view container and then pass it the template reference to render. This is how NgIf works under the hood by checking the truthiness of the value passed into the NgIf and creating or clearing the view.

Now back to the business of the * in structural directives. We didn't have a `TemplateRef` or `ViewContainerRef` in our attribute directives, and the * is the syntactic way to describe to Angular that this directive needs to capture the template and create a view container before the element is rendered. This directive is used like `*delay="1000"`, to denote a delay of 1 second before it's displayed.

Let's put this into use on the Summary components, so open src/app/components/dashboard/dashboard.component.html and update the template where it iterates over the cards:

```
<div class="mdl-cell mdl-cell--3-col" *ngFor="let stock of stocks; index as
    i">
  <summary [stock]="stock" *delay="i * 100" cardTone></summary>
</div>
```

We've extended the NgFor to also create a variable `i` that holds the current index in the loop, and then we multiply the index by 100 and pass it to the Delay directive. This will stagger the display of each card by 100 milliseconds sequentially, and, coupled with the animations on the Summary component, it will also animate in gracefully.

Structural directives are a little trickier than attribute directives because you're working with the Angular views instead of an already rendered element. Thankfully, the use cases for when a structural directive is appropriate are less common.

Most of the directives you'll create are likely to be of the attribute type. I find this to be true in my work, but also generally because NgFor, NgIf, and NgSwitch provide functionality that covers most use cases for structural directives. Most examples of structural directives that I've seen accomplish the same basic tasks as these three built-in directives with some customized abilities. For example, many data table components have their own implementation of NgFor that's better integrated with the data table and can help provide capabilities like pagination.

As you work more with directives, you'll likely need to also spend more time with the Angular APIs related to views and rendering elements. You'll be able to implement more complex scenarios should your needs require them.

We've finished our custom directives, so let's take a look at pipes and how we can craft custom ways to format our data before display.

8.3 *Crafting custom pipes*

Pipes are essentially a way to format data, and depending on the data you have you may find it useful to create your own set of pipes to simplify your templates. Pipes are generally simple and easy to implement, and if they can save you repeated formatting logic, then you should make your own.

Pipes are functions that data is passed through prior to being rendered into the page. Somewhat similar to how components have the OnInit lifecycle hook to handle logic before the component renders, pipes do the same thing for bindings. You can see how Angular processes bindings when pipes are present or not in figure 8.6.

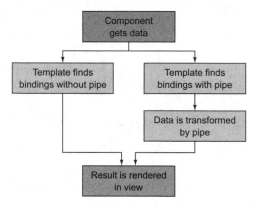

Figure 8.6   Data is passed through a pipe before being rendered in a template binding.

In the chapter example, there are several uses of the Currency and Percent pipes to format data. These are simple but great examples of how pipes can be invaluable. Imagine your application has to support different currencies—the Currency pipe can figure out how each currency is typically formatted.

There are fundamentally two types of pipes: pure and impure. *Pure* pipes maintain no state information, and *impure* pipes maintain state.

Pure and impure pipes are also rendered differently, as you can see in figure 8.7. A pure pipe is only run if the input value passed into the pipe has changed, making it more efficient because it won't run very often. On the other hand, an impure pipe will execute on every change detection run, because an impure pipe has state that might have changed, and that would render a different output regardless of whether the input has changed.

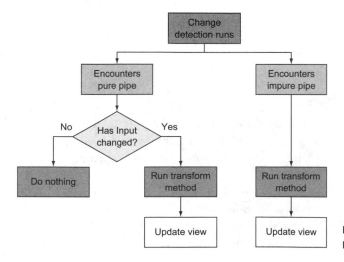

Figure 8.7   How pure and impure pipes are handled by Angular

This is very important to understand if you start to build pipes. Choosing to make a pipe pure or impure can have significant consequences in the way that pipe is executed and potentially on the performance of your application.

We'll build examples of both pure and impure pipes, but you should always try to build a pure pipe. I'd bet that 98% of all custom pipes created are pure—or should be pure. We'll look a little more closely at why this is when we build an impure pipe, but storing state in a pipe is tricky and makes its implementation more complex.

Let's build a pipe that helps us display the change information for a stock, and we'll be making it a pure pipe as well.

8.3.1 *Creating a pure pipe*

Because almost every pipe you create will be a pure pipe, let's start by looking at how to create one for our application. Pipes don't have the same complexities as directives, because they're a way to modify a value prior to it being rendered into the template. Pure pipes are so named because they implement a *pure function*—a function that doesn't maintain any internal state and returns the same output given the same input.

Pure functions are important for performance, because Angular doesn't need to run them with each change detection lifecycle unless the input value has changed. This can save a reasonable amount of overhead for performance reasons.

A pure pipe is implemented as a single function that accepts the value from the binding and any additional arguments that might be passed. This method is called `trans-form` because it takes the input value, does some type of transformation, and returns a result.

We're going to create a custom pipe that takes care of displaying the stock change price and percentage data. Right now, we have this inside of our Summary component template, and we'd like to replace the long line:

```
{{stock?.change | currency:'USD':true:'.2'}} ({{stock?.changeInPercent |
    percent}})
```

with this:

```
{{stock | change}}
```

The original is quite long—imagine writing it in multiple places. We'd easily have issues where the output could be inconsistent, so we want to create a pipe that can make it reusable and cleaner.

Let's make a new pipe called the Change pipe to simplify this snippet. As you'd expect, there's a way to generate a new pipe with the CLI. Using the terminal, run the following command:

```
ng generate pipe pipes/change
```

The new files are generated inside of src/app/pipes. Let's open src/app/pipes/change.pipe.ts and replace it with the code in the following listing.

Listing 8.4 Change pipe

```
import { Pipe, PipeTransform } from '@angular/core';
import { CurrencyPipe, PercentPipe } from '@angular/common';      Imports dependencies
import { StockInterface } from '../services/stocks.service';
```

```
@Pipe({
  name: 'change'        Declares pipe and provides it a name
})                                                              Exports class and implements
export class ChangePipe implements PipeTransform {             the PipeTransform

  constructor(private currencyPipe: CurrencyPipe, private percentPipe:
      PercentPipe) {}

  transform(stock: StockInterface, showPercent: boolean = true): any {
    let value = `${this.currencyPipe.transform(stock.change, 'USD', 'symbol',
      '.2')}`;
    if (showPercent) {
      value += ` (${this.percentPipe.transform(stock.changeInPercent,
      '.2')})`;
    }                                                          Injects Currency and Percent pipes
    return value;
  }
}
```

Implements the transform method, which accepts the stock property and returns a formatted string

This pipe uses the Currency and Percent pipes, and it begins by importing all the dependencies. The `@Pipe` decorator denotes that we're creating a pipe, and we give it a `name` property to define the name of the pipe—this needs to be unique, so consider it carefully.

When the class is defined, it also implements the `PipeTransform` interface to help ensure that we construct the pipe properly. The constructor then injects the Currency and Percent pipes into the class so we can use them.

Finally, the real work happens in the `transform` method, where it accepts one or more arguments. The first is the value that's passed into the pipe and that's always provided by the binding, and it's expected to be a `stock` object. The remaining arguments are optional parameters that might be passed as needed, and they're optional because the interface doesn't require them. In this case, we declare one parameter, `showPercent`, as a Boolean that declares whether we want to add the percentage value or not. The method then constructs a string using the desired formatting and returns it to be displayed.

We've implemented the `transform` method as a pure function. Every time you pass the same arguments to it, you'll get the same output. If there's a chance the value can change, it isn't a pure function or a pure pipe.

Now we can put it to use in our Summary component. Open src/app/components/summary/summary.component.html and change the last line with `stock.change` to the following:

```
{{stock | change}}
```

We were able to simplify the long line with two interpolation bindings into a single one. Notice that we aren't passing an argument into it, because by default it will show the change in percentage. You could disable this by changing the pipe call to pass the Boolean value like this:

```
{{stock | change:false}}
```

Creating any pure pipe will follow this basic outline, and the significant changes will be in how you transform the value. Be sure to return a value that's either a string or that can be transformed into a string. You shouldn't return an array or object, for example.

The value of pipe purity becomes more obvious when we create an impure pipe and see how it's called by the application lifecycle. Let's take a look at that now and create two examples to see in what situations they're useful.

8.3.2   *Creating an impure pipe*

Sometimes the way you want to format a piece of data relies on the state of the pipe or the value itself—it implements the `transform` method in such a way that it doesn't always provide the same result given the same inputs.

Due to this design, an impure pipe is executed with every change detection lifecycle regardless of whether the input itself has changed. This is the only way to know if the final binding result has changed (remember, it might be dependent on some additional state that changes the result) and whether Angular needs to update the rendered view.

The Async pipe is provided by Angular as an impure pipe and has a good use case. It allows you to pass in an observable or promise to the pipe, and when a value is returned asynchronously, the result will be evaluated. It essentially listens for the `async` event to fire (depending on the type) and then displays that value directly. You can use that to call an API that returns a promise, pass the promise into the binding with the Async pipe, and the value will appear after the API returns the value.

To get a better sense of just how an Async pipe behaves, I find it helpful to implement one that logs how many times it's been called to the console, and the resulting output is what you'll see in figure 8.8. This tells you the number of times that change detection has run for the component that contains this pipe.

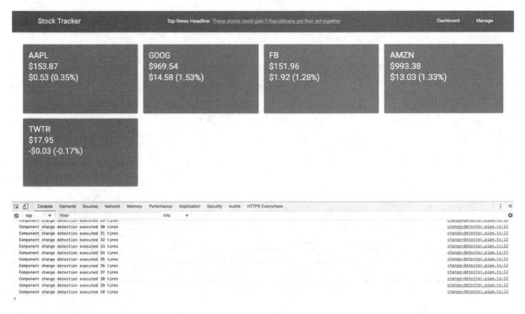

Figure 8.8   Change Detector pipe that alerts to every time a component is checked for changes

Start by generating a new pipe using the terminal. We'll create a new pipe called ChangeDetector:

```
ng generate pipe pipes/change-detector
```

Open the newly generated pipe at src/app/pipes/change-detector.pipe.ts. Replace it with the content found in the following listing.

Listing 8.5   ChangeDetector pipe

```
import { Pipe, PipeTransform } from '@angular/core';

@Pipe({
  name: 'changeDetector',          Decorates the pipe and sets pure to false
  pure: false
})
export class ChangeDetectorPipe implements PipeTransform {
  count: number = 0;          ◄─────────────────  Holds a stateful value

  transform(value: any, args?: any): any {
    this.count++;
    console.log(`Component change detection executed ${this.count} times`);

    return value;
  }
}
```

Implements transform method that simply increments and logs each call — annotates the `transform` method.

This pipe doesn't transform any values by default. We first set the `pure` property to `false` in the decorator to tell Angular that this pipe is impure and must be always reevaluated. Then we store a property that contains a numeric value to hold the number of times it's been called. Lastly, the `transform` method increments the count, logs out a message, and returns the value unchanged.

If this were a pure pipe, it would only increment the count when the value of the binding changed, but this will run many more times. To see exactly how many, let's put it on the App component.

Open src/app/app.component.html and update the line that contains the title to this:

```
<span class="mdl-layout-title">{{'Stock Tracker' | changeDetector}}</span>
```

This binds the string `'Stock Tracker'` into the ChangeDetector pipe, and if you open the console it should log out a lot of messages like `"Component change detection executed 32 times"`. The actual number might vary slightly if you've made customizations to your application.

Now imagine that this transform method did some more difficult work. Perhaps you have a large array of items to scan to find how to map a key to a value, and that performance might be suboptimal. You might even have an asynchronous call to handle. These are examples of potential pitfalls when creating impure pipes, as you see in figure 8.9.

The news item in this pipe is loaded asynchronously from an **API**, making it an impure pipe waiting for data unrelated to the input to resolve.

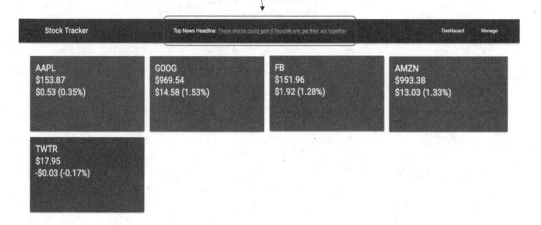

Figure 8.9 **Example of an impure pipe that loads news at the top of the page by maintaining state in the pipe itself**

I find this example provides a nice illustration of what happens, but what about an example of something that accomplishes a task? We can build another impure pipe that takes a value and then makes an HTTP request to load news, as you see in figure 8.9.

Generate a new pipe with the following command and then replace the contents of src/app/pipes/news.pipe.ts with the code from the following listing:

```
ng generate pipe pipes/news
```

Listing 8.6   Impure News pipe

```
import { Pipe, PipeTransform } from '@angular/core';
import { StocksService } from '../services/stocks.service';

@Pipe({
  name: 'news',
  pure: false
})
export class NewsPipe implements PipeTransform {
  cachedSource: string = '';
  news: string = 'loading...';

  constructor(private service: StocksService) {}

  transform(source: string, args?: any): any {
    if (source !== this.cachedSource) {
      this.cachedSource = source;
      this.service.getNewsSnapshot(source).subscribe(news => {
```

Marks pipe as impure

Sets properties with stateful values

transform method makes API request to load latest news item

```
        this.news = `<a href="${news.url}" target="_blank">${news.title}</
      a>`;
      });
    }

    return this.news;
  }
}
```

transform method
makes API request to
load latest news item

This pipe is declared again as an impure pipe, and it has two stateful properties to hold the source and the resulting news title.

The `transform` method is more complex. It's run with every change detection run, so we create a barrier by first checking if the input source has changed or not, since we cache the last provided source. If the value changed (or is provided for the first time), we make an HTTP request to load the news data. As soon as that data has returned, we update the value of the `news` property with the `title` and it will get rendered out.

You may wonder how Angular knows when the API request has completed. Well, because we're using the Angular HttpClient service under the hood, Angular is aware of when that response has finished, and that triggers another round of change detection. Because this is an impure pipe, it's run again, and the `news` value will be rendered.

We need to put this into our template to have it run, so open src/app/app.component.html and add some extra lines to the header, as you see bolded in the following listing.

Listing 8.7   App header with News pipe

```
<header class="mdl-layout__header">
  <div class="mdl-layout__header-row">
    <span class="mdl-layout-title">{{'Stock Tracker' | changeDetector}}</
    span>
    <div class="mdl-layout-spacer"></div>
    <span>Top News Headline: <span [innerHTML]="'cnbc' | news"></span></span>
    <div class="mdl-layout-spacer"></div>
    <nav class="mdl-navigation mdl-layout--large-screen-only">
      <a class="mdl-navigation__link" [routerLink]="['/']">Dashboard</a>
      <a class="mdl-navigation__link" [routerLink]="['/manage']">Manage</a>
    </nav>
  </div>
</header>
```

Here we just add a place to render out the top news headline. There are several values you can pass if you'd rather get a different news source:

- `the-wall-street-journal`
- `bloomberg`
- `cnbc`
- `financial-times`
- `the-new-york-times`

Now when you preview the application you should see the news headline appear at the top of the page with a link to the article. Every time the App component is rendered (which is once per load), it will request the news from the API. This could be dangerous to put onto another type of component that's rendered more often or repeatedly in the same page.

What's important about this example is that it would have been much better to implement this as a component than inside of a pipe. There's not a lot of reason to make it a pipe, in fact.

Although impure pipes are interesting, I'm certainly of the mindset that you should avoid them if you can. Even the Async pipe is problematic to use in production because it makes error handling difficult. They were made to help in a small set of use cases and are perhaps mostly useful for development, but they make application logic more challenging and difficult to predict.

Summary

You've successfully created several directives and pipes! These are useful skills to help with your code reuse and to keep your code focused on specific tasks. Here are the key takeaways from this chapter:

- Directives come in three flavors: attribute, structural, and components.
- Attribute directives are the most common to create and are great for modifying an existing element.
- Structural directives are less common and are meant to be used to modify the existence or structure of DOM elements.
- Pure pipes are the most useful and allow you to transform a value before output using a pure function.
- Impure pipes allow you to maintain state inside of a pipe, but they're run with every change detection check and are to be avoided if possible.

Forms

9

Just about every application uses forms in some way, if only to do something simple like log in or manage settings. HTML comes with a number of form elements by default, such as inputs, selects, and buttons, and Angular provides a way to use these native elements and add some power to them. We've used forms in several previous examples, but in this chapter we'll dig into them much more completely.

Angular provides two approaches to building forms: *reactive forms* and *template forms*. I'll discuss the differences at length shortly, though they're largely in whether you define the form in your controller or in the template. You're not limited to choosing only one or the other form, but typically applications will try to remain consistent with one of them.

With template forms, we'll see how to describe your forms primarily using the NgModel directive, which is used to define the form structure. With reactive forms, you declare the form structure yourself in the controller, and the template renders it out.

As complex as forms can become, the basics are fairly standard in all areas. There are form controls (fields that hold values like inputs, selects, and so on), and there are form buttons (like Save, Cancel, or Reset). The same holds true when working with forms in Angular—the basics remain consistent regardless of how complex the form becomes.

There are often situations where a form requires the use of additional third-party components to help, such as a date picker or range slider. Browsers may implement some newer form controls, but they're rarely standard, and other browsers might not support them at all. Although we're not going to focus on creating custom components that act like form controls, there are many great libraries that provide you additional features, or you can certainly build your own custom form controls by reviewing the documentation. I personally avoid creating these unless absolutely necessary, which it rarely is.

9.1   *Setting up the chapter example*

We're going to build a new application that helps us manage invoices and customers. Imagine you're a freelancer or small business owner and you have customers to manage. This application would be a good tool for keeping track of sending invoices and making sure you get paid (which is pretty important, right?).

The forms themselves are intentionally not complex, but they do demonstrate most of the needs for forms succinctly. You can take the examples you see in this chapter and translate them into larger, more complex forms without having to learn additional concepts. The only difference tends to be the scale.

The application is also designed for the mobile form factor, which is a nice little twist from our previous examples. It uses the Covalent UI library, from Teradata, which extends the concepts and Angular Material Design library. If you weren't aware, mobile browsers tend to have the best support for the latest HTML5 input types, such as search or number fields, which we will use for our example. I recommend using Chrome for this chapter.

Chrome has a useful device emulator in the developer tools, as shown in figure 9.1, and I suggest that you use it while you're building and using this application. It allows you to emulate the dimensions of various mobile devices and get a sense of how your application would look on those sizes. It doesn't really emulate the device in a true way, but it does provide an easy way to preview.

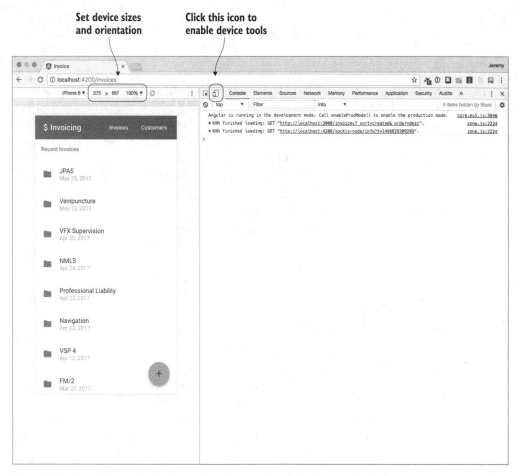

Figure 9.1   Use device tools in Chrome developer tools to simulate mobile devices.

Like other examples, this one is available on GitHub, and you can get the source code by cloning the repo. Make sure to check out the right tag when we start so you can code along, or look at the latest master for the final version:

```
git clone https://github.com/angular-in-action/invoice
cd invoice
git checkout start
```

Otherwise, you can download the archived files from https://github.com/angular-in-action/invoice/archive/start.zip and unzip the files.

When you start the application, you'll notice a number of services and components are there already. I've provided the majority of the code ahead of time so we can focus on the key features for forms. Even the form components are there, with standard HTML forms in place. They don't currently do anything when you try to save them, which is what we'll be updating and implementing in this chapter.

You'll need npm install for all the dependencies, and then you run ng serve to start the local development server. That isn't all, though. This app has a local API server that we need to run also. You'll need to open another terminal session and run the following:

```
npm run api
```

This will start up a local server that provides our app data. As you save and edit records, the data will persist into a local file called db.json, which is important for our app.

There may be a few warnings in the browser console when you run the example—you can safely ignore those. They refer to features that aren't necessary for the chapter example.

Now, before we get into the forms, let's review the rest of the app.

9.1.1   Review the app before starting

There are six routable views in this application. Let's talk briefly about some of the ones that don't contain forms. We'll focus only on two of the routes in the chapter; we'll build one of the forms with template-driven forms and the other with a reactive form. Let's take a look at several of the screens of the application.

Figure 9.2 shows some of the screens for the application, such as the list, detail, and form views. There are two list views, one for customers and one for invoices. These are both fairly simple in that they load a list from the API and render it. They also include a button that will take you to a form to create a new record. You can see these two in the Invoices and Customers components.

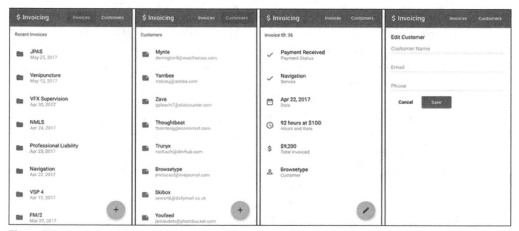

Figure 9.2   Invoicing application screens, emulated in a mobile device size. From left to right: list of invoices, list of customers, invoice detail view, and customer form.

The two detail views for a customer and invoice are also quite similar in that they simply show the relevant data for a given record. There is a button that allows you to edit that record as well. You can preview these in the Invoice and Customer components.

Finally, the two views we'll work on are the form views. The customer or invoice form will let you create or edit an existing record, and the form fields needed are already provided with standard HTML. We'll be updating these forms and the controllers to handle the save, delete, and cancel events. These can be found in the InvoiceForm and CustomerForm components.

Inside of the components you'll see a few new things. The `TdLoading` directive is a feature from the Covalent library to display a loading indicator while data is being loaded. The `MdInput` directive will make an input Material Design–compliant. There are several other elements that start with `Md-`, which are all from the Material Design library and are UI components for structure or controls. It's best to review the Covalent and Material Design documentation for additional questions you may have about the use of these tools. Please note the specific version being used in the package.json file and make sure you're looking it up correctly.

There are also services for the customers and invoices APIs. You may want to review them as a way to extend one service to create another. Both the Invoices and Customers services extend the Rest service, which implements the basic API calls needed. The specialized instances (Invoices and Customers) provide a single property that's used by the Rest service to construct URLs.

All right, let's create the customer form using the template-driven approach.

9.2   *Template-driven forms*

We've already used template-driven forms in several of our examples, and the key marker is when you see the `NgModel` directive on a form control. AngularJS developers will be familiar with the patterns described in this section.

Template forms are named primarily because the form controls are defined in the template of the component. In this case, you can think of the template as having the final say about what is part of the form or not. For example, if you have an `input` element in the page that is part of the form that is wired up into the form controls, then it will also be defined in the controller.

The primary goal of a form is to be able to synchronize the data in the view with data in the controller so it can be submitted to be handled. Secondary goals are to perform tasks like validation, notify about errors, and handle other events like cancel.

Because the form is primarily defined in the template layer, it also means that validation errors are managed primarily through the template. We'll look at how to add validation and alert the user about invalid fields.

In figure 9.3 you can see the customer form that we'll be building in this section. The three fields will be part of the form data and will allow us to capture the input for processing.

To get started, we need to start working with our form controls and wire them up so that they bind the model between both the controller and the template using `NgModel`.

9.2.1   *Binding model data to inputs with NgModel*

Let's take a single form control to begin with and see what it takes to turn it into something Angular can use. In the CustomerForm component, you should see this input:

```
<input mdInput placeholder="Customer Name" value="">
```

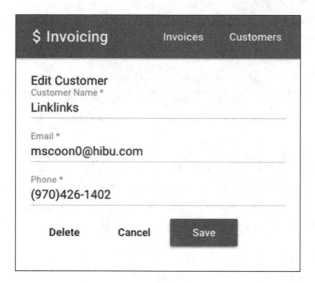

Figure 9.3 Customer form with three fields to bind data to

Right now it's just a normal form element (with the `MdInput` to make it Material Design), but by adding the `NgModel` directive we can turn it into an Angular form control. In the process, we can also remove the `value` attribute, as it's no longer needed:

```
<input name="customer" mdInput placeholder="Customer Name"
    [(ngModel)]="customer.name">
```

The `NgModel` directive is part of the Forms module and will ensure that the value of the form control is set based on the `customer` property value from the controller. But it also sets the value into the controller when it's changed in the view. If you look at the controller, there is no such property, and `NgModel` will create it for you.

You should recall the `[()]` syntax from earlier chapters, but to refresh your memory, it's a way of doing two-way data binding in Angular. That means the controller will now have a property called `customer`, and if the view or controller changes that value, the other will instantly be updated as well. AngularJS developers will know this concept well, and it exists in Angular as well.

Let's go ahead and wire up all of the form controls with `NgModel`. In the Customer-Form template, we'll need to modify the existing form controls, as you see bolded in the following listing. Open src/app/customer-form/customer-form.component.html and update it.

Listing 9.1 CustomerForm using NgModel

```
<md-card-content>
  <md-input-container>
    <input name="customer" mdInput placeholder="Customer Name"
    [(ngModel)]="customer.name">                      Form control using NgModel
  </md-input-container>
  <md-input-container>
```

```
   <input name="email" mdInput type="email" placeholder="Email"
     [(ngModel)]="customer.email">  ◀────┐
  </md-input-container>                     │ Form control using NgModel
  <md-input-container>
    <input name="phone" mdInput type="tel" placeholder="Phone"
      [(ngModel)]="customer.phone">  ◀────┐
    </md-input-container>                    │ Form control using NgModel
{{customer | json}}  ◀──── Displays the customer content in template temporarily
</md-card-content>
```

In these form controls, we now have them wired up to do two-way binding using NgModel. Notice that we're also setting the model values as part of the customer property, so the data is stored in one object. Except for a form that has only one control, it's highly recommended to always use models like this. It will help us later to have all the customer data stored on the same object instead of on different properties of the controller.

So far, this won't change anything significant about our form that you can see, but it will be adding new properties to the customer model as you change the input values behind the scenes. If you watch the customer interpolation binding, you will see that as values are changed in the form inputs, the model is updated.

There are a couple of notes to make about using NgModel. First, you always use it with the two-way binding syntax—it doesn't work otherwise. Second, inputs should always have a name when using NgModel, because it requires that information internally. Last, you notice the value attribute was omitted because NgModel will overwrite it and it's best to just leave it off.

Save these changes and then go to the customer's list, select one, and click the edit icon in the bottom right to view the form. You should ensure there are no errors by looking at the browser console as well, in case you typed something incorrectly.

This is great, because our primary object is largely complete. We simply add NgModel, and our form elements are now being tracked in both the template and controller as changes are made. The next step is to start validating these form fields. Using the power of NgModel, we can track the validity of a form field and report meaningful errors to the user.

9.2.2 *Validating form controls with NgModel*

HTML already provides some built-in form validations that can be put onto form elements, such as required or minlength. Angular works with these attributes and automatically will validate inputs based on them.

Let's take the example of our customer name input field. All we need to do is add the additional required attribute to validate the input to force validation for this field:

```
<input name="customer" mdInput placeholder="Customer Name"
    [(ngModel)]="customer.name" required>
```

When the form control has an invalid value, we can also inspect the state of a field and render out messages about what is incorrect, as shown in figure 9.4.

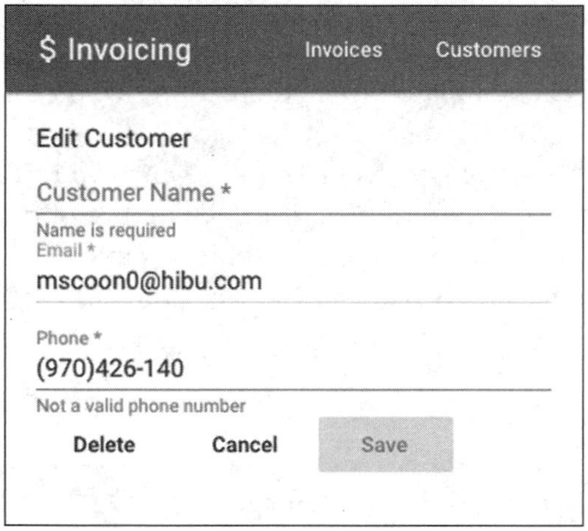

Figure 9.4 Customer form with validation errors

It's time to set up the validation for all the fields and also to look at how to access the state of those fields. Update the CustomerForm template snippet as you see bolded in the following listing.

Listing 9.2 CustomerForm validating fields with NgModel

```
<md-input-container>
  <input name="customer" mdInput placeholder="Customer Name"
    [(ngModel)]="customer.name" required #name="ngModel">      ◄─── Adds validation
  <md-error *ngIf="name.touched && name.invalid">                   attributes and
    Name is required                                                template variable
  </md-error>                                                       to form control
</md-input-container>
<md-input-container>
  <input name="email" mdInput type="email" placeholder="Email"
    [(ngModel)]="customer.email" required #email="ngModel">
  <md-error *ngIf="email.touched && email.invalid">         Uses form control
    A valid email is required                                validation to conditionally
  </md-error>                                                 show error message
</md-input-container>
<md-input-container>
  <input name="phone" mdInput type="tel" placeholder="Phone"
    [(ngModel)]="customer.phone" required #phone="ngModel" minlength="7">
  <md-error *ngIf="phone.touched && phone.errors?.required">    ◄─── Form control
    Phone number is required                                         exposes what
  </md-error>                                                        specific error
  <md-error *ngIf="phone.touched && phone.errors?.minlength">   ◄─── is found.
    Not a valid phone number
  </md-error>
</md-input-container>
```

The form controls now each have a required attribute and a local template variable. The phone number also has a `minlength` attribute, because we expect a phone number to be at least seven digits. We've used local template variables in the component chapter to access values from other controllers inside of the template, and that's precisely the same thing here. For example, `#name="ngModel"` is a way to define the template variable `name` to be a reference to the `NgModel` result, which is the form control data. Remember, template variables are only valid within the template they're defined in, so you can't reach them from your controller.

This form control data is a FormControl type from Angular, which you can view in the API docs to see more about what it can do for you. It has a number of properties, such as `valid`, `invalid`, `pristine`, and `dirty`. These are Boolean values that you can easily use to determine whether something is true or false. See table 9.1 for the most useful form control properties.

Table 9.1   Form control validation properties

Property	Meaning
valid	The form control is valid for all validations.
invalid	The form control has at least one invalid validation.
disabled	The form control is disabled and can't be interacted with.
enabled	The form control is enabled and can be clicked or edited.
errors	An object that either contains keys with validations that are `invalid`, or null when all are `valid`.
pristine	The form control has not yet been changed by the user.
dirty	The form control has been changed by the user.
touched	The form control has been in focus, and then focus has left the field.
untouched	The form control has not been in focus.

The `MdError` element is from the Material Design library and shows a little validation error when the `NgIf` is true. For example, `*ngIf="email.touched && email.invalid"` will show the error when the form control is `invalid`, and the user has left focus on that field. (As a side note, if the value was loaded from a database but was `invalid`, the preceding validation would fail, so you should consider the needs of your application.) This is nice because the error doesn't appear immediately, but only when the user tries to leave the field with an invalid value. You can use different combinations of the properties in table 9.1 to determine when to show a validation error. When you're creating a new item, all the required fields will be `invalid`, but it won't show validation errors until the user has tried to edit them.

Notice how the validation message for the phone number has two different validations: `required` and `minlength`. We're then able to look at the control's error object to determine whether a specific validation failed and show the appropriate message. In this case, if the user leaves it blank, it will prompt it to say the field is required, but if the user only inputs four characters, it will show that it expects at least seven digits.

It's also useful to note that Angular will apply various CSS classes to a form control based on its validation state. They mirror the properties in table 9.1, but have the ng- prefix. For example, an invalid form control will have the ng-invalid class applied. This is useful if you want to craft your own styling for valid or invalid controls without any special work. We're not doing that here, but you could certainly take advantage of them. Some Angular UI libraries may come with support for them out of the box.

Though this validation is helpful, it's still possible to submit the form with invalid values. We'll prevent this from happening in a moment, but first I want to wrap up validation by creating our own validation directive.

9.2.3 Custom validation with directives

The validation for our phone number is somewhat lacking. We really would want it to enforce not just the length but also that the content matches a known phone format. Unfortunately, even the tel input type doesn't do that for us, so we'll have to implement our own custom validation using a directive. Our best effort so far has been to enforce a minlength validation, but that only cares about the number of characters, not the actual value.

Although there is the pattern validation attribute in HTML, which allows you to declare a regular expression to validate the input, it's not very usable and doesn't work in all browsers.

We'll need to create two things to make this happen: a customer validator function and a directive that uses the validator function. Start by creating a new directory at src/app/validators; then create a file inside it named phone.validator.ts, and add the code from the following listing.

> **Listing 9.3 Phone validator**

Regular expression to validate typical phone number

```
import { AbstractControl, ValidatorFn } from '@angular/forms';

const expression = /((\(\d{3}\) ?)|(\d{3}-))?\d{3}-\d{4}/;

export function PhoneValidator(): ValidatorFn {
  return (control: AbstractControl): { [key: string]: any } => {
    const valid = expression.test(control.value) && control.value.length <
      14;
    return valid ? null : { phone: true };
  };
}
```

Returns a function to handle validation (annotation pointing to `export function PhoneValidator(): ValidatorFn {`)

Defines a function that returns a ValidatorFn type (annotation)

Validates the control value against expression (annotation)

This is a bit terse, so let's look at it step by step. First, we're defining a regular expression that should validate the primary phone number formats. You could select a different expression if your needs require. Then we're exporting a function that will return a function. The ValidatorFn interface expects that this returned function will accept a control as a parameter and return either null or an object with validation errors.

Our PhoneValidator function will return the real validation function to use during the validation. It accepts a single argument, which is the form control. For the most part, you only care about the control.value property, which holds the current value of the form control. Then inside of the validation function, it tests the current value against the expression and returns either null, to mean it's valid, or an object if it's invalid, with a property explaining what is invalid.

If it returns an object, it expects you to give it a property with a value. Here it's a Boolean, but it could be any value you want to expose. Normally, I find Boolean is suitable unless you want to also provide the error message as a string. You can access the value in the local template `control.errors` property.

To use this validator we need to create a directive. Using the Angular CLI, generate a new directive like so:

```
ng generate directive validators/phone
```

Now open src/app/validators/phone.directive.ts and add the code found in the following listing to it. This will take the validator function we created a moment ago and make it possible to apply it to an element as an attribute.

Listing 9.4   Phone validator directive

```
import { Directive } from '@angular/core';
import { Validator, AbstractControl, NG_VALIDATORS } from '@angular/forms';
import { PhoneValidator } from './phone.validator';

@Directive({
    selector: '[phone][ngModel]',     ◄───  Selector designed to apply to elements
                                             with phone and NgModel attributes
    providers: [{ provide: NG_VALIDATORS, useExisting: PhoneDirective, multi:
    true }]   ◄───  Way to define this directive as part of Angular's list of validators
})
export class PhoneDirective implements Validator {     ◄───
    private validator = PhoneValidator();

    validate(control: AbstractControl): { [key: string]: any } {   Method that form
        return this.validator(control);                            controls will call to
    }                                                              validate value
}
```

Creates instance of validation function   Implements the Validator interface

This is also a bit terse, but what we're doing is implementing the necessary pieces to wire up the directive to Angular's list of validators and implement the same interface. We start by defining the selector to expect to have both phone and `NgModel` attributes on the form control. This means if you just put `phone` as an attribute, it won't use this directive for validation, because `NgModel` is required.

The directive also has a `providers` array and uses a multiprovider, which allows a single token (like `NG_VALIDATORS`) to have multiple dependencies. `NG_VALIDATORS` contains a list of default validation dependencies, and this extends that list by adding one more of our own. This isn't very common, but it's required in this situation.

Our directive then exports a class, which implements the `Validator` interface. This expects that there will be a `validate` method defined in the class, which we have done. We also have a property that holds an instance of our `validator` function that we imported, and then inside of the `validate` method we call our custom validator and pass in the control.

There's a bit of juggling of the form control in this custom validation process, but when you look at these two files together, it should be clearer how they relate to one another. To implement this new `validator` directive, we need to update our `phone` form control, as you see in the following listing.

Listing 9.5 Updated phone form control

```
<md-input-container>                              Adds the phone directive
  <input name="phone" mdInput type="tel" placeholder="Phone"
    [(ngModel)]="customer.phone" required phone #phone="ngModel">
  <md-error *ngIf="phone.touched && phone.errors?.phone">
    Not a valid phone number                      Looks for
  </md-error>                                      validation errors
</md-input-container>                              of phone type
```

The form control removes the `minlength` attribute and replaces it with the `phone` attribute. This makes the form control now aware of the phone validation, and when the number isn't a correct phone number we can tell by looking at the `errors.phone` property. Recall our `validator` function returns an object with `{phone: true}`, so this is where we see it returned to us. We also removed the additional error message for it being required, as our new validation covers that scenario as well.

To review, when we add the `phone` attribute, the `NgModel` will validate using the Phone validator directive. Internally, the Phone validator directive registers itself with the default list of validators that `NgModel` knows about by declaring the multiprovider (a special kind of provider that can be registered more than once) for `NG_VALIDATORS`. It then implements a `validate` method, which calls the `validator` function we created at the beginning. There are a few steps here, but that's the price we pay for the flexibility provided by Angular's platform.

Congrats! You've now got a custom validation directive that you can reuse on any form control, or you can create additional ones for different scenarios. Now we need to wrap up this form by handling events to either submit, cancel, or delete.

9.2.4 *Handling submit or cancel events*

We've got all the data and validation we would like on this form, so now it's time to handle the various events that might happen with it. The most important is to handle the submit event, but also we want to allow the user to cancel from saving the edits or delete the record if it exists.

The controller already implements all the methods we need to handle these scenarios, so we just need to write up our form to call them properly. You can review the methods in there and see how they work.

The first thing we should do is update our form element. Angular does another thing to forms that isn't visible by default. It automatically implements an `NgForm` on a form even if you don't declare a directive (unlike how you have to declare `NgModel`). When it does this, it essentially attaches an `NgForm` controller that then maintains the form controls in the form.

NgForm provides a couple of features we'll need; the first is that it can tell us if the entire form is valid (not just an individual field) and help us implement an event binding for submitting the form. Find the `form` element at the top of the CustomerForm template and update it to have these additional values shown in bold:

```
<form *ngIf="customer" #form="ngForm" (ngSubmit)="save()">
```

First we create another template variable and reference the NgForm controller. This is the same idea we used for our form controls with NgModel, except this local template variable will reference the entire form. Then we have an (`ngSubmit`) event handler to call the save method.

Now we just need to update our buttons at the bottom to call the correct methods. The following code in bold contains the pieces to add to the buttons in the `card actions` element near the bottom:

```
<md-card-actions>
  <button type="button" md-button (click)="delete()" *ngIf="customer.
    id">Delete</button>
  <button type="button" md-button (click)="cancel()">Cancel</button>
  <button type="submit" md-raised-button color="primary" [disabled]="form.
    invalid">Save</button>
</md-card-actions>
```

The first two buttons are standard buttons, so we just use the `click` event binding to call the appropriate method. The delete button is hidden if we're creating the record by checking whether there is an ID, which is only set after creation. The submit button doesn't have an event binding, because that's already being handled by `ngSubmit`. But we do bind to the `disabled` property and look at the `form.invalid` property to determine if the entire form is invalid.

That about wraps up template-driven forms. Everything about our form was described in the template, primarily by adding `NgModel` directives to our form controls. Using local template variables that referenced the `NgModel` of a control, we could inspect the validation errors for a field and show appropriate error messages. We also were able to build a custom validator for phone numbers that works like any default validation attribute. Finally, we handled the submit event and checked the validation of the overall form before enabling the submit button. Not too bad for a modest amount of code! The final version of the customer form can be seen here in the following listing.

Listing 9.6   Final customer form template

```
<div *tdLoading="'customer'">
  <form *ngIf="customer" #form="ngForm" (ngSubmit)="save()">
    <md-card>
      <md-card-header>Edit Customer</md-card-header>
      <md-card-content>
        <md-input-container>
          <input name="customer" mdInput placeholder="Customer Name"
    [(ngModel)]="customer.name" required #name="ngModel">
          <md-error *ngIf="name.touched && name.invalid">
            Name is required
```

```
        </md-error>
      </md-input-container>
      <md-input-container>
        <input name="email" mdInput type="email" placeholder="Email"
  [(ngModel)]="customer.email" required #email="ngModel">
        <md-error *ngIf="email.touched && email.invalid">
          A valid email is required
        </md-error>
      </md-input-container>
      <md-input-container>
        <input name="phone" mdInput type="tel" placeholder="Phone"
  [(ngModel)]="customer.phone" required phone #phone="ngModel">
        <md-error *ngIf="phone.touched && phone.errors?.required">
          Phone number is required
        </md-error>
        <md-error *ngIf="phone.touched && phone.errors?.phone">
          Not a valid phone number
        </md-error>
      </md-input-container>
    </md-card-content>
    <md-card-actions>
      <button type="button" md-button (click)="delete()" *ngIf="customer.
  id">Delete</button>
      <button type="button" md-button (click)="cancel()">Cancel</button>
      <button type="submit" md-raised-button color="primary"
  [disabled]="form.invalid">Save</button>
    </md-card-actions>
  </md-card>
  </form>
</div>
```

Now it's time to implement the other form for creating or editing an invoice in the reactive form style. It will approach the form from the controller first and have less logic in the template to manage.

9.3 Reactive forms

The alternative to template-driven forms, *reactive* forms, is the other way to design your forms in Angular. The name *reactive* comes from the style of programming known as reactive, where you have immutable data structures and your views never mutate them directly. That means no two-way binding is allowed.

The basic idea is that your form has a copy of the original model that it uses while the user is editing the form, and upon saving, you trigger an action like saving it to the database and update the original model. Template-driven forms only have one shared model, and because values are being constantly synced between the two, there may be timing issues of values changing in multiple places.

One of my favorite aspects of reactive forms is that you can use an observable to watch a particular form control for changes. I might do this to handle a task like autocomplete, for example. It's been useful for me on several occasions, and template-driven forms don't have a good way to do this.

Reactive forms still have a template, because you need to define the markup associated with the form. The main difference in the template is you won't use `NgForm` or `NgModel` on any of the form controls; instead we'll use a different directive to link a particular form control in the template to the corresponding form control declared in the controller.

There are a few other differences in the way that reactive forms behave. Because template-driven forms employ two-way binding concepts, they're inherently asynchronous in their handling. During the rendering of a template-driven form, the `NgModel` directive is building the form up for you behind the scenes. This takes more than one change detection cycle, though, causing potential race conditions where you expect a form element to be registered but it hasn't yet. This doesn't happen with reactive forms, because you define the form in your controller, so it's not dependent on change detection cycles.

The challenges with timing of template-driven forms tend to only appear when you try to access form controls or the form itself too early, and require you to wait until the `AfterViewInit` lifecycle hook to ensure the view has fully rendered. The Angular documentation covers some details about the differences and virtues of each approach as well and is worth reviewing: https://angular.io/guide/forms.

Setting aside some of the internal mechanical differences, let's focus on what reactive forms look like. In a template-driven form the `NgModel` builds the form controls, but with reactive we need to define our form programmatically in the controller. When you settle on using one form approach, it's not easy or advisable to mix them in the same form, though you could in different forms.

In this section, we'll build the InvoiceForm component form, and you can see the result in figure 9.5. It has more fields, but visually isn't all that different from the last form. Let's start by building the entire form for our InvoiceForm component. We already have the markup ready to go, so we need to define it for Angular.

9.3.1 *Defining your form*

The first step is to define the form for our invoice, and this is done to ensure that the controller is aware of all of the aspects of the form. This will define a separate model that exists just for the form. When we load the invoice data from the API, we'll load it into the form, rather than directly bind the form to it like we saw with `NgModel`.

Angular provides a service called FormBuilder, which is a helpful tool to build a reactive form. We'll use this to build the description of our form. It lets us define each of the form controls and any validations we want to apply to them.

We'll be editing the InvoiceForm component in this section, so start by opening src/app/invoice-form/invoice-form.component.ts and update the constructor like you see in listing 9.7. This only includes the top portion of the file—to focus on the changing pieces, which are in bold.

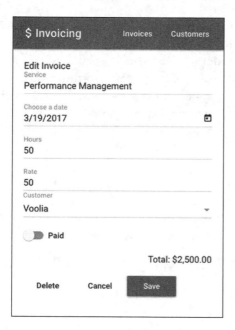

Figure 9.5 Invoice form with more controls, built in reactive style

Listing 9.7 Using FormBuilder to define the form

```
export class InvoiceFormComponent implements OnInit {
  invoiceForm: FormGroup;         ◄─────┐
  invoice: Invoice;                     │ Creates a property to hold the resulting form
  customer: Customer;
  customers: Customer[];
  total = 0;

  constructor(
    private loadingService: TdLoadingService,
    private invoicesService: InvoicesService,
    private router: Router,
    private dialogService: TdDialogService,
    private customersService: CustomersService,
    private formBuilder: FormBuilder,
    private route: ActivatedRoute) {                   Defines the form
                                                       by creating a group
      this.invoiceForm = this.formBuilder.group({   ◄──┘
        id: [''],
        service: ['', Validators.required],           Defines a property
        customerId: ['', Validators.required],   ◄──  that has a validation
        rate: ['', Validators.required],
        hours: ['', Validators.required],
        date: ['', Validators.required],              Defines a property
        paid: ['']   ◄──────────────────────         without validation
      });

  }
```

To begin, we set a property on the controller to hold our form. It's of the `FormGroup` type, which is an object designed to hold various form controls together. Then inside of the constructor, we'll use the FormBuilder service to build a group of controls.

It accepts an object that contains properties with the name of the control set to an array that holds at least one value. The first value is the value it should hold, which we're defaulting to empty for all of them. For some properties, we only define the default value. For other properties, we can add additional items to the array that must be validator functions. We'll create a custom one in a little bit, but for now we're assigning the required validation to each.

That's all we need to do to define our form. But it will always be a blank form, so when we're editing a record we need to load the data into the form. We do this in the `OnInit` lifecycle hook where we load the data. In the following listing, you can see the snippet for the data loading and add the bolded line that sets the form state based on the data.

Listing 9.8   Setting the form state

```
this.route.params.map((params: Params) => params.invoiceId).
    subscribe(invoiceId => {
  if (invoiceId) {
    this.invoicesService.get<Invoice>(invoiceId).subscribe(invoice => {
      this.invoiceForm.setValue(invoice);        ◄─┐  Use setValue to update
      this.invoice = invoice;                       │  the form state.
      this.loadingService.resolve('invoice');
    });
  } else {
    this.invoice = new Invoice();
    this.loadingService.resolve('invoice');
  }
});
```

The `invoiceForm` has a `setValue` method, which takes a data model and sets properties based on that. Otherwise, it's a new form, and the default values were already declared earlier in the controller when we defined the form. In the case where we're editing and have an existing invoice, it gets set into the form after it's been loaded from the API.

Now we need to update our template so the form controls are aware of this form and its data.

9.3.2   *Implementing the template*

The form controls in our template are currently unaware of our reactive form, and this step is about linking the form controls in the template and form controls defined in the controller. Form controls in a template exist like a normal HTML form by default. But for this all to work right, they need to know about the form and its current state so they can display properly.

The InvoiceForm template has a couple of UI components from Material Design: a date picker and a slide toggle. These act like normal form elements, and you can learn more about them in the documentation.

Much as we used `NgModel` to link a form control to the form, we'll use a different directive called `FormControlName`. This will indicate which form control should be bound into that element, based on the name provided when we built the form.

Open src/app/invoice-form/invoice-form.component.html and make the additions to the form controls, as you see in bold in the following listing, to wire up the controls.

Listing 9.9 InvoiceForm template with form controls

```html
<div *tdLoading="'invoice'">
  <form *ngIf="invoice" [formGroup]="invoiceForm">          ◄── Defines the form group on
    <md-card>                                                    the form element
      <md-card-header>Edit Invoice</md-card-header>         Adds a formControlName that
      <md-card-content>                                     maps to the control name
        <md-input-container>
          <input name="service" mdInput type="text" placeholder="Service"
      formControlName="service">                           ◄──
        </md-input-container>
        <md-input-container>
          <input mdInput [mdDatepicker]="picker" placeholder="Choose a date"
      formControlName="date">                               ◄──
            <button type="button" mdSuffix [mdDatepickerToggle]="picker"></
      button>
        </md-input-container>
        <md-datepicker #picker></md-datepicker>             Material Design date picker
        <md-input-container>                                 works with a normal input field.
          <input name="hours" mdInput type="number" placeholder="Hours"
      formControlName="hours">
        </md-input-container>
        <md-input-container>
          <input name="rate" mdInput type="number" placeholder="Rate"
      formControlName="rate">
        </md-input-container>
        <div>
          <md-select name="customerId" placeholder="Customer"
      formControlName="customerId">
            <md-option [value]="customer.id" *ngFor="let customer of
      customers">{{customer?.name}}</md-option>
          </md-select>
        </div>
        <div class="toggler">                               Slide toggle has a Boolean state.
          <md-slide-toggle formControlName="paid">Paid</md-slide-toggle>  ◄──
        </div>
        <div class="total">
          Total: {{total | currency:'USD':true:'.2'}}
        </div>
      </md-card-content>
      <md-card-actions>
        <button type="button" md-button>Delete</button>
        <button type="button" md-button>Cancel</button>
        <button type="submit" md-raised-button color="primary">Save</button>
      </md-card-actions>
    </md-card>
  </form>
</div>
```

The first step is to use the `FormGroup` directive to bind the form we declared to the form element. If you miss this step, the form won't know about the model you defined. Then we just linked the form controls with the name used when we built the form, and at this point the form will now render properly. We'll have to work out the details of saving in a little bit, but otherwise it's a fully functional form.

Now I think it would be nice for us to display the invoice total in the page so users know the invoice total based on the rate and hours input. We can do this by observing form controls, so let's see how we can use that.

9.3.3   *Watching changes*

Unlike in template-driven forms, our reactive form controller has the source of truth for the form state, and it gives us the ability to observe a form or a single control for changes. This lets us run logic that might be useful, such as validation or saving progress.

In our case, we want to display the total invoice amount at the bottom, and that requires multiplying the `hours` and `rate`. Each form control exposes an observable that we can use to subscribe to changes, and we'll use it to get both `hours` and `rate` values.

The template already has a place for the total at the bottom, but it shows 0 all the time. Although we could try to do math directly in the interpolation binding, it gets a little bit messy and harder to test. We'd rather handle this in the controller.

Using the form, we can get a specific control using `invoiceForm.get('hours')`. You pass a string that's the name of the form control, and you get the instance of that control. This instance provides a number of properties and capabilities, one of which is the `valueChanges` observable.

Let's make this work by adding a little bit to the end of the `OnInit` method. You can see the snippet to add here in the following listing.

Listing 9.10   Observing state changes in the form

```
Observable.combineLatest(
  this.invoiceForm.get('rate').valueChanges,
  this.invoiceForm.get('hours').valueChanges
).subscribe(([rate = 0, hours = 0]) => {
  this.total = rate * hours;
});
```

This snippet might be new to you, but we're using the `combineLatest` operator from RxJS. This operator takes two observables, which are references to the stream of value changes of the `rate` and `hours` controls, and merges them into one. We can then get the latest values from the stream and multiply them to get the current total.

Imagine you had more complex math here, such as adding in taxes, or perhaps there was another value to plug in. Doing math in the interpolation binding directly would quickly get out of hand, and this provides you direct access to run calculations when values change. This is also a pattern of reactive, because in this case you're reacting to changes in the form state and updating the total.

When you use `invoiceForm.get('rate')`, you're also able to access the same properties from table 9.1 (form control status properties). You can check whether the control is `valid`, `pristine`, `touched`, or what errors exist. This might be helpful for you to do additional validation or checks.

We can also implement our own validator functions as we did before and see how to plug them into the form.

9.3.4 Custom validators with reactive forms

Previously, when we implemented custom validation, we created both a validation function and a directive. With reactive forms, we only need to create the validation function and then add it into the form when we create it with FormBuilder.

We'll update our validation messages as well to use the validation rules we defined, as you see in figure 9.6.

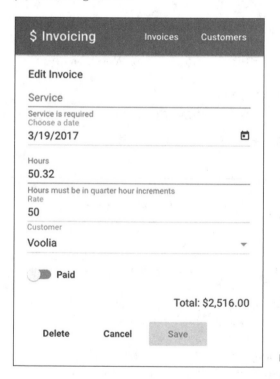

Figure 9.6   Validation rules in the invoice form

Imagine our invoicing application had the restriction that hours had to be always rounded to the quarter hour—like 1 hour, 1.25, 1.5, 1.75, or 2. It should not allow values like 1.1 or 1.7. This is fairly common when invoicing by time, and the way we enforce this is to validate the `hours` input and see if it's valid by quarter hour.

We'll build a validator function like we did previously, but we won't have to wrap it up in a directive. Start by making a new file at src/app/validators/hours.validator.ts, and add the code from the following listing to it.

Listing 9.11   Hour validator

Directly
exports the
validator
function

Determines if
the number
is a valid
figure and
returns
validation

```
import { AbstractControl, ValidatorFn } from '@angular/forms';

export function HoursValidator(control: AbstractControl) : { [key: string]:
    any } {
  return (Number.isInteger(control.value * 4)) ? null : { hours: true };
}
```

This is very succinct, but in contrast to the previous validator, we're directly exporting the validation function. When we created a custom validator earlier for a directive, we needed a function to return a validator function, whereas here we export the validator function directly. When the validator function runs, it multiplies the value by 4 and checks if it is an integer. That means any valid hourly increment will multiply an integer by 4 and return null for valid. Otherwise, it returns the object with the key and Boolean.

Now we need to make our form aware of this validation function, and that's done when we construct the form using FormBuilder. In the component controller, update the form definition like you see in the following listing. You'll need to import the HoursValidator function into the file.

Listing 9.12   Using HoursValidator

```
this.invoiceForm = this.formBuilder.group({
  id: [''],
  service: ['', Validators.required],
  customerId: ['', Validators.required],
  rate: ['', Validators.required],
  hours: ['', [Validators.required, HoursValidator]],     ← Adds custom validator
  date: ['', Validators.required],                           to the control
  paid: ['']
});
```

Because we're directly constructing the form, we just need to pass the custom validation function into the control. Notice how the hours control also now has an array for the second item in the array. That's because if you have multiple validators, they need to be grouped here. The form control takes the default value, synchronous validators, and asynchronous validators as a third array item.

We haven't looked at async validators, but the only difference is that they might take a moment to run. Imagine you needed a validator that checked whether a username was already taken; that probably requires making an API call. The only difference when you implement an async validator is that you need to return a promise or observable, and Angular handles it.

We'd also like to show validation errors in the template, so we'll need to add the same type of error messages we saw earlier. But the way we access the form elements to check their validity is slightly different.

Open the template again and update the fields with error messages, as you see in the following listing.

Listing 9.13   Validation messages

```
<md-card-content>
  <md-input-container>
    <input name="service" mdInput type="text" placeholder="Service"
    formControlName="service">
    <md-error *ngIf="invoiceForm.get('service').touched && invoiceForm.
    get('service').invalid">          ◄─────  Use invoiceForm to get the
      Service is required                      form control reference.
    </md-error>
  </md-input-container>
  <md-input-container>
    <input mdInput [mdDatepicker]="picker" placeholder="Choose a date"
    formControlName="date">
    <button type="button" mdSuffix [mdDatepickerToggle]="picker"></button>
    <md-error *ngIf="invoiceForm.get('date').touched && invoiceForm.
    get('date').invalid">
      Date is required
    </md-error>
  </md-input-container>
  <md-datepicker #picker></md-datepicker>
  <md-input-container>
    <input name="hours" mdInput type="number" placeholder="Hours"
    formControlName="hours">
    <md-error *ngIf="invoiceForm.get('hours').touched && invoiceForm.
    get('hours').invalid">
      Hours must be in quarter hour increments
    </md-error>
  </md-input-container>
  <md-input-container>
    <input name="rate" mdInput type="number" placeholder="Rate"
    formControlName="rate">
    <md-error *ngIf="invoiceForm.get('rate').touched && invoiceForm.
    get('rate').invalid">
      Hourly rate is required
    </md-error>
  </md-input-container>
  <div>
    <md-select name="customerId" placeholder="Customer"
    formControlName="customerId">                         At time of writing,
      <md-option [value]="customer.id" *ngFor="let customer of   select did not
    customers">{{customer?.name}}</md-option>              support validation.
    </md-select>
  </div>
  <div class="toggler">
    <md-slide-toggle formControlName="paid">Paid</md-slide-toggle>
  </div>
  <div class="total">
    Total: {{total | currency:'USD':true:'.2'}}
  </div>
</md-card-content>
```

Here we've added the same MdError to display errors, except we use invoiceForm.
get('rate') to access the form control. The same properties from the earlier table
are still available to you, but instead of having a local template variable to get a reference to it, we reference it from the form itself.

Now that we have the form validated as we would like, we need to be able to submit it. Let's see how that's done with reactive forms now.

9.3.5   *Handling submit or cancel events*

The final step is to submit the form when it's ready. The steps are almost identical, except we manage the data in a different way before we submit it to the service. The `NgSubmit` event binding is still available for us to capture submit events to handle, so we'll use that again.

Open the InvoiceForm component template again and update the form element like you see here in bold:

```
<form *ngIf="invoice" [formGroup]="invoiceForm" (ngSubmit)="save()">
```

While you have the template open, let's also wire up the buttons at the bottom. Add the bolded parts to your buttons:

```
<md-card-actions>
  <button type="button" md-button (click)="delete()" *ngIf="invoice.
    id">Delete</button>
  <button type="button" md-button (click)="cancel()">Cancel</button>
  <button type="submit" md-raised-button color="primary"
    [disabled]="invoiceForm.invalid">Save</button>
</md-card-actions>
```

Here we're implementing the click handlers on the delete and cancel buttons, and also disabling the save button unless the form is valid. Notice how we're using the `InvoiceForm` properties to determine the form state, similar to how we used `NgForm` with template-driven forms.

The last step is to update the save method in the controller so it gets its data from the form. Because the data was bound into the form when we loaded the component, we need to extract it back out before we save. Update the save method as you see here in bold:

```
save() {
  if (this.invoice.id) {
    this.invoicesService.update<Invoice>(this.invoice.id, this.invoiceForm.
    value).subscribe(response => {
      this.viewInvoice(response.id);
    });
  } else {
    this.invoicesService.create<Invoice>(this.invoiceForm.value).
    subscribe(response => {
      this.viewInvoice(response.id);
    });
  }
}
```

You can see that when we need to get the data back out of the form, we can look at the `invoiceForm.value` property. This gives us an object representing the same form model with the values for each field. We pass this into the service to either create or update a record and see our values being saved correctly.

We're now finished with our invoice form, and you can see both the controller and template in listings 9.14 and 9.15 to ensure you have everything correct.

Listing 9.14   InvoiceForm component controller

```
import { Component, OnInit } from '@angular/core';
import { ActivatedRoute, Params, Router } from '@angular/router';
import { TdLoadingService, TdDialogService } from '@covalent/core';
import { FormBuilder, FormGroup, Validators } from '@angular/forms';
import { InvoicesService, Invoice, CustomersService, Customer } from '@aia/
    services';
import { Observable } from 'rxjs/Observable';
import 'rxjs/add/observable/combineLatest';
import { HoursValidator } from '../validators/hours.validator';

@Component({
  selector: 'app-invoice-form',
  templateUrl: './invoice-form.component.html',
  styleUrls: ['./invoice-form.component.css']
})
export class InvoiceFormComponent implements OnInit {
  invoiceForm: FormGroup;
  invoice: Invoice;
  customer: Customer;
  customers: Customer[];
  total = 0;

  constructor(
    private loadingService: TdLoadingService,
    private invoicesService: InvoicesService,
    private router: Router,
    private dialogService: TdDialogService,
    private customersService: CustomersService,
    private formBuilder: FormBuilder,
    private route: ActivatedRoute) {

      this.invoiceForm = this.formBuilder.group({
        id: [''],
        service: ['', Validators.required],
        customerId: ['', Validators.required],
        rate: ['', Validators.required],
        hours: ['', [Validators.required, HoursValidator]],
        date: ['', Validators.required],
        paid: ['']
      });

  }

  ngOnInit() {
    this.loadingService.register('invoice');
    this.loadingService.register('customers');

    this.customersService.query().subscribe(customers => {
      this.customers = customers;
```

```
      this.loadingService.resolve('customers');
    });

    this.route.params.map((params: Params) => params.invoiceId).
      subscribe(invoiceId => {
        if (invoiceId) {
          this.invoicesService.get<Invoice>(invoiceId).subscribe(invoice => {
            this.invoiceForm.setValue(invoice);
            this.invoice = invoice;
            this.loadingService.resolve('invoice');
          });
        } else {
          this.invoice = new Invoice();
          this.loadingService.resolve('invoice');
        }
      });

    Observable.combineLatest(
      this.invoiceForm.get('rate').valueChanges,
      this.invoiceForm.get('hours').valueChanges
    ).subscribe(([rate = 0, hours = 0]) => {
      this.total = rate * hours;
    });
  }

  save() {
    if (this.invoice.id) {
      this.invoicesService.update<Invoice>(this.invoice.id, this.invoiceForm.
       value).subscribe(response => {
        this.viewInvoice(response.id);
      });
    } else {
      this.invoicesService.create<Invoice>(this.invoiceForm.value).
       subscribe(response => {
        this.viewInvoice(response.id);
      });
    }
  }

  delete() {
    this.dialogService.openConfirm({
      message: 'Are you sure you want to delete this invoice?',
      title: 'Confirm',
      acceptButton: 'Delete'
    }).afterClosed().subscribe((accept: boolean) => {
      if (accept) {
        this.loadingService.register('invoice');
        this.invoicesService.delete(this.invoice.id).subscribe(response => {
          this.loadingService.resolve('invoice');
          this.invoice.id = null;
          this.cancel();
        });
      }
```

```
      });
    }

    cancel() {
      if (this.invoice.id) {
        this.router.navigate(['/invoices', this.invoice.id]);
      } else {
        this.router.navigateByUrl('/invoices');
      }
    }

    private viewInvoice(id: number) {
      this.router.navigate(['/invoices', id]);
    }

}
```

Listing 9.15 InvoiceForm component template

```html
<div *tdLoading="'invoice'">
  <form *ngIf="invoice" [formGroup]="invoiceForm" (ngSubmit)="save()">
    <md-card>
      <md-card-header>Edit Invoice</md-card-header>
      <md-card-content>
        <md-input-container>
          <input name="service" mdInput type="text" placeholder="Service"
      formControlName="service">
          <md-error *ngIf="invoiceForm.get('service').touched && invoiceForm.
      get('service').invalid">
            Service is required
          </md-error>
        </md-input-container>
        <md-input-container>
          <input mdInput [mdDatepicker]="picker" placeholder="Choose a date"
      formControlName="date">
          <button type="button" mdSuffix [mdDatepickerToggle]="picker"></
      button>
          <md-error *ngIf="invoiceForm.get('date').touched && invoiceForm.
      get('date').invalid">
            Date is required
          </md-error>
        </md-input-container>
        <md-datepicker #picker></md-datepicker>
        <md-input-container>
          <input name="hours" mdInput type="number" placeholder="Hours"
      formControlName="hours">
          <md-error *ngIf="invoiceForm.get('hours').touched && invoiceForm.
      get('hours').invalid">
            Hours must be in quarter hour increments
          </md-error>
        </md-input-container>
        <md-input-container>
```

```
        <input name="rate" mdInput type="number" placeholder="Rate"
    formControlName="rate">
        <md-error *ngIf="invoiceForm.get('rate').touched && invoiceForm.
    get('rate').invalid">
            Hourly rate is required
        </md-error>
      </md-input-container>
      <div>
        <md-select name="customerId" placeholder="Customer"
    formControlName="customerId">
            <md-option [value]="customer.id" *ngFor="let customer of
    customers">{{customer?.name}}</md-option>
        </md-select>
      </div>
      <div class="toggler">
        <md-slide-toggle formControlName="paid">Paid</md-slide-toggle>
      </div>
      <div class="total">
        Total: {{total | currency:'USD':true:'.2'}}
      </div>
    </md-card-content>
    <md-card-actions>
      <button type="button" md-button (click)="delete()" *ngIf="invoice.
    id">Delete</button>
      <button type="button" md-button (click)="cancel()">Cancel</button>
      <button type="submit" md-raised-button color="primary"
    [disabled]="invoiceForm.invalid">Save</button>
    </md-card-actions>
  </md-card>
 </form>
</div>
```

That covers the majority of what you need to know about both reactive and template-driven forms. There are certainly more minor features that exist for additional cases, but this foundation should get you building forms, and you can learn about other features as you go.

9.3.6   *Which form approach is better?*

That is a trick question, to my mind, though you probably want a bit more of an explanation. Rather than tell you to use one and never the other, I'll share from my experience why I use both.

Excluding the mechanical differences of the two form libraries, I find the most important aspect is how they approach defining the form. The patterns they employ can work in most situations.

Most of the time I suggest reactive forms. I like the guarantees reactive provides and the way you define the model and let the template react. I prefer my templates to reflect state, not create state. By that I mean how NgModel creates the controls for you behind the scenes and binds data up to the controller. If you need an answer, I would recommend reactive forms, if you really pinned me down.

But you may have noticed this is the first time we've seen reactive forms in the book. Sometimes it's simpler to use NgModel, especially when it's a single form field. In simple scenarios, I find template-driven forms to be more approachable with low overhead, but when a form becomes more complex, then I recommend reactive forms.

I think the most important thing is to be consistent in your applications. Although you can mix and match as much as you like, there's a mental drawback to that when you write and test them.

Before I close out the chapter, let's see how to implement your own form controls in cases where your application needs controls that don't exist out of the box or in libraries.

9.4 *Custom form controls*

There are scenarios where your application requires a different form control that isn't defined in HTML or in a third-party library. All form controls have a few basic requirements, and Angular already implements them for the built-in HTML form elements.

Regardless of whether you use reactive or template-driven forms, there has to be some logic to write up the native HTML element (or custom component) with the forms library. There are essentially two places to track the current value of a form control: in the form and the control. Angular provides the ControlValueAccessor interface as a way to implement a custom control that works with forms, which we'll use in conjunction with the Angular Material library components to create our own custom control.

In our application, there are several candidates for creating custom form controls, but we'll be transforming the current hours input field from the invoice form into a custom form control. We'll implement some basic features that make it easier to use, but also encapsulate the internal logic of the control.

As you see in figure 9.7, the hours form field now has several buttons underneath that help you dial in the value by smaller increments. As you change the values, the form element will continue to validate and update the total invoice value at the bottom, as you would expect.

Our first step is to create a new component to house our custom control. To do this, use the CLI as you see here:

```
ng generate component hours-control
```

Once the component is created, open the src/app/hours-control/hours-control.component.ts file and replace the contents with what you see in listing 9.16. There's a lot happening in this file, so we'll look at the various pieces closely.

Figure 9.7   New `hours` custom control that connects with Angular forms

---

Listing 9.16   HoursControl controller

```
import { Component, forwardRef } from '@angular/core';
import { ControlValueAccessor, NG_VALIDATORS, NG_VALUE_ACCESSOR, FormControl
       } from '@angular/forms';
import { HoursValidator } from '../validators/hours.validator';

@Component({
  selector: 'app-hours-control',
  templateUrl: './hours-control.component.html',
  styleUrls: ['./hours-control.component.css'],
  providers: [{
    provide: NG_VALUE_ACCESSOR,
    useExisting: forwardRef(() => HoursControlComponent),
    multi: true
  }, {
    provide: NG_VALIDATORS,
    useExisting: forwardRef(() => HoursControlComponent),
    multi: true
  }]
})
export class HoursControlComponent implements ControlValueAccessor {

  hours = 0;
  validateFn = HoursValidator;
  onChange = (v: any) => {};
```

Declares providers

ControlValueAccessor interface is used by all form controls

Properties to house the value, validation function, and change event

```
update() {
    this.onChange(this.hours);        Changes binding to
}                                     update the form control

keypress($event) {
    if ($event.key === 'ArrowUp') {
        this.setValue(.25);
    } else if ($event.key === 'ArrowDown') {    Event handler for
        this.setValue(-.25);                    key press
    }
}

setValue(change: number) {
    this.hours += change;             Method to set value
    this.update();                    from button clicks
}

validate(control: FormControl) {
    return this.validateFn(control);    Validation handler
}

writeValue(value: any) {
    if (value !== undefined) {
        this.hours = value;           Handles writing a value
    }                                 into the control
}

registerOnChange(fn) {
    this.onChange = fn;               Wires up change handler
}

registerOnTouched() {}  ◄——— Empty method to satisfy interface
}
```

There's a lot happening here in a short amount of space, so let's break things down. The HoursControl component implements the ControlValueAccessor interface, which ensures that your form control is designed to work correctly with Angular forms. It requires that a control implements the three methods found at the end of the controller: writeValue, registerOnChange, and registerOnTouched.

The writeValue method is used by Angular to pass a value into the form control from the form itself. This is similar to binding a value into the component, though it works with the form controls like NgModel, and it passes the value from the form into the control.

The registerOnChange method accepts a function that the form library will pass in that your control needs to call whenever the value changes. It stores this function on the onChange property of the controller, and the default noop function is defined so the component compiles correctly. In other words, it gives you a method to call that passes the current form value up to the form.

The registerOnTouch method isn't implemented here, but it allows you to accept a method to handle touch events. This might be useful on controls that have some kind of touch impact, such as a toggle switch. But there isn't much for us to implement for a form control that takes a number input.

In the component metadata, we see some providers are declared. Recall that we did something similar when we created our directive for validation. Here we have to declare two providers—the first is to register this component with NG_VALUE_ACCESSOR. This marks this component as a form control and registers it with dependency injection so Angular can access it later. The second is to register the component with NG_VALIDATORS. This control has validation internally, so we need to register the control on the validators provider for Angular to access later.

Because the control has a validate method, Angular can call this method to determine whether the control is valid or not. This is the same as with creating a Validator directive as we did earlier in listing 9.4. In this case, though, we import the HoursValidator function and reuse it inside the component.

The rest of the methods are there to handle the internal actions of the control. The update method is responsible for calling the change event handler, which will alert the form that the control's internal state value has changed. The keypress method is just a nice feature that allows us to bind to the keyup event, and if the user pressed up or down arrows, it will increment or decrement the current value by 0.25. Finally, the setValue method is called by the row of buttons to add or subtract from the current value.

In summary, this component really has three roles. First, it implements an internal model to track the current value of the control (the number of hours) and allows that value to be manipulated by buttons or keypresses. Second, it provides validation and ensures the number provided is to a quarter of an hour. Third, it wires up the necessary methods for Angular forms to be made aware of the current state of the control.

Next we need to look at the template, so let's go ahead and implement it so we can see everything together. Open src/app/hours-control/hours-control.component.html and replace its contents with the code from the following listing.

Listing 9.17 HoursControl template

```
<md-input-container>
  <input name="hours" mdInput type="number" placeholder="Hours"
    [(ngModel)]="hours" hours (keyup)="keypress($event)"
    #control="ngModel" (change)="update()">
  <md-error *ngIf="control.touched && control.invalid">
    Hours must be a number in increments of .25
  </md-error>
</md-input-container>
<div layout="row">
  <button type="button" md-button flex (click)="setValue(1)">+ 1</button>
  <button type="button" md-button flex (click)="setValue(.25)">+ .25</button>
  <button type="button" md-button flex (click)="setValue(-.25)">- .25</
    button>
  <button type="button" md-button flex (click)="setValue(-1)">- 1</button>
</div>
```

Shows or hides error messages

Binds hours using NgModel, adds directive to validate, and event bindings

Buttons in a row to add or subtract hours

In our template, we encapsulate the entire form control that we want to provide, which includes the buttons and the original input box. Because we're still accepting text input, we use a standard `input` element. But we're also setting up the `NgModel`, a validation directive (which we'll create next), and two event bindings for `keyup` and `change`.

This control has built-in error validation and uses the same Angular Material patterns we saw earlier in the chapter. It shows a message if the control is invalid, and if the control has been focused on. It's nice that the validation messaging is built in, because it doesn't need to be implemented later. If you have the same controls in many places with the same validation, this might be useful. If you want to ensure that this control is more reusable, with different validation types, this might not be ideal.

The last set of elements is the buttons that add or subtract from the current state. When they're clicked, the internal hours model is updated, and the form is alerted to the change as well.

There's a bit of CSS that we need to add for the control to look correct, so open src/app/hours-control/hours-control.css and add the code from the following listing.

Listing 9.18   HoursControl stylings

```css
:host {
    width: 100%;
    display: block;
}
md input container {
    width: 100%;
}
button {
    padding: 0;
    min-width: 25%;
}
```

This makes sure that a few pieces of the control play nicely with the UI library, since we've changed the way it usually expects elements to be laid out.

You probably noticed that we have a validation directive for hours on the input, but we haven't created a directive version of this validator yet. That's simple to do, and we need to do so before we use this control. Create a new directive by running the following command:

```
ng generate directive validators/hours
```

Then open the directive file at src/app/validators/hours.directive.ts and replace its contents with the code in the following listing.

Listing 9.19   Hours validation directive

```typescript
import { Directive } from '@angular/core';
import { Validator, AbstractControl, NG_VALIDATORS } from '@angular/forms';
import { HoursValidator } from './hours.validator';

@Directive({
```

```
                                                    ┌─────────────────────────────────┐
                                                    │ Ensures selector applies to elements
                                                    │ with the hour and NgModel attributes
                                                    └─────────────────────────────────┘
    selector: '[hours][ngModel]',        ◄─────────┘
    providers: [{ provide: NG_VALIDATORS, useExisting: HoursDirective, multi:
      true }]
})
export class HoursDirective implements Validator {
  private validator = HoursValidator;

  validate(control: AbstractControl): { [key: string]: any } {
      return this.validator(control);
  }
}
```

This directive looks almost identical to the one we created earlier, except it references the `HoursValidator` function. I recommend reviewing the details from listing 9.3 for specifics if you have any questions.

Now we have everything we need to use our new control. This control is meant to be used in the InvoiceForm component, so open the template found at src/app/invoice-form/invoice-form.component.html and replace the existing hours input element with our newly created form control, as you see here in bold in the snippet of the whole template:

```
<md-datepicker #picker></md-datepicker>
<app-hours-control formControlName="hours"></app-hours-control>
<md-input-container>
  <input name="rate" mdInput type="number" placeholder="Rate"
      formControlName="rate">
</md-input-container>
```

Because this is a custom form control, we can use it with reactive forms or template-driven forms without issue. Congratulations! You've created your own control and can now make as many as you want.

But wait—there are a couple of caveats to building your own controls, and to this particular example. Custom controls seem like a great idea, but they can also be a lot of work to build properly. For example, does your custom control work well on mobile or touch devices? Does it have proper support for screen readers and other accessibility requirements? Does it work in multiple applications or is it too custom for your application? These are important questions to ask, and also to verify whether your controls work for the largest set of users. One of the major reasons I advocate using an existing UI library is that the good libraries will have solved these issues ahead of time for you.

Before going off to build a custom control, see if you can think clearly about the user experience and determine whether an existing control could be used instead of a new one. Users tend to struggle more with custom form elements that they haven't seen before, so it can be very practical to adjust the application slightly so it can use already existing controls before you make a new one.

Because this chapter is using a specific UI library, I've implemented the form controls in a way that fits with that library. Therefore, it's limited to being used only with Angular Material, which may limit the use of your control. On the other hand, if you can expect to always use Angular Material (or the UI library of choice), then the custom control may be saving you a lot of repetition.

At the time of writing, the Angular Material library doesn't support creating your own form controls that work nicely with the input container. (See https://github.com/angular/material2/issues/4672.) This is why I ultimately encapsulated the entire form control and surrounding markup. It makes the example more verbose than you might need, so you should consider how to simplify your form controls if possible.

This example uses a standard `input` element inside, which is why `NgModel` was used, but in many custom form controls you may not have an input, so you wouldn't use `NgModel`. In those cases, you simply make sure that as the control state changes (such as a toggler that goes from true to false), you call the change handler so the form knows the state changes.

That wraps up forms, both reactive and template-driven, as well as creating your own controls. Forms are very important to most applications, and you should now have the tools to craft feature-rich and usable forms.

Summary

We've built two forms, in both the reactive and template-driven styles in this chapter. Along the way we also managed to learn about most of what forms have to offer. Here's a brief summary of the key takeaways:

- Template-driven forms define the form using `NgModel` on form controls.
- You can apply normal HTML validation attributes, and `NgModel` will automatically try to validate based on those rules.
- Custom validation is possible through a custom validator function and directive, which gets registered with the built-in list of validators.
- The `NgForm` directive, though it can be transparent, exposes features to help manage submit events and overall form validation inspection.
- Reactive forms are different in that you define the form model in the controller and link form controls using `FormControlName`.
- You can observe the changes of a form control with reactive forms and run logic every time a new value is emitted.
- Reactive forms declare validation in the controller form definition, and creating custom validations is easier because they don't require a directive.
- Ultimately, both form patterns are available to you. I tend to use reactive forms, especially as the form gets more complex.
- Creating a new form control requires implementing the `ControlValueAccessor` methods and registering it with the controls provider.

Testing your application

10

This chapter covers

- The value of testing your Angular applications
- How to set up and create unit tests to test individual pieces
- Unit test strategies for directives, services, components, and pipes
- How to implement e2e tests to test the application as a whole
- Additional testing strategies

All the applications we've built could benefit from testing. Some developers dread writing tests, whereas others are probably wondering why I didn't cover testing from the start. I consider testing essential, though it requires a set of new concepts and tools, which is why I waited till now.

Angular was designed to be highly testable, and projects created using the Angular CLI automatically set up basic testing scaffolding and tools for us to use. We'll use the CLI provided tools and configuration in this chapter. Developers with experience using other tools can choose to set up something else on their own and use the ideas and concepts from this chapter with those tools.

When developers talk about *testing*, they often mean *unit tests*. If you aren't familiar with unit tests, these are ways of testing individual pieces (units) of your application in isolation. For example, we'll test a single component without being rendered in the entire app and a pipe without being used in a template. If we compare unit tests to making a car, it would be analogous to testing each part, such as the wheel, electronics, engine, and so on, on its own, before it's assembled as a whole car. This is the first type of testing we'll look at in detail.

End-to-end (e2e) testing, also called *integration* testing, is a way of testing the application as a whole. In contrast to isolating each unit individually, these tests are used to ensure that everything works together in concert. In our car analogy, it would be like running a test drive and asserting that all the parts were indeed working well together.

If you've never tested your code in the past, writing good tests will decrease the level of effort required to maintain an application and give you more confidence that it's behaving as expected. Different projects have different requirements, but performing *no* tests generally means that you're either manually testing everything with every change or that people can't depend on your application. Depending on who determines the testing strategy for your application, you should be sure to argue for taking the time and effort to write quality tests to ensure that everything is working.

Testing is such a big topic in Angular that there's an entire book devoted to it, called *Testing Angular Applications* (Manning, 2018). I cover a lot of the basics here very quickly, but there's more to dive into, and I suggest you take a look at it. You can find it at https://www.manning.com/books/testing-angular-applications.

In this chapter, we'll focus on how to write unit tests for components, services, pipes, and directives. We'll also create a few e2e tests that navigate and check elements on pages. It will be very hands on, so to get us going, let's set up the example.

10.1 Testing tools and setting up the chapter example

The stock tracker application makes an appearance once again, because it has the best mix of things to test. We're going to use the version from chapter 8 where we created custom pipes and directives, so we can test them too.

We won't modify the behavior of the application (except for a couple of examples where the tests show us ways to improve our code)—we'll only be adding code into the various test files. The Angular CLI already generated the test files for us when we generated a new component, pipe, directive, or whatever, so we'll just need to implement the tests.

This code lives in a different repo, and you can get it using Git like this:

```
git clone https://github.com/angular-in-action/testing
cd testing
git checkout start
```

Otherwise, you can download the archived files from https://github.com/angular-in-action/testing/archive/start.zip and unzip the files.

As usual, you'll need to run `npm install` to download all the dependencies, and then you can run `ng serve` to start the local development server. I've cleared out all the tests so they'll run, just so you can run the commands easily. It will mention an error like "Executed 0 of 0," but once we create a test, that will go away—so you can ignore it for now.

Let's take a look at the various testing tools that are used by Angular out of the box.

10.1.1 Testing tools

Angular provides an opinionated set of tooling choices for creating and running tests. Some tools apply to only unit or e2e tests, whereas some apply to both. Tests have to run in a real browser, because that's the environment where web applications execute, so there are a few pieces of technology that enable tests to execute JavaScript code.

Jasmine is the first tool. It's a framework for writing tests. Jasmine is JavaScript (or TypeScript in our case), but it's capable of connecting with a browser to execute tests using the browser's JavaScript engine. When we write our tests in this chapter, you'll always be using the Jasmine framework. A *test* ultimately consists of any code required to set up and tear down the specific test case, and then a set of expectations that verify that your code behaves as expected. For example, you'll transform some text with a pipe to see if it returns the expected result. You can learn more about Jasmine at https://jasmine.github.io/.

Next we have Karma, a tool originally created by the Angular team to help execute unit tests. Karma can control any type of framework, but it's already configured to control Jasmine out of the box with the Angular CLI. It can do some interesting things, like run your tests on multiple browsers at once and provide features for continuous integration tools. You can learn more about Karma at https://karma-runner.github.io/1.0/index.html.

Protractor is the next tool. It's geared at helping run e2e-type tests by helping manage the way that tests run (like Karma), but also by providing an additional testing framework that you use with Jasmine to test and control the browser like a real user might. It's built on WebDriver, a specification for how to control a browser through automation. Learn more at www.protractortest.org.

You may have noticed that all these tools require a browser, and you have some options on which browsers to use. I generally recommend using Chrome for local development, because it's set up out of the box, but you should also read about how to use each of these tools to test on different browsers to be more certain things work. Not all browsers support the same features or behave in exactly the same ways, so keep that in mind.

There are a few other minor tools used behind the scenes; they're plugins for these primary tools. This chapter doesn't intend to cover all the potential ways these tools can be configured. We're going to focus on what works out of the box, and you can expand to more complex scenarios as your needs change.

10.2 Unit testing

I'll begin with unit testing, because it's likely that you'll write more unit tests than other types of tests. They're the lowest-level test you can write for your application—they verify that the smallest pieces work as expected. Remember from earlier the analogy of testing each component of the car before it's assembled to ensure that quality parts are being used in the vehicle.

You can write unit tests in a wide variety of ways, but Angular has some general guidelines that work in most scenarios. Fundamentally, there are two ways to write unit tests:

- Creating truly isolated unit tests in which you construct the entities yourself
- Rendering a test bed module to render the entity with Angular and verify behavior

Truly isolated unit tests are best for pipes and, often, services, where you create a new instance of the class outside of Angular. That means you wouldn't have access to using dependency injection, and you'll see how you can either mock or manually inject dependencies. These tests are extremely fast and reduce the surface area of your tests to the lowest level. If you can write a test using this approach, it's recommended that you do so.

Test bed module testing is more involved, but it's more appropriate for components and sometimes directives when you need to verify how things are rendered in the context of an Angular application. In this case, you're essentially creating a temporary Angular application that has the minimal amount of stuff needed to run. As you can imagine, these are a little bit slower to run but provide more capabilities for building tests.

10.2.1 Anatomy of unit tests

All unit tests share a few basic concepts, so let's start by taking a closer look at the basic anatomy of a unit test. Each test has a few pieces, some of which are optional. This all comes from the Jasmine testing framework as well, so if you need any more context about a certain part, you can always review the Jasmine documentation.

The parts are as follows:

- `describe`—A container for a set of tests that cover the same overall entity, such as describing the test suite for a pipe.
- `it`—A container for a single test that is used to describe a single feature, such as testing a specific component method that handles saving.
- `expect`—A way to assert that a value meets expected requirements, such as the response from a method must equal true.
- `beforeEach/beforeAll`—These are a way to execute code before each individual test, or before all tests, such as setup logic to construct a new instance of the entity for each test. They only apply within the Describe block in which they're defined.
- `afterEach/afterAll`—These allow you to execute after each test or all tests, such as cleaning up anything between tests or resetting any shared state. They also apply only within the Describe block in which they are defined.

In most tests you'll use all of these, with the exception of the `afterEach/afterAll` blocks. You'll want to ensure that each test is set up with a clean instance of the object you want to test, and the `beforeEach` tends to be the most practical way to do that.

Let's start writing some tests to see everything in action. We'll focus first on a pure pipe so we can see the most basic type of test and how these pieces work together.

10.2.2 *Testing pipes*

Pipes are often the easiest thing to test, especially pure pipes. Because they're simple classes that implement a single function, we can easily run them without creating a full Angular application.

I think it's best to jump right into a test and walk through the basic steps. We'll start by writing a test for our Change pipe, which can be found at src/app/pipes/change. pipe.ts. The pipe is pure, and the only difficult aspect is that it injects two other pipes as services. Open up the test spec file at src/app/pipes/change.pipe.spec.ts and replace its contents with what's shown in the following listing.

Listing 10.1   Change pipe test

```
import { ChangePipe } from './change.pipe';              Imports dependencies
import { CurrencyPipe, PercentPipe } from '@angular/common';   from our application

describe('ChangePipe', () => {        Creates a describe block for the pipe tests
  const currencyPipe = new CurrencyPipe('en-us');
  const percentPipe = new PercentPipe('en-us');
  const pipe = new ChangePipe(currencyPipe, percentPipe);
  const stock = {                       Defines variables
    symbol: 'abc',                      and constructs an
    lastTradePriceOnly: 10,             instance of the pipe
    change: 1,
    changeInPercent: 0.05
  };

  it('create an instance', () => {      Pair of it blocks to describe a single test
    expect(pipe).toBeTruthy();
  });

  it('should transform a stock value', () => {
    expect(pipe.transform(stock)).toEqual(`$1.00 (5.00%)`);
    stock.change = -3.45;
    stock.changeInPercent = -0.0345;
    expect(pipe.transform(stock)).toEqual(`-$3.45 (-3.45%)`);
  });
});
```

Expect statements to validate a particular value meets expectations

This test begins by importing the required pieces to construct the Change pipe, and because it depends on the Currency and Percent pipes, those are imported as well. Then you create the describe block to wrap the rest of the file, because all the rest will be inside of the context of the Change pipe. Notice the describe block takes two parameters: a string and a function. The string is used in the test suite logging to help pinpoint how tests ran, and the function is executed when the test is slated to run.

Inside of the describe block, you set up a number of variables that are used to manually create an instance of the Change pipe. When constructing these entities individually, you have to create them using the new operator to instantiate the instance, and pass any configuration into the object constructor. There's also a variable to hold a sample stock object that you'll use later to verify behavior.

The first `it` block describes a simple test to ensure that the pipe was created successfully. It's often useful to have a simple test that verifies that nothing threw an error during creation. Notice that the `it` statement takes two parameters, a string and a function, just like the `describe` block. In this case, when the test runs, the string is added to the `describe` block in the console output so you can track the `describe` block and the specific test that passes or fails.

Inside of the `it` block, there's a single `expect` statement. This is the test statement that will trigger a success or failure. If the pipe was incorrectly constructed, it will mark this test as failed and provide the relevant error message.

The next `it` block tests the `transform` method by passing the sample `stock` object and expecting it to equal a particular string. I also changed the values of the `stock` object and tested it with a negative value to verify that case as well. You could write a large series of assertions to test various scenarios, which is useful when there's more complexity in the `transform` method.

Now you need to run the test, which you do from the command line by running the `ng test` command. This will open up a new browser window that will show the results of the tests (similar to what you see in figure 10.1), as well as the results in the command line. Congratulations, you've written your first test!

This test tests every line of the Change pipe, which we can view by generating a test coverage report. You can generate a coverage report by running the test command with the `-cc` flag, like this:

```
ng test -cc
```

It will generate a new directory called coverage, and you can view the report in the browser. That allows you to see what lines of code were executed or not in a visual format and can help identify areas that you've missed. But it doesn't necessarily mean your tests are comprehensive. You might test the code in such a way that it only executes with a passing condition, but it might fail if you provide different parameters. Keep an eye out for this as you write tests.

There isn't anything particularly special about testing an impure pipe, except that you have to keep track of some state. You can look at the final version of the chapter example to view the other pipe tests and see a few more examples in action.

10.2.3 *Testing services, stubs, and mocking HTTP requests*

Services are the other type of entity that can sometimes be tested by creating an isolated entity yourself. We'll do that for our service, though you'll start to see why this can be a tricky thing to do for many of your tests.

Some services have few, if any, dependencies. In this case, our Stocks service has just one: the HttpClient service from Angular. The trick is that I have to manually construct the HttpClient service as well, which is possible, but is the kind of thing that can get out of hand if you have a lot of dependencies. We'll look at how to use testing modules in the next section, and you can also see the final version of this project, which has the testing module version of this test in the comments.

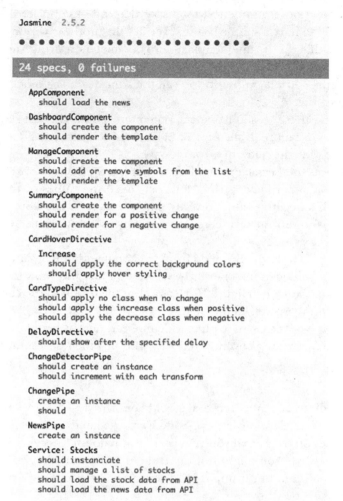

Figure 10.1   The complete test spec report from the chapter example

Because this service uses the HttpClient service, we also have to provide a solution to mocking HTTP requests. We don't want to make real HTTP calls during our unit tests, because they're slow, unpredictable, and require a real API to be available. Luckily, Angular provides a way to intercept HTTP requests and lets us send back a mock response body that we can test. Because Angular tests the HttpClient service extensively, we want to trust that Angular's tests are more than sufficient to ensure the HttpClient service is working, but this lets us test to ensure that the way we're using the HttpClient service is correctly implemented.

Before we create this test, let's take a look at the mock objects I've included ahead of time. The file src/app/services/stocks.mock.ts contains several variables that have values we can reuse throughout the application. A snippet of the file appears in the following listing. You'll need to have actual objects that match the expected responses from the API, so I've stored them in this file. You'll import the various mocks many times over the remaining tests.

Listing 10.2 Stocks mock data sample

```
export const MockSymbolsList: string[] = ['AAPL', 'GOOG', 'FB', 'AMZN',
    'TWTR'];                                        Mock object holding a list of symbols
export const MockNewsResponse: any = {
    "author": "Kelli B. Grant",               Mock object for a news item
    "title": "Happy about hitting that $435M Powerball jackpot?
     Congratulations — now here's your tax bill",
    ... more data
};
export const MockStocksResponse: any[] = [      Mock object for the full stocks data
    {
        "symbol": "AAPL",
        ... more data
    },
    {
        "symbol": "GOOG",
        ... more
    }
```

We'll use these objects in various tests, depending on the things we're testing. They're real objects that I've included in the project so that there are known pieces of data we can use to test against. They're JSON objects, so they're the same as the raw data used, and not a mock of anything more.

Now let's get to the test. Open up src/app/services/stocks.service.spec.ts and replace its contents with the code from the following listing. This test will create an instance of the service, intercept HTTP requests, and provide mock responses.

Listing 10.3 Stocks service test

```
import { TestBed, inject } from '@angular/core/testing';
import { HttpClientTestingModule, HttpTestingController } from '@angular/
    common/http/testing';
import { StocksService } from './stocks.service';
import { MockStocksResponse, MockSymbolsList, MockNewsResponse } from './
    stocks.mock';

describe('Service: Stocks', () => {                      Describes block
  const baseUrl = 'https://angular2-in-action-api.herokuapp.com';   and shared
  let service, http;                                     variables for test

  beforeEach(() => {
    TestBed.configureTestingModule({
      imports: [ HttpClientTestingModule ],
      providers: [ StocksService ]
    });                                                  Creates test module and get

    service = TestBed.get(StocksService);
    http = TestBed.get(HttpTestingController);
  });
```

```
afterEach(() => {
  http.verify();
});
```
Checks no Http requests are pending after test

```
it('should instantiate', () => {
  expect(service).toBeTruthy();
});
```
Simple test to verify creation

```
it('should manage a list of stocks', () => {
  expect(service.get()).toEqual(MockSymbolsList);
  service.add('TEST');
  expect(service.get()).toEqual([...MockSymbolsList, 'TEST']);
  service.remove('TEST');
  expect(service.get()).toEqual(MockSymbolsList);
});
```
Tests the symbol manipulation methods

Tests the load of data for stocks by mocking Http request/ response
```
it('should load the stock data from API', (done) => {
  service.load(MockSymbolsList).subscribe(result => {
    expect(result).toEqual(MockStocksResponse);
    done();
  });

  const request = http.expectOne(baseUrl + '/stocks/snapshot?symbols=' +
   MockSymbolsList.join(','));
  request.flush(MockStocksResponse);
});
```

```
it('should load the news data from API', (done) => {
  service.getNewsSnapshot('abc').subscribe(result => {
    expect(result).toEqual(MockNewsResponse);
    done();
  });

  const request = http.expectOne(baseUrl + '/stocks/news/
   snapshot?source=abc');
  request.flush(MockNewsResponse);
});
});
```
Tests the load of news data the same way

There's a lot more going on in this test, but most of it has to do with the setup required for mocking Http. The describe block starts by declaring some variables that are contained in these tests only. Then the beforeEach block constructs a testing module, so that we can properly instantiate the services using dependency injection (it's usually difficult to try to manually set up a test for things that inject dependencies). We'll talk more about this testing module in the next section, but for now consider it a helpful way to create a temporary Angular module and then get a reference to the services for the test to consume.

The afterEach block is used to run a test to verify that there are no extra HTTP requests that haven't been properly resolved. This is helpful to avoid a test making an HTTP request that wasn't expected, because that could indicate an issue with a test or that the methods called weren't fully tested.

Then we have a simple test that checks that the service was instantiated, and another one to test the manipulation of the symbols. If the service failed to load, that's probably because of a change in the dependencies or a coding error that will get caught here. The symbol manipulation methods are easy to test because they mutate the list of symbols. The test starts by testing that the service gets the expected default list of stocks, adds a new item and validates that it was retained, and finally removes it with verification.

MOCKING HTTP REQUESTS

The last two tests are very similar because they both deal with making HTTP requests. Let's walk through the first one closely, and the second one will also become clear as we go.

When we declare the `it` block, we start by also passing the `done` parameter into the test function. We'll use this to tell the test when it has finished—otherwise it would be out of sync. What we'll be doing is triggering an HTTP request using our service, and then later calling a service that will fire the response, allowing us to handle some setup before the HTTP request is made.

The first step is to make an HTTP request using the service, as you see here:

```
service.load(MockSymbolsList).subscribe(result => {
  expect(result).toEqual(MockStocksResponse);
  done();
});
```

This is saying that we want to call the `load` method, subscribe to the response, and when it returns, verify that it matches our expectations. Finally it calls the `done` function to tell the test it has finished. This will make the observable subscribe immediately, but since we imported the `HttpClientTestingModule`, it won't fire a request yet allowing the code after this block to execute.

Then we use the `HttpTestingController` (part of the `HttpClientTestingModule`, which we injected in the `beforeEach` earlier), and we declare that we expect one URL to be called. We build the expected URL, pass it to `http.expectOne`, and then the test will know to look out for this URL. If it fails to be requested for some reason, the `afterEach` would verify that it wasn't called and throw an error. That's the first line of the following code, and the second line tells the test to finally `flush`, or resolve, any pending requests for this URL, and takes an argument with the payload to send:

```
const request = http.expectOne(baseUrl + '/stocks/snapshot?symbols=' +
    MockSymbolsList.join(','));
request.flush(MockStocksResponse);
```

Because our service should have made this request, at this point the result should be returned like a real response. The subscribe method would emit the `MocksStockResponse` object (because that's what the `flush` method sends), and then the test would verify the match to complete the test. The news test follows the same pattern.

That completes our test for the service. You could extend this suite to test different edge cases, such as the server sending back a 500 status error, or the server sending back an invalid body. Those additional tests would help you identify weaknesses in the service. As it stands, this service mostly assumes that everything works correctly and could be made more resilient.

STUBBING A SERVICE

Before we write tests for components, we will want to stub the Stocks service. This will help simplify our other tests because our stub won't call HTTP, and that allows us to avoid having to do the HTTP mocking in every component that calls the service for data.

Stubs can be created and used in a variety of ways. Angular allows us to substitute a mock in place of the real thing using dependency injection, making mocks very easy to use. It's even possible to stub entities other than just services, though they're less common and not covered in this chapter.

There are many perspectives on how and what to stub, and I don't want to get into that debate here. I typically suggest keeping it simple and only building what's necessary at first. Stubs are additional code to maintain, because they need to stay in sync with your service, so keep them simple and light. Some argue that you should stub any dependency for a particular test, but you should realize that comes with a cost to build and maintain.

Let's create our stub by adding a new file to src/app/services/stocks.service.stub.ts and including the content from the following listing. It will craft a new class that uses the mock data and expose the same methods as the real service.

Listing 10.4   Stub Stocks service

```
import { Observable } from 'rxjs/Rx';
import { HttpClient } from '@angular/common/http';
import { MockNewsResponse, MockStocksResponse, MockSymbolsList } from './
    stocks.mock';
import { StocksService } from './stocks.service';

export class StubStocksService extends StocksService {        ← Extends the
                                                                real service
  constructor() {
    super({} as HttpClient);        Calls parent constructor, passing in a
  }                                  stub for the HttpClient dependency

  load(symbols: string[]) {
    return Observable.of(MockStocksResponse);
  }                                              Mocks the load and getNewsSnapshot
                                                 methods by returning an observable
  getNewsSnapshot(source: string) {             like HttpClient
    return Observable.of(MockNewsResponse);
  }
}
```

This stub is crafted by extending the Stocks service, so that we don't have to implement all the methods. This allows us to focus on writing code only for the methods that we need to change. Because we're extending the method, we also need to call the super method in the constructor to pass in the dependencies. What's of interest here is that we're passing a blank object but casting it as the HttpClient service, so the compiler is happy, but it doesn't need to use the real thing. We create the same behavior as well for getNewsSnapshot.

The Stocks service defines the add, remove, and get methods, which don't need to be stubbed because they work just fine as they are without side effects. Often you can get away with using the real service or its methods in your tests. Here's a list of some common side effects of a service and why you would stub them:

- *Asynchronous*—If there are async events, tests have to be written in a way that handles that behavior. This can make them harder to test, but writing a stub for these can eliminate that.
- *External dependencies*—When an entity requires an external dependency (such as the Http service), it may require jumping through additional hoops to set up, and that can be avoided by stubbing it.
- *Internal state*—Sometimes services or entities have internal state that you need to manipulate in your tests, but the service doesn't expose. A stub can expose additional logic to allow you to mutate that state.
- *Redirects*—Anytime an entity tries to redirect the user away from the current context, this usually breaks the test. Stubbing can prevent the location changes. This is usually a challenge for tests that deal with user authentication, for example.

Carefully consider whether you need a stub before creating one. Most applications will benefit from having stubs for at least some of the services, but not everything makes sense as a stub. Imagine, for example, that you have a service that reads and sets from localStorage; the scope of this service is very focused and doesn't have any of the side effects given in the preceding list, so it's a good candidate for something that might not need to be stubbed.

If you prefer to always use strict typing with TypeScript, you may run into issues if the stub doesn't implement the exact same interface as the real service. You can rectify this by writing the stub to return values with the same types, or you can loosen the type safety of your code in the tests.

10.2.4 *Testing components and using testing modules*

Components are the building blocks of your application, and they have two key parts that we're interested in testing: the controller and the view. We can test individual methods in the controller (such as methods that load data from a service), but we also want to validate behaviors on the template (such as whether the correct data was displayed). Because our tests are comprised of testing both things, setting up a component test requires an additional step.

When we want to test a component, we need to start by creating a test module that's a miniature Angular application with the bare minimum required to set up and run. The more you import and include in the test module, the slower it will be to run the test, and the less isolated the test becomes. Technically, you could bootstrap the normal Angular application before each test, but that's in opposition to the concepts of unit testing and will make your tests significantly slower.

Setting up the test module happens in a `beforeEach` statement of your test and is quite similar to defining a regular Angular module. You're able to declare a list of providers, imports, declarations, and so forth, and then can get some references to the target component for easy testing.

To see this in action, let's write our first test for a component. The Manage component is a good one to start with, so open the src/app/components/manage/manage.component.spec.ts file and include the code from the following listing.

Listing 10.5   Manage component test

```
import { ComponentFixture, TestBed } from '@angular/core/testing';
import { FormsModule } from '@angular/forms';

import { ManageComponent } from './manage.component';
import { StocksService } from '../../services/stocks.service';
import { StubStocksService } from '../../services/stocks.service.stub';
import { MockSymbolsList } from '../../services/stocks.mock';

describe('ManageComponent', () => {
  let component: ManageComponent;
  let fixture: ComponentFixture<ManageComponent>;     // Sets some variables for
  let el: HTMLElement;                                 // the set of tests to use

  beforeEach(() => {
    TestBed.configureTestingModule({
      imports: [
        FormsModule,
      ],
      declarations: [                                  // Creates a testing
        ManageComponent                                // module with
      ],                                               // minimal
      providers: [                                     // dependencies
        { provide: StocksService, useClass: StubStocksService }
      ]
    });
  }))

  beforeEach(() => {
    fixture = TestBed.createComponent(ManageComponent);
    component = fixture.componentInstance;             // Gets access to the
    el = fixture.debugElement.nativeElement;           // values needed for
    fixture.detectChanges();                           // testing the component
  });

  it('should create the component', () => {
    expect(component).toBeTruthy();
  });
```

```
it('should add or remove symbols from the list', () => {
  expect(component.symbols).toEqual(MockSymbolsList);
  component.stock = 'ABC';
  component.add();
  expect(component.symbols).toEqual([...MockSymbolsList, 'ABC']);
  component.remove('ABC');
  expect(component.symbols).toEqual(MockSymbolsList);
});
```
Tests for controller behavior

```
it('should render the template with a list of stocks', () => {
  const items = el.querySelectorAll('td.mdl-data-table__cell--non-
    numeric');

  for (let i = 0; i < items.length; ++i) {
    expect(items[i].innerHTML).toContain(MockSymbolsList[i]);
  }
});
});
```
Tests for view behavior

This test contains the usual `import` block, which contains the `ComponentFixture` and `TestBed` objects from Angular. These are what we'll use to create the test module and bootstrap the component. When the Angular CLI generates component tests, it will create the test with a test module for you, similar to what you see here. The `describe` block contains a few variable references, which we'll assign values to later. Then you'll need to add any additional pieces into the test module that your component requires. In this example, we require the Forms module, because we use NgModel, and the Stocks service, and the stub service is injected as the Stocks service.

The `TestBed.configureTestingModule` method will set up a module with the base Angular services (like default pipes and directives), and returns a `TestBed` object. If you're not using the Angular CLI, you might need to call the `compileComponents` method (see the Angular documentation for details).

The next `beforeEach` block uses the `TestBed` to create an instance of the component to test and assigns the instance of the component and the native DOM element to variables. The `fixture.detectChanges` method is used to manually trigger change detection and make sure that the components reflect their current state—otherwise the state might not be accurate. The first test is another simple check to see if the component was created correctly.

The second test exercises the component methods that are used to manipulate the list of symbols. The Manage component implementation is calling the mock service instead of the real one in this case, because we declared that in the testing module providers. The test is simple: It checks the default array of symbols against the mock values, adding and then removing an item, and checks whether the list of symbols is built as expected. I like to call this kind of test a *controller unit test*, because it directly uses the controller methods.

The final test looks at the rendered view to see if the component has displayed data as expected. It uses the DOM element to query for all the rows and verify that each of the symbols is being displayed in the DOM. I like to refer to this kind of test as a *view unit test*, because it observes the rendered output of the view. Sometimes a test does both things, but I attempt to keep them focused.

That summarizes the primary tenets of a component test, the creation of a testing module, including or stubbing dependencies, rendering the component, and testing either the controller or view.

STUBBING DIRECTIVES OR COMPONENTS AND USING DEBUGELEMENT

There are times where you don't want a directive or child component to render in the test. In this example, our Delay directive gives us a little bit of trouble because it delays the rendering of items, and our tests either have to wait for it to complete or work around it some other way. But we can stub the Delay directive and have it display immediately. We'll get the test coverage that the Delay directive works when we test it directly.

We want to test the Dashboard component, which loads a few things. In order to focus on just the Dashboard component, we'll also stub the Summary component, because it has animations that can get in the way.

There's also another way to look at the rendered view, by using the Angular `DebugElement`. Instead of using the native DOM element directly, the `DebugElement` gives us a few additional options, the most powerful of which allows us to query the element based on a directive instead of only CSS selectors. We'll see how to use that in this example.

Let's create our test for the Dashboard component. Open up the src/app/components/dashboard/dashboard.component.spec.ts file and replace it with what's shown in the following listing. We'll stub the Summary component and the `Delay` directive, and query using the `DebugElement` and a directive.

> **Listing 10.6   Dashboard component test**

```
/* tslint:disable:no-unused-variable */
import { ComponentFixture, TestBed } from '@angular/core/testing';
import { By } from '@angular/platform-browser';
import { DebugElement, Directive, Input, TemplateRef, ViewContainerRef,
    Component } from '@angular/core';

import { DashboardComponent } from './dashboard.component';
import { CardTypeDirective } from '../../directives/card-type.directive';
import { CardHoverDirective } from '../../directives/card-hover.directive';
import { StocksService } from '../../services/stocks.service';
import { StubStocksService } from '../../services/stocks.service.stub';
import { MockSymbolsList } from '../../services/stocks.mock';

@Directive({
  selector: '[delay]'
})
class StubDelayDirective {
  @Input() set delay(ms: number) { this.viewContainer.
    createEmbeddedView(this.templateRef); }
  constructor(private templateRef: TemplateRef<any>, private viewContainer:
    ViewContainerRef) { }
}
```

Creates a stub Delay directive

```
@Component({
  selector: 'summary',
  template: '<div class="mdl-card">{{stock}}</div>'
})
class StubSummaryComponent {
  @Input() stock;
}
```

Creates a stub
Summary component

```
describe('DashboardComponent', () => {
  let component: DashboardComponent;
  let fixture: ComponentFixture<DashboardComponent>;
  let de: DebugElement;

  beforeEach(() => {
    TestBed.configureTestingModule({
      declarations: [
        DashboardComponent,
        StubSummaryComponent,
        StubDelayDirective,
        CardTypeDirective,
        CardHoverDirective,
      ],
      providers: [
        { provide: StocksService, useClass: StubStocksService }
      ]
    });
  });
```

Declares the stubs and some directives

```
  beforeEach(() => {
    fixture = TestBed.createComponent(DashboardComponent);
    component = fixture.componentInstance;
    de = fixture.debugElement;
    expect(component.stocks).toBeFalsy();
    fixture.detectChanges();
    expect(component.stocks).toBeTruthy();
  });
```

Gets an instance of the
DebugElement and test
component initialization

```
  it('should create the component', () => {
    expect(component).toBeTruthy();
  });

  it('should render the template', () => {
    expect(de.query(By.css('.mdl-cell')).properties.innerHTML).not.
      toContain('Loading');
    expect(de.queryAll(By.directive(StubSummaryComponent)).length).
      toEqual(MockSymbolsList.length);
  });
});
```

Queries the
view by CSS or
directive

I've put the Delay directive stub inline for this test, because I won't use it anywhere else. I find it useful to keep it localized unless you're reusing the stub in multiple places, like the Stocks service. All this stub does is implement a directive that immediately renders the view without the delay, but it does have the same selector to ensure that it's used in the component. The real Delay component causes a problem with tests because it doesn't render immediately, and if we waited for it to finish it could take a while, depending on the number of items.

Likewise, we declare the Summary component stub inline because it isn't used anywhere else, and it's a simple component that implements the smallest interface for the component. The component accepts a single input (it would not compile if we didn't add the input), and there's an expectation that there's an element with the `mdl-card` class on it.

Because this is an isolated test, we declare the stubs as part of the test module and also include the real version of other directives that don't have an asynchronous nature to them. If we didn't include them, the test would complain about not being able to render those directives. In the `beforeEach`, we also put a couple of `expect` statements that check that the stocks are loaded after the component has rendered.

The primary test here runs two expect assertions against the view. The Dashboard component doesn't have a lot of methods to test the controller with, except the `OnInit`, which loads data. Because that's checked in a `beforeEach` block, we can focus on the view. The test uses `DebugElement` from the `TestBed` instance, and uses the query capability to inspect the element based on a CSS selector. The first query checks that the Loading text doesn't display any more. The second query looks for all elements that are of the stub Summary component type (remember, components are directives). These queries use the `By` object to construct the selector for you based on directive or CSS selector. `DebugElement` also gives you access to element properties like the `innerHTML` property.

I recommend choosing to use either the native DOM element or `DebugElement` approach to inspect the component views. Mixing them works all right, but consistency is a good goal.

TESTING COMPONENTS WITH INPUTS AND ANIMATIONS

Sometimes our components have inputs, and we need to handle those in our tests. For example, the Summary component accepts an input of the stock value, and we want to ensure that it renders as expected, even if the stock price has gone up or down.

The Summary component also has an animation to allow it to fade in, and our testing module needs to be able to handle that scenario. Angular allows us to bypass the animations so they don't interfere with fast-running tests.

Most of the Summary component test is familiar by now, so we'll focus only on the new pieces. Open src/app/components/summary/summary.component.spec.ts and use the code from the following listing.

Listing 10.7   Summary component test

```
import { ComponentFixture, TestBed } from '@angular/core/testing';
import { NoopAnimationsModule } from '@angular/platform-browser/animations';    ◄── Imports the
                                                                                    NoopAnimationsModule
import { CurrencyPipe, PercentPipe } from '@angular/common';
import { SummaryComponent } from './summary.component';
import { CardTypeDirective } from '../../directives/card-type.directive';
import { ChangePipe } from '../../pipes/change.pipe';
```

```
describe('SummaryComponent', () => {
  let component: SummaryComponent;
  let fixture: ComponentFixture<SummaryComponent>;
  let el: HTMLElement;

  beforeEach(() => {
    TestBed.configureTestingModule({
      imports: [
        NoopAnimationsModule        ◄─── Imports the NoopAnimationsModule
      ],
      declarations: [
        SummaryComponent,
        ChangePipe,
        CardTypeDirective,
      ],
      providers: [
        CurrencyPipe,
        PercentPipe
      ]
    });
  });

  beforeEach(() => {
    fixture = TestBed.createComponent(SummaryComponent);
    component = fixture.componentInstance;
    el = fixture.debugElement.nativeElement;
  });

  it('should create the component', () => {
    expect(component).toBeTruthy();
  });

  it('should render for a positive change', () => {
    component.stock = { symbol: 'abc', lastTradePriceOnly: 10, change: .25,
      changeInPercent: 0.025 };        ┌─┐ Sets the input and runs
    fixture.detectChanges();           └─┘ change detection

    const content = el.querySelector('.mdl-card h4').innerHTML;   ┌ Tests the
    expect(content).toContain('ABC');                            │ rendered view
    expect(content).toContain('$10.00');
    expect(content).toContain('$0.25 (2.50%)');
  });

  it('should render for a negative change', () => {
    component.stock = { symbol: 'abc', lastTradePriceOnly: 8.34, change:
      -1.43, changeInPercent: -0.0243 };
    fixture.detectChanges();

    const content = el.querySelector('.mdl-card h4').innerHTML;
    expect(content).toContain('ABC');
    expect(content).toContain('$8.34');
    expect(content).toContain('-$1.43 (-2.43%)');
  });
});
```

The NoopAnimationsModule is used to support the animations dependencies that are required by the component, but when it runs, the animations don't animate. This is good for test cases, because animations take time and slow down the test. If you want to test animations, you'll probably want to do that using e2e style testing.

In order to handle testing the input, we treat it just like a normal property. In fact, it is a normal property, except it has the ability to receive data from a binding when used. During our test we're focused primarily on how it works, and not on whether the binding works. We tested the binding in our Dashboard component, so we can trust that it will have a binding. In the test, we set the stock property to a known value and then run change detection to update the view.

Then we check the view by inspecting the content of the view and checking whether the values rendered as expected based on the stock data. We have another test to verify that different stock data still renders the result as expected.

TESTING COMPONENTS WITH THE ROUTER

There's one last component to test, the App component, and it contains a router outlet that we need to handle in our tests. The App component also has the navbar, which renders out the latest news item that we'd like to test. It's not much different from any other component in how we need to test it. Anything that this component directly uses will need to be imported or stubbed in some way, and that includes setting up the router and using the stub service.

Let's take a look at the App component test and see what's different for a component containing a router outlet. Open src/app/app.component.spec.ts and replace its contents with those in the following listing.

Listing 10.8   App component test

```
import { TestBed, ComponentFixture } from '@angular/core/testing';
import { RouterModule } from '@angular/router';
import { APP_BASE_HREF } from '@angular/common';

import { AppComponent } from './app.component';
import { ChangeDetectorPipe } from './pipes/change-detector.pipe';
import { NewsPipe } from './pipes/news.pipe';
import { StocksService } from './services/stocks.service';
import { StubStocksService } from './services/stocks.service.stub';
import { MockNewsResponse } from './services/stocks.mock';

describe('AppComponent', () => {
  let component: AppComponent;
  let fixture: ComponentFixture<AppComponent>;
  let el: HTMLElement;
  beforeEach(() => {
    TestBed.configureTestingModule({
      imports: [
        RouterModule.forRoot([]),        ◁——  Sets up the Router module, provides an
      ],                                        empty list of routes, and sets base href
      declarations: [
        AppComponent,
        ChangeDetectorPipe,
        NewsPipe,
```

```
    ],
    providers: [
      { provide: StocksService, useClass: StubStocksService },
      { provide: APP_BASE_HREF, useValue: '/' }
    ]
  });
});

beforeEach(() => {
  fixture = TestBed.createComponent(AppComponent);
  component = fixture.debugElement.componentInstance;
  el = fixture.debugElement.nativeElement;
  expect(component).toBeTruthy();
  fixture.detectChanges();
});

it('should load the news', () => {
  expect(el.innerHTML).toContain(MockNewsResponse.title);
});
});
```

> Sets up the Router module, provides an empty list of routes, and sets base href

> Tests whether the view rendered the News pipe correctly

This test is set up just like the rest, with the exception that it has the Router module set up. The Router module makes the router outlet and router link directives available for the test module to render. It also requires us to provide the APP_BASE_HREF, but override it with a value. It can be any valid path, but almost always you'll want to use /.

Then, inside of the test, we check that the component has the mock news title rendered somewhere in the view. This is quick way to verify that the News pipe has run and used the stub Stocks service to return the mock news data.

That wraps up the tests for our components in this example. As you build more complex components, the tests will also become more complex. This is a good reason to create many smaller components instead of a few large ones, so keep that in mind. Also, if you have good separation of concerns (such as data access is in services, and rendering views is in components), you can more easily stub those different aspects and write tests to focus on a smaller surface area.

10.2.5 *Testing directives*

Directives can be the trickiest thing to test because they're modifiers of elements. Directives are tested by attaching them to an element or component and verifying that the view has changed accordingly. They can be attached to a real component from your application, but I prefer to make a stub component for the test to simplify the testing scenarios.

We'll test with two different approaches. The first is to create the directive ourselves by passing in a constructed component. The second is to allow the testing module to construct it for us.

The reason you might opt to construct it yourself is that you can call elements on the directive directly that way. Otherwise, the directive isn't easily accessible to you in the testing module.

We're going to look at two of the three directives to test in this section. The third doesn't provide anything new, but you can review the test in the GitHub repository. The first test will be for the CardHover attribute directive, and the second will be for the Delay structural directive.

Let's start with the CardHover directive. In this test, we'll create the directive ourselves, but we'll still need a testing module to set up the stub component. Recall that this is to help us encapsulate the logic needed to determine if a card is being hovered, and also to modify the default colors of the Summary component. Open src/app/directives/card-hover.directive.spec.ts and use the code from the following listing to complete the test.

Listing 10.9   CardHover directive test

```
import { Component, ElementRef } from '@angular/core';
import { By } from '@angular/platform-browser';
import { TestBed, ComponentFixture } from '@angular/core/testing';
import { CardHoverDirective } from './card-hover.directive';

@Component({
  template: `<div cardHover class="mdl-card decrease">Content</div>`
})
class MockComponent {}

describe('CardHoverDirective', () => {
  let directive: CardHoverDirective;
  let card: HTMLElement;

  beforeEach(() => {
    TestBed.configureTestingModule({
      declarations: [
        MockComponent,
      ]
    });
  });

  beforeEach(() => {
    const fixture = TestBed.createComponent(MockComponent);
    card = fixture.debugElement.query(By.css('[cardHover]')).nativeElement;

    directive = new CardHoverDirective(new ElementRef(fixture.debugElement.
      nativeElement));
    directive.ngOnInit();
  });

  it('should apply the correct background colors', () => {
    expect(card.style.backgroundColor.replace(/ /g, '')).
      toContain('rgb(255,171,64)');
    card.classList.remove('decrease');
    card.classList.add('increase');
    directive.ngOnInit();
    expect(card.style.backgroundColor.replace(/ /g, '')).
      toContain('rgb(63,81,181)');
    card.classList.remove('increase');
    directive.ngOnInit();
    expect(card.style.backgroundColor).toEqual('');
  });
```

- Creates stub component with CardHover directive
- Creates the testing module for the mock component
- Gets references to the fixture and card
- Creates the directive instance and runs OnInit lifecycle method
- Tests for checking the background color based on classes

```
it('should apply hover styling', () => {
  directive.onMouseOver();
  expect(card.style.top).toEqual('-2px');
  directive.onMouseOut();
  expect(card.style.top).toEqual('');
});
});
```

> **Tests for checking mouse events**

There are a lot of familiar aspects to this test when you compare it with a component, but the differences are important. First, we create a stub component that has the expected classes and structure, as well as the directive applied. The testing module is created and set up so that the stub component can be properly instantiated.

In the next `beforeEach` block, we do two important tasks. First we get the compiled component from the testing module, and then we create a new instance of the Card-Hover directive. Notice that the directive expects a parameter that contains an `ElementRef`, which is a wrapper around the component native DOM element. The directive exists outside of the testing module, so we have to call the lifecycle methods directly ourselves, like `directive.ngOnInit`.

Now that we have the directive ready, we can test it by looking at the rendered card and seeing if the background color matches the expected values based on the current classes applied to the card. We're directly manipulating the element and then running the `ngOnInit` lifecycle hook again in order to simulate the change. Notice that we don't use the fixture to run change detection, because we've bypassed the testing module by creating the directive ourselves.

The last test calls the two mouse event methods directly and verifies that when they fire, the card styling is as expected. Any methods that you need to test can be called directly like this, but only if you can get the reference of the directive when you create it manually.

Although we've tested this directive by creating it ourselves, using a testing module to set things up is usually preferred. That ensures things are plumbed and can make life a little easier, but at the cost of calling directive methods directly. You may want to create a set of tests that call the directive directly if you want to validate the internals of a method, and then use a testing module for the rest.

HANDLING ASYNCHRONOUS TASKS IN TESTS

The last test we'll write also shows us two ways we can handle asynchronous tasks in our tests. We'll be testing the Delay directive, which waits to render the component for a certain number of milliseconds. Unlike the way the Http service allows us to mock the response and handle it in the test, we need to use one of two options from Angular that help ensure that tests have executed everything properly even when things happen async.

Angular provides a way to fake async events, specifically intervals and timeouts, and provides a way to wait for async events to finalize before continuing execution. We'll write the same test twice using both approaches so you can see them side by side. By default, Jasmine assumes that tests are synchronous but does provide an optional done callback object that you can use to handle async tasks, but with Angular's testing utilities, that shouldn't be necessary, and using the two options demonstrated here is recommended.

The Delay directive test is located at src/app/directives/delay.directive.spec.ts. Open it and replace its contents with the code from the following listing.

Listing 10.10   Delay directive test

```
import { Component } from '@angular/core';
import { TestBed, ComponentFixture, fakeAsync, async, tick } from '@angular/
    core/testing';
import { DelayDirective } from './delay.directive';

@Component({
  template: `<div *delay="delay"><h1>DELAYED</h1></div>`
})
class MockComponent {
  delay = 10;
}

describe('DelayDirective', () => {
  let fixture: ComponentFixture<MockComponent>;
  let el: HTMLElement;

  beforeEach(() => {
    TestBed.configureTestingModule({
      declarations: [
        MockComponent,
        DelayDirective
      ]
    });
  });

  beforeEach(() => {
    fixture = TestBed.createComponent(MockComponent);
    el = fixture.debugElement.nativeElement;
  });

  it('should show after the specified delay using fakeAsync', fakeAsync(() =>
    {
    expect(el.innerHTML).not.toContain('DELAYED');
    fixture.detectChanges();
    tick(10);
    expect(el.innerHTML).toContain('DELAYED');
  }));

  it('should show after the specified delay using async', async(() => {
    expect(el.innerHTML).not.toContain('DELAYED');
    fixture.detectChanges();
    fixture.whenStable().then(() => {
      fixture.detectChanges();
      expect(el.innerHTML).toContain('DELAYED');
    });
  }));
});
```

Annotations:
- Creates a stub component with the delay directive
- Creates testing module with stub and directive
- Uses the fakeAsync handler to make test synchronous
- Uses the async handler to handle waiting for async calls to return

In this example, we're creating a stub component and ensuring that it implements the Delay directive. We're setting the delay to 10 milliseconds, so it doesn't make for a long delay when running the test. If we made this 1 second, it would halt test execution for 1 second—not desirable. The testing module is then configured by declaring both the mock component and Delay directive.

The first test uses the `fakeAsync` handler to wrap the execution of the test. It works by returning a synchronous function for the test to run and also exposes the additional `tick` object. Inside of the `fakeAsync` handler, you can run expectations to validate that on initialization, the directive doesn't display the content of the component, and then call `tick` to trigger any timer events. We pass `tick(10)` to trigger the timer events at 10 milliseconds, which is the value configured in our mock component. If you have multiple timer events, you can use `tick` to step through the different timer events and verify behavior between each step. The `tick` function is only available inside of the `fakeAsync` handler.

The second test uses the `async` handler, which handles telling the test to wait until some async activity has resolved. Here we use `fixture.whenStable().then()` to handle waiting the 10 milliseconds for the component to fully render, since the directive delays the rendering. Inside of the `then` promise handler, we run our expectation to see that the component has rendered. The drawback to this approach is that the timeout waits for however long the delay is set, and if you had a lot of tests doing similar things, this would slow your tests down considerably.

I recommend using `fakeAsync` when you can, but note that it doesn't help you deal with HTTP calls. When you use asynchronous calls in your code, be sure to consider how to best test that and avoid making lots of nested or simultaneous asynchronous calls, if possible. These increase test complexity and probably also make your component more difficult to implement.

That wraps up the unit tests for this application. It now has 25 tests, and if you run the code coverage analysis, it claims to have tested 100% of the code. An experienced developer knows that this doesn't mean the tests cover every scenario or edge case, because many of these tests could be expanded to validate more error conditions, for example.

Now we'll step out of unit testing and focus on how to test the whole application at once using e2e to mimic a real user launching the application.

10.3 *e2e testing*

Just because all the units of your application are working smoothly in isolation doesn't necessarily guarantee they'll work together as a whole or with real-world data sources. e2e testing is the way you can test your application as a whole by controlling it like a real user would.

e2e is meant to emulate the same experiences from the user perspective, where they click links, type in input fields, and otherwise engage with the application. It's important to keep your mind focused on this as you write e2e tests, because this means you should only write tests in a way that are realistic options for users. For example, when you navigate between pages, you should have the test click the link in the navbar instead of changing the URL in the browser.

I find the best way to think about e2e testing is to consider several of the paths through the applications that are important for a user to be successful with your application. For example, if your application is based around creating invoices, consider testing the primary paths for users to create, edit, manage, or delete their invoices. You may also want to focus on key paths such as signing up for the service, login flows, and other similar critical tasks.

It may not be obvious at first, but there's a larger cost to creating and maintaining e2e tests. These tests may sound like the most comprehensive type of tests to write, but the reality is they're much more difficult to write and maintain than unit tests. They also don't provide clear guarantees like unit tests—a failure in an e2e test might or might not mean there's an issue. They can be hard to repeat consistently because they have more variables, such as a real back end and state changes that are controlled in unit testing. e2e tests are also much slower to execute than unit tests, because they require loading the entire application, so expect them to require more time.

I like to caution that e2e tests are difficult because you have to control so many variables, not because they're inherently difficult to write. Imagine you're testing an application for a forum. You'll need a test user you can rely on who can log in and post messages. But what happens when this test user posts? Does it appear on the site? Perhaps you can run the tests on a test or staging environment instead of the real production site, but that requires having a test or staging site available. Considerations like these make it challenging to orchestrate the tests. The larger the system, the more important it is to consult with all parties involved in the application about how this testing can be set up and managed.

Given these potential challenges, you may be less interested in testing flows that aren't vital or are rarely used. The cost might be simply too much for you to worry about testing parts of the site that are used 1% of the time.

Let's forge ahead anyway and write a few e2e tests for our stock application. We're lucky that our application is simple and stateless. Every time we reload, the application is reset, but that's not typical for most applications, so keep that in mind as well.

Angular CLI provides built-in scaffolding for running e2e tests using Protractor, a tool that uses the WebDriver API to remotely control a browser. Protractor was written for AngularJS and has a few features that aren't supported for Angular 2+ applications (consult the Protractor documentation to see more details, at http://protractortest. org). Remember that if you try to use something from Protractor that doesn't work, it might be a feature that only works for AngularJS.

When the Angular CLI generates a project, it creates a directory called e2e that contains a basic set of tests that work for the default app. We'll update it in a moment with four tests that will verify that both the Dashboard and Manage pages load correctly, and then test adding and deleting a stock.

Before we write the tests, we're going to create something called a *page object*, which is a way to define aspects of the pages you want to test in a way that allows you to write cleaner-looking tests. We'll have to write things that are similar to CSS selectors, called *page locators*, which are responsible for finding elements on the page to interact with.

Protractor provides two important objects to use for finding elements: element and by. Using them in various combinations, you can find a single element on the page, find multiple ones, find a list and then select a specific item from it, and more. The element object returns an element inside a wrapper (similar to what jQuery does to an element) and exposes helpful methods to do things like click the element. element also accepts an argument that should use the by object, which helps you construct something like an element query. You can use by.css('.someClass') to locate an element by a CSS selector. This is called a *page locator*.

Let's see this in action by writing some code. Create a new file at e2e/dashboard.po.ts and use the code from the following listing. This is the DashboardPage object, and it's simple. The larger the page, the more things it might contain.

Listing 10.11 DashboardPage object

```
import { element, by } from 'protractor';        ◁──┐ Imports the element and
                                                      │ by objects from Protractor
export class DashboardPage {
  navigateTo() {
    return element(by.linkText('Dashboard')).click();    ◁ Method to click
  }                                                          Dashboard link

  getCards() {
    return element.all(by.css('.mdl-cell'));    ◁ Method to find all
  }                                                 summary cards
}v
```

As a standalone piece of code, this might seem a little strange at first, but it's pretty straightforward. Protractor gives us the element and by objects, which are used to find elements on the page. element is like an element wrapper object, and the by object exposes several methods to find elements based on criteria like a CSS selector, link text, button name, or input name. These are the fundamental calls you'll be making to interact like a real user.

We're defining a class that gives us a few methods that help us navigate or select elements. First, the navigateTo method looks for the Dashboard link in the navbar and triggers a click event on it, which triggers the navigation to the page. The getCards method looks for all elements on the page that have the mdl-cell class, which happens to be all the cards that contain stock items.

Let's go ahead and create another one of these for ManagePage. Create another file at e2e/manage.po.ts and include the code from the following listing.

Listing 10.12 ManagePage object

```
import { element, by } from 'protractor';

export class ManagePage {
```

```
navigateTo() {
    return element(by.linkText('Manage')).click();
}
```
⟵ **Navigates to ManagePage**

Gets list of cells with symbols ⟶
```
getSymbols() {
    return element.all(by.css('.mdl-data-table__cell--non-numeric'));
}
```

```
getRemoveButton(index) {
    return element.all(by.buttonText('Remove')).get(index);
}
```
⟵ **Finds the remove button by an index value**

```
getAddInput() {
    return element(by.name('stock'));
}
}
```
⟵ **Finds the add stock input**

There are a couple more things in this page object, because we have the ability to add and remove stocks on this page. The class starts with a `navigate` method that clicks the Manage link in the navbar. The next method, `getSymbols`, finds all the table cells that contain a stock symbol. Then the `getRemoveButton` method accepts an index value and will click the Remove button of the symbol based on that row. Finally, `getAddInput` finds the stock name input field.

There are more options for what Protractor provides in its API, so I suggest you consult the documentation for full details. Harnessing the page locators can give you many options on how to find elements on the page to engage with.

All right—now we can write the test. The idea is that our tests are easy to read and the code reads very similar to the user's actions; they should cover user expectations as they use the application. Open up the e2e/app.e2e-spec.ts file and replace its contents with the code from the following listing.

Listing 10.13   App e2e tests

```
import { DashboardPage } from './dashboard.po';
import { ManagePage } from './manage.po';
import { protractor, browser, by, element } from 'protractor';

describe('Stock App', () => {
    let dashboard: DashboardPage;
    let manage: ManagePage;

    beforeEach(() => {
        dashboard = new DashboardPage();
        manage = new ManagePage();
        browser.get('/');
    });
```
⟵ **Creates new instances of page objects and starts on home page**

```
    it('should load the dashboard default list', () => {
        dashboard.navigateTo();
        dashboard.getCards().then(stocks => {
            expect(stocks.length).toEqual(5);
        });
    });
```
⟵ **Checks default behavior for dashboard**

```
it('should load the manage stocks view', () => {
  manage.navigateTo();
  manage.getSymbols().then(symbols => {
    expect(symbols.length).toEqual(5);
  });
});
```

Checks default
behavior for manage

```
it('should add a new stock and be updated in dashboard', () => {
  dashboard.navigateTo();
  dashboard.getCards().then(stocks => {
    expect(stocks.length).toEqual(5);
  });

  manage.navigateTo();
  manage.getAddInput().sendKeys('MSFT', protractor.Key.RETURN);
  expect(manage.getSymbols().last().getText()).toEqual('MSFT');

  dashboard.navigateTo();
  dashboard.getCards().then(stocks => {
    expect(stocks.length).toEqual(6);
  });
});
```

Tests whether
adding a new
item persists
and renders
in dashboard

```
it('should remove a stock and be updated in dashboard', () => {
  dashboard.navigateTo();
  dashboard.getCards().then(stocks => {
    expect(stocks.length).toEqual(5);
  });

  manage.navigateTo();
  manage.getRemoveButton(0).click();
  expect(manage.getSymbols().first().getText()).not.toEqual('AAPL');

  dashboard.navigateTo();
  dashboard.getCards().then(stocks => {
    expect(stocks.length).toEqual(4);
  });
});
});
```

Tests whether
removing an
item persists
and renders
in dashboard

Notice how the test is written using the same describe, beforeEach, and it blocks we used in unit tests. That's because we're using Jasmine as the testing framework for describing tests, which helps keep things familiar. During the beforeEach phase, we construct a new page object for the manage and dashboard pages, and then tell the browser to load the main page.

The first test checks that the dashboard itself loads with the expected number of cards. It does this by navigating to the page and querying for the list of cards. Notice how it's a promise, because there may be some time waiting for tasks to trigger. Protractor is usually smart enough to wait for the page to settle down before executing code, and then we run our expectation in the callback. The second test is similar, except it goes to the manage page and checks the list of symbols.

The third and fourth tests manipulate state and verify that it renders properly after adding or removing a symbol. They both start by verifying that the dashboard has the expected number of cards and then navigate to the manage page. The tests either add or remove a symbol and then navigate back to the dashboard to verify whether it's reflected the change.

Often you'll break apart your tests based upon features. In this application, there's one primary feature: to view and manage a list of stocks. If you had additional features, like creating an account, a login process, or perhaps a news page, each of those would probably be best organized into its own file.

This gets us through the basics of writing e2e tests and demonstrates their primary role and value. Though they have some drawbacks and can be challenging to maintain, they test the system as a real user would and allow you to codify the primary user flows and objectives into a suite of tests.

Before closing the chapter, I want to cover a few common questions that people ask about testing in real-world scenarios. All too often developers don't invest in tests or get hung up on the proper approach to testing. Although the answers are my opinions, I think they're useful to consider.

10.4 Additional testing strategies

When I teach about testing, sometimes the response by students is that testing is a lot of work. Many questions boil down to asking whether testing is worth the effort. Assuming you believe that testing is important as I do, how do you decide which strategy and tests to implement and which can you safely ignore?

Depending on your experience and project requirements, you likely have a number of questions, such as these:

- How much testing is enough?
- When do I write the tests?
- What do I write, e2e or unit tests?
- What if I don't have time to write tests?
- What about other types of testing?

I can't give you definitive answers that will apply to all projects, but I'd like to offer you some of my strategies for testing. There are many strategies and perspectives on testing. The two extremes are as follows:

- People who argue for writing tests for every line of code before you even create the actual code
- People who argue that tests are a waste of time and slow down development

On this spectrum, I fall closer to the former, but I also recognize that some tests have little value and that there are alternative ways to ensure code behavior. You'll find most of my perspectives to be pragmatic and between the extremes.

10.4.1 *How much testing is enough?*

This is the kind of question that's asked a lot, but few know how to answer it. Sometimes people want specific code coverage metrics and consider that enough, whereas others want tests to cover the important aspects of the application. I don't believe in a magic formula, but I think there's a simple way to determine whether you have enough testing.

Imagine your application is currently being used by 100 people on average per day. The application is relatively simple, has been in use for at least a few months, and has only had a couple of bug reports. You may feel confident in the application and its behavior—but that's your gut, which shouldn't be how you decide whether you have enough testing.

What you should do instead is employ usage metrics and error-logging tools to analyze the data to see whether users are successful using your application or receive errors. Use data to inform you about the quality of your application and to get insights into how people use it. You can use something like Google Analytics to track users and report metrics to you; it requires some setup and paying attention to the reports. There are many great tools out there—look for web analytics and error-tracking tools that fit your needs best.

Developers are notorious for IWFM syndrome (*it works for me*). I imagine you've been guilty of this syndrome, as have I. This is why your gut feeling about quality is really an excuse to ignore testing instead of measuring quality. You have to remember that your users are using different computers, browsers, and network connection speeds than you.

When you use data to measure, you can better understand your users and capture errors as they happen. Also, users are more likely to leave your application than to report a bug, so just because nobody complains doesn't mean it's working right.

10.4.2 *When do I write tests?*

Which came first, the chicken or the egg? The test or the implementation? Strategies like TDD (test-driven development) propose that you should write your tests before you implement any actual code. Other approaches advocate writing the implementation first and then figuring out how to write tests to support the implementation.

Writing tests before implementation aims to ensure that you think through the implementation clearly before you write it. The assumption is that you'll imagine the implementation correctly in your mind, write the test first, and then write the implementation. To me, the biggest drawback here is that it assumes that you can clearly imagine the implementation—and if you're wrong, you have to rework your tests.

Writing the implementation and then writing the tests aims to save you time because you focused on the implementation first, and then the tests. You may not have to plan as carefully before you start coding, and therefore it's often faster. The biggest drawback there is that you can miss nuances and write tests that confirm flawed behavior. For example, if your code doesn't handle an edge case and you don't write a test to check it, the tests will still pass.

My take on it is somewhere in the middle. I tend to write a test as I build a specific piece of functionality, but I don't worry about always writing it ahead of time. That's often because I'm also working with APIs that have complex responses, and they're being developed simultaneously with my work. I suggest you don't wait until the end and then go back and write a bunch of tests. When you do that, you tend to write tests that verify your implementation, and that could mean you write tests that verify buggy behavior if you don't think about the potential cases properly.

10.4.3 *What do I write, e2e or unit tests?*

I've heard the argument that an application doesn't need different types of tests if you write one type really well. This perspective typically means that the developer is confident in creating a particular type of test and doesn't feel like other types are going to be as valuable.

I believe you should write at least some e2e tests, but focus mostly on unit tests. Keep in mind the role of each type of test and write the type that best verifies that behavior. For example, if you want to verify that the API is returning the data as expected, you need to write e2e tests. Likewise, if you want to be sure that a pipe works given a wide range of input values, a unit test is most sensible.

e2e tests can be challenging because they're run against a real data source, and if you're creating or deleting objects from the database, you have to handle that properly without messing up the system. If an e2e test fails, it can leave test data in the system and not properly clean up.

In short, favor unit tests unless it becomes too complex—then create e2e tests. e2e tests should focus on user flows, and unit tests should focus on the specific entity's behavior.

10.4.4 *What if I don't have time to write tests?*

Usually this argument only comes if you're writing a fairly small application by yourself and you know the code very well. The reality is that your memory is limited, and it's hard to be confident in making changes that won't break anything else without doing extensive manual testing.

If you think about this a little differently, you probably don't have time to waste *not* having tests, if you think about the potential loss of time spent testing the application manually, or the cost of support for dealing with customer-reported bugs.

Perhaps you finish a project and have to come back to it after a few months, or even years. Your memory about that project will have faded considerably, and your coding style will likely have changed. Without tests, you're changing the code blindly and hoping for the best. I think of it as *cowboy* coding.

I don't like dealing with support issues or manually testing my application. When I fix a bug, I try to write a test to verify that the bug won't happen again. I suggest you make it a habit, too, and you can slowly add tests where you don't have them.

I know that sometimes projects are just proof-of-concepts and that sometimes clients don't have enough budget to cover the time to properly test the app. But proof-of-concepts tend to turn into production applications, and customers keep coming back for changes, and soon the app grows out of control. I encourage you to fight for the time or budget to make testing a priority. Your future self (and boss or client) will thank you.

10.4.5 What about other types of testing?

There are other testing types, not covered here, that could be useful for you. These include things like *usability* testing (observing your users accomplishing a set of tasks to see if they can do so easily), *cross-browser compatibility* testing (analyzing how the application renders in various browsers and noting any differences), and *performance* testing (analyzing the efficiency of the application, how long it takes to load, and other factors that influence actual and perceived performance).

There are so many things you can test that you could easily spend all your time writing tests and not improving the application. Instead of telling you which types of testing you need to adopt, I offer the following thoughts for your consideration:

- *Automate slow or manual processes*—This is usually related to testing, but it can also apply to other aspects, like building the application. For example, if you're spending significant energy trying to validate that code runs properly in different browsers, you'd likely be better off in the long term building a testing infrastructure that can automatically run your tests in more than one browser (such as using a selenium grid service).

- *Test areas that cannot fail*—Think about the process of login or sign up. If those fail, you lose users very fast, and that can be a major issue. You might consider how to constantly test for failure, such as doing automated tests that attempt to log in a user every five minutes and report on failure.

- *Track errors and activity*—Very few users will bother to report bugs or contact support, even on a paid product. You can't assume that users will let you know about errors, so you should consider tracking errors in your application (front end and back end) so you can see what issues users are facing and figure out how to fix them.

- *Add other types of testing as necessary*—There's no need to start a new project and build every type of testing possible. Instead, apply new types of testing when pain points are found. For example, if you get reports that some pages look different in different browsers, you might employ *visual diff* testing that helps automate what the pages look like so you can identify when things are inconsistent or change.

- *Test based on users and outcomes*—Understand your users and what outcomes you expect them to have, and figure out what tests help increase your confidence that users' needs are being met. If you expect the outcome for users is that they'll sign up for your service, then test the marketing and signup pages extensively.

Testing is a big subject that extends far beyond Angular. Web applications have many potential areas to test and validate. Good applications will find the right mix of testing across the spectrum to test the most critical and weakest areas first and then extend that test coverage over time.

Summary

We've taken a whirlwind tour of testing in this chapter, and gotten a realistic amount of testing done to our stock tracking application:

- Unit tests and e2e tests are the two primary types of tests you can write for Angular. Unit tests are written to verify that the individual parts of the application work in isolation, and e2e tests verify that the application works together as a whole.
- Pipes are usually the easiest to unit test because they're usually pure functions that are easy to pass arguments to.
- Services can be easy to test, especially if they have minimal dependencies. Manually constructing a service for testing is preferred if possible, and it's best to also write stub services for other tests to use.
- Components are the major building blocks that you'll be testing—by either testing the controller methods directly or testing how the view is rendered—and they depend on using testing modules to instantiate a lightweight Angular application.
- Testing directives is very similar to components except that you're testing how they modify a component by observing changes to the rendered component.
- e2e tests can be written to interact with the application as a typical user would, by clicking or typing into fields. e2e tests are challenging to maintain, so they should be designed to test the most critical features first.
- There are many other types of testing and considerations, but most general web-development practices can be applied easily to an Angular application and are recommended to be added when necessary.

Angular in production

So, you've built your application—now what? That's a loaded question, but we'll try to unpack it in this chapter. You could do or focus on a lot of things, but not everything is necessary in all projects. There are many general web development things you can do, such as enabling gzip on your server, and there are things specific to Angular, such as ensuring you run the build using Ahead-of-Time compilation.

The way we've been developing our application by running `ng serve` is perfectly acceptable for development but unacceptable for production. The dev server isn't designed to handle real web traffic, can expose vulnerabilities, and can easily crash without warning. You'll want to use a hardened web server for hosting your application.

You may be writing applications for customers, or for the enterprise. I have experience in both spaces to share. In an enterprise environment, for example, often there are different constraints or greater separation of responsibilities across different teams.

I'll cover many important production topics, but remember, there's always room to improve and there are nearly infinite ways to orchestrate tooling for building your application. This chapter focuses on the primary things that most applications should do and gives you a good foundation of knowledge to apply to any unique or customized environments you might be working in.

11.1 Building Angular for production

Throughout this book we've been doing only development builds of our application. That won't serve us well when we want to deploy our application in a real environment—it has a lot of extra code, isn't optimized, and needs cleanup. Our goal is to optimize the final built assets for our application so that it's as small and efficient as possible. We want to also ensure that the files can be downloaded as quickly as possible.

Keep in mind that Angular is constantly evolving, and new releases will add additional capabilities and changes to the platform and tooling. I expect everything in this chapter to remain accurate in principle over time, but a number of specifics will in fact change, so keep an eye on the releases and take advantage of improvements as they arrive.

11.1.1 Production build

The CLI provides for a *production build* option, which adds a number of steps to optimize the final code generated by the build. During development, we do everything as quickly as possible, but at the cost of larger file sizes. This works just fine because you're working on a local server, where sending 5 MB isn't too slow—but that would be unbearably slow for anyone using a 3G mobile connection.

You can run a production build by running the following CLI command:

```
ng build --prod
```

The CLI will build the assets and put them into a directory called dist. These files are now ready to be deployed as a set of static assets to your target server. I'll cover some details about that later, but the CLI makes it surprisingly simple to generate these assets.

When it does a production build, a few important things happen (note that this list may change over time as the CLI tool evolves):

- *Uses production environment*—If you've used the environment configuration targets, it will automatically use the production version during build.
- *Uses minification*—Files are minimized by running them through a tool to reduce the number of bytes required to perform tasks.
- *Bundles assets*—Instead of having every file loaded individually, it splits them into smaller bundles. These bundles are grouped by purpose, such as vendor files placed in one, polyfills in another, the application in another, and so on.
- *Sets the base* href—If you plan to deploy the application outside of the root directory for a domain, you'll have to set the base href to match the file path. You can configure that by passing the --base-href flag.

- *Filename hashing*—To prevent issues with caching, files are named with a unique hash, so that when you deploy a new version, the browser doesn't ignore the update and use its internal cache.
- *File copying*—Any static assets like CSS, images, or fonts are copied over into the dist directory.
- *Tree shaking*—The bundles themselves are optimized by tree shaking, a process in which unreachable or uncalled code is removed from the bundle. Due to ES2015 modules, the tooling can determine exactly which lines of code are executed or not, and "shake out" the unused bits. This is a tricky feature, and as of this writing there are some known issues to be fixed.
- *AoT*—Ahead-of-Time compilation is enabled to pre-compile the component templates, helping to speed up initial render time and allowing Angular to not ship a lot of additional code required to compile.

You can disable some of these by using flags, such as `aot=false`, and you can review the CLI documentation for other flags to enable other things, such as translations or alternative output directories.

11.1.2 Optimizing for target browsers

Have you put together a plan for which browsers you want to target? If not, you should figure out what versions of which browsers you plan to support. In the age of evergreen browsers, it becomes important to continuously evaluate which browsers you support and figure out what deficiencies they may have.

Polyfills are included by default in projects to bridge the gap in missing features, and you can customize what's used. If you have a good grasp on the browsers you support and on what features your application uses, you can customize the polyfills.

The file src/polyfills.ts contains a list of polyfills that get imported into the project. Some might be needed, but others might not be. You'll have to evaluate your codebase to see for sure, but check to see if you can remove any of them to optimize the bundle size.

11.1.3 Progressive Web Apps

Progressive Web Apps (PWAs) are a specific category of apps that have a few features. They're designed to help provide fast-loading web apps for mobile experience that can also work offline. You can read more about them at https://developers.google.com/web/progressive-web-apps.

At the time of writing, Angular is still working on the tooling for making a PWA using Angular. Angular's site dedicated to this work (http://mobile.angular.io) is worth following. As this goes from an alpha state to a stable feature, you can expect the tooling to be available through the CLI (as it already is, somewhat). The site should provide you with the instructions on how to try it out yourself.

The goal is to make it simple for Angular applications to be deployed as PWAs, and the Angular documentation is already a working example of this idea. Supporting PWA in Angular is a major boost for applications that need to work in mobile environments.

11.1.4 *Internationalization (i18n)*

Angular has built-in support for providing local translations of your application, but it's quite lengthy to go through, and not every application may need it. The Angular documentation on internationalization (https://angular.io/guide/i18n) is quite thorough, and this is an area that the Angular community expects to invest in and improve upon in the coming years. Because it's covered so well in that guide, I'll talk more about the concepts and less about the implementation.

Translations are difficult and time consuming, but unavoidable for many. Angular can't provide you support to actually do the translation work—as in the work required to convert one language to another—but it is designed to fit into a typical translation workflow. The basic idea is that all your text messages—anything inside the template that is written language—can be extracted out of the application, translated, and then recompiled for different languages.

Here are the typical steps to implement i18n in an application. Typically, the sooner you set up your i18n process, the easier it will be to implement and maintain:

1 Identify and format any static messages in your application. There are several ways to do this depending on your preference and how your translation should be managed.

2 Extract the messages from the application using the CLI (ng xi18n), which will generate a file in the Xliff 1.2 (default), Xliff 2, or XMB format.

3 A translator does the manual work of taking the list of original language messages and translating them into the other language. Expect this step to take time, and you'll have to identify the person for this work (it might be you, someone on your team, or someone external to your team).

4 Using the CLI, build a new version of the application and define the translation file to use during compilation (ng build --i18n-file). This will output a full build with the translation messages replaced inside the templates.

As of this writing, one major limitation is that translations can't be dynamically loaded into a running application. These messages are hard-coded during the build into the resulting output. If you have multiple languages, you'll have to build it once for each language, passing the appropriate i18n file. This is certainly a potential area for improvement, so I refer you again to the documentation to see if it has become more flexible.

11.1.5 *Using alternative build tooling*

Although space prohibits my covering all scenarios here, many people are producing various alternative build tools for Angular, ranging from using different module loaders (such as SystemJS) to different tree-shaking optimizers (such as Rollup).

These all attempt to optimize various aspects of the build process while rolling their own solutions. Some are quite good for specific use cases. The larger your project, or the more important it is that a certain aspect is optimized, the more you may want to consider additional tooling.

Although choosing to go your own route with build tooling is certainly a viable option, for most scenarios I highly suggest you use the CLI. This is a time-saving tool that's growing with the Angular platform.

I originally set up my own tooling before the CLI was available, and it was a lot of work to maintain. I might have had full control over certain things, but at the cost of much more time and effort. I've also worked with projects that have maintained their own tooling using Grunt or Gulp, and I found that they add a lot of code to a project to manage the same tasks that the CLI provides. Invariably, there tends to be only one person who understands the build tooling, making it hard for others to understand what is happening.

If you have custom needs, consider using the Angular CLI as part of the process instead of duplicating its behaviors, especially those related to how it builds the application. If you want to do additional processing after the build, better to do it after the CLI has run.

At the time of writing, the CLI is being reworked into more of a software development kit (SDK) so that it can be better integrated into custom solutions and tooling. I expect that this will evolve into an even more powerful set of tools that provides greater flexibility and opens many more options.

11.1.6 *Server-side rendering or pre-rendering*

Some applications have important needs such as search engine optimization (SEO), meaning they need to be easily crawled by search engines. Or perhaps being able to quickly see the content of the page is important (as is the case with our forum and chat application example from chapter 7).

Angular has a package called platform-server that provides a way to render Angular on the server. Like the PWA support, at the time of writing it's still in active development. You can find out more about it at https://github.com/angular/universal. The goal of such an approach is to render pages of your application on the server, which would be best for crawlers and for users. Users would see the page content sooner than they do today, because the rendered version would still bootstrap Angular after the initial content has displayed.

Think of how a blog post might appear where you could begin to read, but until Angular finished loading the rest of the assets in the background, the ability to click links would be delayed. Angular is smart enough to capture those events and replay them after the background loading has finished, so it doesn't prevent users from interacting—it's largely about getting content displayed before the bootstrapping of Angular.

This could be tremendously beneficial for many applications, and of not much value to others. Your use case will determine its usefulness for you, but expect server-side rendering to be an important feature of the Angular platform in coming releases. As of Angular 4, the rendering is all part of the official build process, but still has a number of roadmap tasks to tackle.

11.1.7 *Build pipelines*

Gone are the days when you simply upload a file to a remote server and let it run. Most applications, including those built with Angular, require build tooling and orchestration for how to build a production version. Today, we have extensive tooling to help with processes, known as *continuous integration and delivery* (CI/CD). There are many ways to approach the build orchestration problem, but the basics usually include a chain of tools that automatically run to validate a particular build of your application, run tests, build it for production, and push it into production.

Angular itself uses a number of tools to aid in the automated testing of the framework, and because it's an open source project, it can do so freely. Many tools provide free accounts for open source projects or trial accounts if you'd like to try them. I'm not going to focus on any specific tool here, but instead on the kinds of things you should consider putting into your own pipelines.

There isn't much special about Angular related to build pipelines, except that Angular has plans to surface a set of tools from the Google ecosystem that would be a great option for applications to leverage when the tools are stable. Pay attention to release notes and project announcements, because the addition of more CI/CD tools is sure to be a major capability.

11.2 *Angular architecture choices*

If you didn't start out planning your application's architecture before you wrote code, you missed an opportunity to think about design choices that will help you later on. It's better late than never to review your architecture and consider what potential choices you can make to either simplify or optimize.

This section covers what could be considered a list of best practices for writing your application, and you should follow these approaches in most scenarios. They all have an impact on the quality, performance, or stability of your application.

Most of these are also choices you have to make continuously as you build the application. They're not steps you take once but principles that you should apply as you build and maintain the application.

11.2.1 *Lazy load routes*

When it comes to making your application quick to load and run, *lazy loading* your routes is likely to be the most important step you can take. One of the biggest measures of performance is time for the application to load and become ready for the user to interact with.

There are a number of milestones along that path, but the faster your users can start to use your application, the more likely they are to stay around. This is especially true on mobile devices where slow loading and rendering causes user retention to drop quickly after a few seconds.

When you look at your application, think about how every route is structured. You likely want to bundle your default route without lazy loading it, but most every other route is probably a good candidate to separate out into its own module and lazy load.

Chapter 7, section 7.8 covered lazy loading, so refer back to that for a refresher on the specifics of how it works and how to employ it in your application. My suggestion is to make every route its own feature module (except the default route, like the home page and perhaps the login). When you do that, the build files will be split into many different files for each route, and only the core bundles will be loaded on app load. The rest will be loaded as the user navigates around the application.

Imagine your application has 10 routes and a few shared services and components. The 10 routes could represent something like 60–70% of the code weight for your application (excluding libraries), so you could achieve significant savings by extracting them. Every application will be different, but the more routes you have, the greater the potential savings.

You could also consider preloading the lazy loaded modules, which is a way to download the modules in the background after the initial route has loaded. This means subsequent routes will be faster to render, but it does load the application files. If you're on mobile, that might not be great if you have a very large application or routes that are rarely loaded.

There are also strategies for preloading only specific modules unless they're explicitly used, but that takes a little more custom wiring. Both of these strategies are nicely laid out by Victor Savkin, a former Angular core member, at https://vsavkin.com/angular-router-preloading-modules-ba3c75e424cb.

11.2.2 *Reduce external dependencies*

There are a lot of useful external libraries out there, but everything comes at a cost. There's always a tradeoff, but it's something you should consider carefully. If you include a dependency, be prepared to keep track of how it's used in your application.

In all the earlier chapter examples, I've included some external dependencies, like UI libraries. These libraries provide immense value because we don't have to build and implement those features ourselves. That's the whole reason for including external dependencies.

On the flip side, the more dependencies you include, the larger your application will become. You have little control over these dependencies, and many of us don't spend much time inspecting them carefully, if at all.

There are some tools and techniques that can help you inspect the impact of these dependencies in your application. Most of the time, though, you need to practice common sense and restrict yourself to the most important dependencies. My primary concerns about dependencies follow.

SECURITY CONCERNS

Libraries are often treated as black boxes, and it's always possible that they contain security issues. Keep a close eye on them and review them. Dependencies may also import additional sub-dependencies, and that can make security issues hard to keep track of.

You can look at the Node Security project for help tracking known vulnerabilities in Node modules, at https://nodesecurity.io/opensource. This is a free tool, though it has some paid solutions as well. It looks at your project's package.json file and compares it against its database of vulnerabilities.

QUALITY AND SIZE

Not every dependency is written with production use cases in mind. Many are written because they solved a problem and were published for others to consume. Always measure the impact they have on your application and make sure to evaluate more than one option if it exists—or see if it's better to do yourself.

I often review a dependency by looking at the type and quality of testing it has in place. Unfortunately, many dependencies don't have any testing, or the testing is inadequate. That's because so often things are published quickly as a hobby.

As far as the size impact, you can use a tool called source-map-explorer, shown in figure 11.1, to see the impact of each directory and file on your overall bundle size.

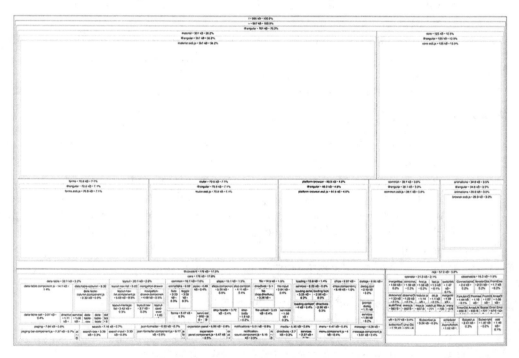

Figure 11.1   source-map-explorer lets you view the size of each part of your bundle to identify potential optimizations.

To use source-map-explorer, you'll need to install it on your system using the following command:

```
npm install -g source-map-explorer
```

Then you'll need to build the application, but make sure you build it with sourcemaps. You can do a production build, but toggle sourcemaps on (which are defaulted to off in production build):

```
ng build --prod --sourcemap=true
```

That will output your files into the dist directory, and then you can inspect the various bundle files by running the following, where the second parameter is the filename you want to analyze:

```
source-map-explorer dist/vendor.4e84f21c95c687f96a48.bundle.js
```

A browser window will open, looking like figure 10.1. The text is quite small in the image, but you can click various files and zoom into the internals of that package. For example, figure 10.1 shows that the Angular Material package from the chapter 8 example is ~35% of the vendors bundle, whereas Covalent is ~18% and RxJS is ~6%. This is helpful to know—you want to see the impact of a module on the size of your bundles. Run this tool against all your bundle output files and see which components are the largest, or how much a polyfill weighs.

COMPATIBILITY AND SUPPORTABILITY

External dependencies aren't necessarily maintained. When there are issues, can you trust they will be fixed? One example is TypeScript, which has added features Angular depends on.

There are a couple of ways to determine supportability, and doing so is largely subjective. I personally like to spend time on the project's site, often GitHub, to see how active it is. Are there many bug reports with no responses? What about commit activity? Just because there hasn't been any activity in the past few months doesn't mean it's been abandoned. Some projects show helpful badges to declare if a dependency is actively maintained or not.

Rather than opening an issue and asking if the project is active, I find it's much better to find a small improvement to make. You can do that by adding a few lines to the documentation or README file, but the goal is to provide some value to the project and make it an easy contribution to merge. There are always documentation improvements to make, so use that as a way to gain a little favor with the maintainer and also figure out how responsive they are.

When it comes to compatibility, you'll need to make sure you have good testing in place. The only way to verify whether things are working is to test, and you want to automate that as much as possible.

Another useful project is Green Keeper, which helps you keep your projects automatically updated with latest versions. It also tries to run your tests with the newer version to help determine if there are any breaking changes—good testing has to be in place for that to be useful. You can find the project at https://greenkeeper.io.

IMPORT MINIMAL ITEMS

When you decide you need an external dependency, often there are ways to optimize how it's used in your application. Well-designed libraries allow you to import only the specific pieces you need instead of the entire library. Any extra imported items may make it into your final build as dead code. It varies by library, but one example is RxJS, which allows you to import the specific items you need instead of the whole library. Likewise, the Covalent UI and Angular Material libraries both allow you to import specific portions of the library as needed instead of the entire bundle. This saves overall code weight, and I like it because you can be specific about what to import.

Long term, this may not be an issue if you're able to optimize your bundle files to drop out any unused code. But it's still a good idea to practice importing the fewest items possible in the meantime and focus on only what you need.

11.2.3 *Stay up-to-date*

When Angular 4 came out, it was possible for almost every application to upgrade without causing any breaking changes to deal with. That's pretty impressive considering the number of changes and improvements made between the Angular 2 and 4 releases.

One of the key improvements was related to the Angular compiler, and due to the way it was optimized under the hood, the size of application bundles decreased significantly. The savings varied by application, but it was estimated that the compiler would reduce the size of components by around 60%. The only thing applications had to do to achieve these savings was update!

As Angular evolves, this type of scenario will continue. The Angular library will evolve and optimize itself, the build tooling will keep getting smarter, and those who use the latest and greater versions will be able to take advantage of those benefits.

As I've stressed, Angular is more of a platform than just a framework. The combination of the tooling, various libraries, and other ecosystem components is being constantly improved. I've sat down with the Angular team to talk about priorities and goals, and optimization is one that comes up consistently.

The takeaway here is to not lock yourself into a version of Angular and forget about upgrading. Keep track of the development notes and enjoy the regular, incremental releases. There is a six-month cycle for major releases that may contain some breaking changes. Angular hopes to minimize the number of breaking changes and provide clear upgrade paths for keeping on the latest versions. This does mean making changes to your applications over time, but if you aren't doing that, you're losing out on all the potential benefits. Plus you might be open to any security issues that have been reported and resolved.

11.3 *Deployment*

There are a lot of potential ways of deploying your application and a lot of opinions about which is best. You may have to work with a specific option because that's what your company or team always uses, or you may be able to choose your own. Either way, a few basics remain consistent. This section looks at a few of these considerations and at a couple deployment approaches. I hope it serves as a helpful guide for you to base your own deployment strategy on.

No matter which server you plan to use, you should make sure a few things are set up to work properly:

- *gzip compression*—Configure your server to send files with gzip compression enabled. gzip is a simple configuration value supported by most browsers that significantly reduces the sizes of files sent over the network. Savings vary, but 30% or more isn't uncommon.
- *Fall back to index.html by rewriting URLs*—Any single page application (Angular or otherwise) needs the server to handle rewriting URLs to serve up the index file even if another file is requested. Imagine you land on example.com/blog/my-post-123. The server will first look for an asset at the /blog/my-post-123 location, but that file doesn't exist because it's just an Angular route. Instead, the server needs to fall back to sending the index.html file so Angular can execute.
- *CORS or reverse proxy*—Many APIs run from a different domain (or even subdomain), and it's easy to enable CORS headers in the API server. Alternatively, you can use a reverse proxy to map URLs so they proxy through your domain to another.

Depending on your server, other optimizations or configurations may be available to you. My suggestions here aren't exhaustive, so it's best to research a bit more about what your server has available.

Once you've run the CLI `build` command, you can take the dist directory and drop it on a server that handles service static files. You should automate the process, but there are a few ways you could deploy it for free on a service like GitHub pages, Heroku, or Firebase.

That's the most common and easiest approach, but sometimes you'll want to wrap it up in a container and deploy it that way. The following example uses the nginx server and builds a container that has your application files. You can create a file called Dockerfile in your project directory and use code from listing 11.1. You also need to have an nginx.conf file in your directory, as you see in listing 11.2.

Listing 11.1 Sample Dockerfile for nginx

```
FROM nginx

COPY ./nginx.conf /etc/nginx/nginx.conf
COPY ./dist /usr/share/nginx/html
```

Listing 11.2 Sample nginx config

```
events {}
http {
  server {
    listen      80;
    server_name  myapp;

    # Redirect to index if file not found
```

```
    location / {
        root    /usr/share/nginx/html;
        index   index.html index.htm;
        try_files $uri$args $uri$args/ /index.html;
    }
    # Additional configurations go here
  }
}
```

The preceding two listings will allow you to build a container that has nginx to serve your application. Assuming you have Docker installed on your machine, you can run the following commands to build and run the container:

```
ng build --prod
docker build . -t myapp
docker run -p 80:8080 myapp
```

There are many ways to configure this Dockerfile, and this is just meant as a basic starter. You can fine-tune the nginx config as well, including handling error pages and adjusting gzip settings.

Because Angular provides you with the built static assets, injecting them into many different server environments is easy.

Congrats! You've designed, built, and now deployed your Angular application! At this point, you can either lie back and enjoy your success or start on your next project!

Summary

This chapter covered a lot of details around building and deploying Angular for production. There's a lot of detail work you can do, and many opportunities for optimizing. Over time, new abilities will be added to the Angular platform that you'll want to take advantage of. Here are the key highlights covered in this chapter:

- Angular CLI provides a production build option that does a number of tasks as it builds your application's final bundle assets. It can optimize and shake out dead code, implement cache-busting names, and provide you a directory with everything your app needs.
- Some best practices to follow include lazy loading your routes and importing only the necessary pieces of libraries. As you add more dependencies to your application, more things can potentially bloat your bundle size or have an impact on your ability to maintain the application.
- Deploying to servers is easy because you get the final rendered assets. You can bundle these static files into a container or include them in other server environments. Be sure you've handled falling back to the index.html file and other server considerations.

Appendix:
Upgrading from
AngularJS to Angular

AngularJS (version 1.x) is one of the most popular and most-used frameworks of all time, and many applications built with it are still running today. It continues to be supported as long as there is a critical mass of developers submitting issues and patches, but the future is certainly to be found in upgrading to Angular (2.x or newer). This appendix talks about the strategies for moving forward with an existing AngularJS application and aims to help clarify the options you have when deciding your next move.

Upgrading to Angular requires an investment and a plan. There are many conceptual similarities between the two, but Angular was a total rewrite from AngularJS and changes some important design patterns. The ability to simply "upgrade" is unfortunately not that simple in most cases and requires some careful consideration.

You have three basic choices: Don't upgrade, rewrite from scratch, or do incremental upgrades. Each option has positives and negatives, so you'll have to weigh out your own needs against them. I've ordered them from the least likely to most likely choice you'll want to make.

I've also diagrammed your options on the spectrum of the application's business value against its complexity. Figure 1 is only an illustration and not necessarily the reality for your application, but it's meant to give you some perspective on how to think about the choices.

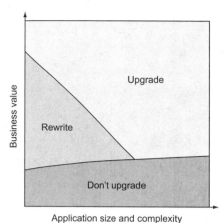

Figure 1   Options for upgrading diagrammed as a function of business value against application complexity

As much as I think everyone should upgrade or rewrite, it's important that you weigh the technical challenges against your business needs. There's always a cost to making a change, and you want to ensure that you accurately estimate and minimize that cost.

Let's start with the first option: Don't upgrade and continue with AngularJS.

A.1   Option 1: Don't upgrade

I feel this is an option that's not often considered, but you *can* decide not to upgrade your app to Angular. This might sound contrary to everything this book is about, and to some degree it is, but existing applications have a host of considerations that might make this the most viable option.

Here's a sampling of the various reasons you might consider just maintaining your existing application instead of upgrading:

- Very large applications might be so complex that the thought of making major changes is very hard to entertain. Be careful not to make an excuse of your application being too large to upgrade, because it's certainly possible to upgrade, but perhaps the application has invested so heavily into the existing design that the cost to change could be difficult to pay.
- Some applications are very stable and don't require a lot of work. There may not even be anyone actively working on it anymore. This is especially true for applications that aren't in the critical path for your business, such as internal tools. Perhaps your efforts are better spent on building or improving more important applications.
- Some applications have to support older browsers, and upgrading to Angular might break support. This has become less of an argument as most old browsers are deprecated, retired by the vendors, or have become evergreen with self-upgrading mechanisms. For example, supporting IE8 today is possible for some applications, depending on what kind of customers you have, but it's also frustrating because that browser is vulnerable and outdated.

I think it boils down to asking one question: Does your application have any strong business or technical reasons not to upgrade? If so, weigh them against the reality of your customers and what's best for them. Customers using outdated or insecure browsers is bad for them, and perhaps the right decision is to not support such scenarios. This might take a change in perspective, however.

If the ultimate decision here is to leave the application and not upgrade, you have to be very aware of the consequences. But you can also expect that AngularJS will be supported as long as there is a critical amount of users working with it. Review the AngularJS site to see if there are any specific timelines or guarantees, but at the time of writing there is no schedule set for stopping AngularJS maintenance.

If you're in an enterprise environment, this can be the easiest choice. It saves you from engaging with the business development cycle, resource planning, and other processes that your company might have in place. But regardless of what role you play or how big your company is, the key is to focus on making a case for why not to upgrade, rather than a case for why to upgrade. Legacy applications are a fact of life, but from experience, I know that the sooner an application is upgraded, the more likely it is to be maintained—otherwise, it tends to drift slowly into oblivion. But perhaps that is the best path.

No matter what, just promise me you won't *start* new projects in AngularJS! Put your knowledge from this book to use and create new applications with Angular.

A.2 *Option 2: Rewrite from scratch*

Your next option is to start over and throw your existing application away. Some developers will love this idea, whereas others will balk at the notion of just tossing all that work.

Rewriting your application has a number of advantages if you decide you're ready to take the leap and upgrade to Angular. Most of these hold true for deciding to upgrade any application over time, but there are a couple of Angular-specific notes here to mention:

- You don't have to deal with any legacy code. AngularJS does a few things that ultimately have been known to cause issues, such as an over-reliance upon two-way data binding. If your application is running older versions of AngularJS, upgrading is likely a bigger task than if you're running the latest and greatest.
- The new application can be rebuilt using best practices that you might have to fight against if you work on upgrading an existing application. You can start fresh with TypeScript even if you didn't have it before.
- It's easier to implement new features or drop old features because you can think of rewriting as an opportunity to reimagine your application's purpose and goals.

Of course, there are also disadvantages to this approach, and they're often overlooked:

- Rewriting means you have to start everything from scratch, including rethinking your build pipeline, redesigning your tests, and so forth.

- If you depended on any libraries for AngularJS, they might not exist for Angular, or they might be different. This increases your level of effort if you have to find an alternative, write your own, or redesign your application.
- It's hard to recreate the exact same application, with the exact same features, by rewriting. Almost certainly some feature will change its behavior, even if very slightly, and this could cause issues for your users.

I prefer this option when the application is small enough to do a rewrite in a reasonable amount of time (what is *reasonable* varies, but a good rule of thumb is weeks, not months). Incrementally upgrading a small application might cost you more time and effort in the end, but do make sure you can account for the stability of your application and not sacrifice the experience for your users.

The main goal of rewriting should be to build the best Angular application that solves your business needs. If you're focused primarily on the technical aspects, there's a chance your efforts will have a negative impact on the business. This is particularly true for enterprise environments, where expectations are typically set and managed by product managers and customers.

This tends to be a problematic choice in the enterprise, at least initially. The prevailing thought is often, "If it's not broken, don't fix it." But you can make a case for the rewrite based on future objectives and outcomes. I've made the argument that if we don't adopt newer technologies today, we'll pay the price later by having to spend more on migrating applications. Again, business objectives should drive decisions, but usually business objectives include being successful long term, so technical choices should support that as well.

A.3   *Option 3: Incrementally upgrade*

The final option is to begin an incremental upgrade process, which means running part of your application using AngularJS and another part using Angular. This is the strategy that allows you to maintain the current application while incrementally changing pieces of the application to Angular.

I believe this is the most common scenario, as any application with business value and some complexity will fit this category. Here are some of the advantages of incremental upgrades:

- You can slowly migrate the application piece by piece, so the existing application remains functional.
- The tooling exists for running the two side by side, and it's flexible enough to allow you several different approaches for how to tackle refactoring.
- It allows developers to focus on building new features with Angular without rewriting older functionality.

Of course, there are a few negatives you should also be aware of:

- You'll end up loading both Angular and AngularJS in your application, which increases the size of your application.

- Poorly written AngularJS applications are harder to migrate and may need some work to make the process easier.
- It's possible to get stuck in the upgrade process and never fully finish if you don't plan and execute correctly. You need to be able to fully commit to seeing it through so you don't give your users a poor experience in the long term.

I believe most applications fall into this bucket, and you'll want to know a bit more about the best ways to approach the upgrade. The Angular documentation covers the upgrade tool quite well, and I don't intend to duplicate that coverage here, but it doesn't discuss some of the approaches that you could use.

I fully recommend that you make sure your AngularJS application is, first, up to date with the latest AngularJS release, and that you follow the style guidelines. If you have some work to do in this area, you should invest in that first.

Once you have a well-designed AngularJS application, there are two great approaches outlined by Victor Savkin, which he calls *horizontal* and *vertical slicing*. He has a series online about upgrading AngularJS applications, starting here: https://blog.nrwl.io/ngupgrade-in-depth-436a52298a00. It outlines additional steps for upgrading, and I recommend it highly. There's also a book listed there, which you may find useful.

Horizontal slicing is the idea that you'll try to upgrade the lowest, most reusable components in your AngularJS application. This includes things like UI components and components that aren't routing components. The idea is that these lower level components are already pretty decoupled, and you can just replace them for a new version written in Angular. It's nice because you can change one component at a time.

Vertical slicing is the approach that changes every component of a given route at the same time. That means the routing component and anything it depends upon will need to be changed at the same time. This is beneficial because you're never mixing Angular and AngularJS in the same route, but it means upgrading each route may require a larger investment in time.

I would suggest vertical slicing in most cases, because mixing Angular and AngularJS in the same route is harder to reason through and debug. Vertical slicing also means you've got an entire page upgraded and working at once, which might take longer for each incremental step but be faster overall by requiring fewer steps.

Summary

Upgrading an AngularJS application to Angular is not a decision to be made lightly. You should carefully consider the options and understand your business and technical requirements:

- You can choose to not upgrade at all, and trust in the support provided for AngularJS. Stable applications that aren't in the critical business path are likely candidates.

- Alternatively, you can rewrite the entire application to Angular in one large step. This may work well for smaller applications or ones that can endure a full refactoring without interruption to the current application development.
- Incremental upgrading is the primary choice for the majority of applications, as it allows you to change components piecemeal from AngularJS to Angular. The strategies of horizontal (working from the lowest components up the tree) and vertical (working on entire routes for each upgrade step) slicing are the best ways to think about how to approach the upgrade.

Index

Symbols

.angular-cli.json file 30
: character 62, 167
@Input( ) decorator 42
@NgModule decorator 33
? operator 41
& operator 68
++ operator 68
| (pipe character) 62
@ symbol 21
# symbol 183

A

access, limiting with route guards 177–182
afterAll block 245
AfterContentChecked lifecycle hook 84
AfterContentInit lifecycle hook 84
afterEach block 245, 250
AfterViewChecked lifecycle hook 84
AfterViewInit lifecycle hook 84, 222
Angular CLI (command-line interface) 6–7
Angular expression 41
AngularJS platform
    Angular vs. 4
    upgrading to Angular 287–292
        disadvantages of 288–289
        rewriting from scratch 289–290
        upgrading incrementally 290–292
Angular Material library 10
Angular platform 1–24
    AngularJS vs. 4
    benefits of using 2
    component architecture of 11–20
        JavaScript modules 17–20
        key characteristics of components 13–15
        Shadow DOM 15–17

templates 17
    desktop capabilities 8–9
    JavaScript and
        observables 21–22
        overview 20–21
    mobile capabilities 8–9
    TypeScript and 23–24
    UI libraries 9–11
animations
    overview 81
    testing components with 258–260
AoT (Ahead-of-Time) compiler 65, 277
APP_BASE_HREF 261
App component 86–87
AppComponent class 32
applications
    basic scaffolding of 29–31
    bootstrapping 33–35
    building 25–53
        components 38–50
        services 36–38
    components of 31–32
    modules of 32–33
    rendering 31–35, 64–65
    routing 50–53
    testing 242–274
        e2e testing 265–270
        strategies for 270–274
        tools for 244
        unit testing 244–265
AppModule 183
aria attributes 72
asynchronous tasks, handling in tests 263–265
Async pipe 203
async validators 228
attribute bindings 72–73
attribute directives, creating 192
auxiliary routes 173

293

RELATED MANNING TITLES

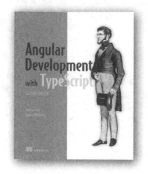

Angular Development with Typescript, Second Edition
by Yakov Fain and Anton Moiseev

> ISBN: 9781617295348
> 475 pages, $49.99
> June 2018

Testing Angular Applications
by Jesse Palmer, Corinna Cohn, Michael
   Giambalvo, Craig Nishina

> ISBN: 9781617293641
> 235 pages, $44.99
> April 2018

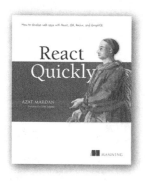

React Quickly
*Painless web apps with React, JSX, Redux,
and GraphQL*
by Azat Mardan

> ISBN: 9781617293344
> 528 pages, $49.99
> August 2017

React in Action
by Mark Tielens Thomas

> ISBN: 9781617293856
> 300 pages, $44.99
> March 2018

For ordering information go to www.manning.com